Phillies N
The 100 Greatest
Phillies of All-Time

An exploration of the 100 greatest players ever to wear red pinstripes and more!

Written by Ian Riccaboni
Edited by Barbara Morris
Contributions by Pat Gallen

PhilliesNation.com is more than a blog. It is a web site, television show, and online and offline meeting point for the most fanatical Phillies fans to share ideas, absorb information, and rant with impunity.

Phillies Nation, LLC is not affiliated with the Philadelphia Phillies or Major League Baseball.

All statistics updated through September 8, 2015.

For my beautiful wife, Sarah, who has believed in me at every turn; my brother Bill for putting a Wiffle Ball bat in my hand at age two and teaching me how to love baseball; Pat Gallen for assuring me I could do this; my parents Rich and Shelly; the Riccabonis, Morrises, Garcias, Gerbrachts, Wernetts, and Rogers; Chris Kobela for never saying no to going to a game; and the readers of Phillies Nation.

Table of Contents – Top 100 Phillies Entries

Table of Contents – Top 100 Phillies Entries, Continued

Table of Contents – Top 100 Phillies Entries, Continued

Table of Contents – Bonus Content

Transactions That Shaped the Phillies

In Their Own Words

Table of Contents – Bonus Content, Continued

Bonus Countdowns

Prologue

For 132 years, the Philadelphia Phillies have been delighting, disappointing, and dazzling lifelong fans from across the Delaware, Lehigh, and Schuylkill Valleys in Pennsylvania to Atlantic and Cape May Counties in New Jersey, and down to the furthest reaches of Dover, Lewes, and Rehoboth Beach, Delaware. Each year, as flowers began to bloom and the grass turned greener, men, women, and children would begin to flock to the ballpark, first to Recreation Park then to the Philadelphia Baseball Grounds followed by the Baker Bowl, Shibe Park, Connie Mack Stadium, Veteran's Stadium, and currently Citizens Bank Park, a veritable baseball cathedral for folks throughout the Philadelphia region.

Every year since the opening of Veteran's Stadium in 1971, the Phillies have welcomed over one million fans per year. The names on the back of the jerseys have changed while the name on the front has endured. It is the undeniable dedication of fans from the tristate area to the name on the front of the jersey that has made the name on the back of the jersey so meaningful.

As we at Phillies Nation have found out, that loyalty, passion, and dedication carries over into discussion, whether it be on sports talk radio or throughout our website, PhilliesNation.com. Shortly after the completion of the 2008 World Series, site patriarch Tim Malcom began a noble quest: to identify the 100 greatest Phillies in the history of the franchise. Tim's list was comprehensive, sparked much debate, including everyone from Randy Lerch to Mike Schmidt.

Much has changed in the six years since Tim compiled his list. Tim left Phillies Nation just a few months after the final entry was complete, the Phillies would continue their most successful run in franchise history by winning three more division titles, and Phillies Nation saw many changes in personnel and in media space. Who would have thought then that we would soon expand into another media realm with our own weekly cable television show?

We owe the success this site has had in our 11 years to our readers. And six years later, we owe our loyal and engaged readership a revised Top

100, one that incorporates all of the advantages Tim did not have and one that is far enough away from the conclusion of the franchise's historic run to assess it properly.

The research sources that we have at our disposal that Tim did not are many. They include very much improved and more user-friendly *Baseball Reference* and *FanGraphs* sites that make assessing turn-of-the-19th-century players in context a little easier. There has also been a significant explosion in use, and acceptance, of wins above replacement level (WAR) as a tool of comparison among players. With statistics playing such an important role in analyzing and talking about baseball, this list has been compiled with a high degree of consideration for both traditional and advanced analytics.

In this book, you will be introduced to players who have not played in 80, 90, or in some cases, over 100 years. These players made the list over players you or your parents may have watched play at Connie Mack or at the Vet. This may jar you. Yet, part of those jarring feelings are what make lists like these, and baseball, so special: Everybody's perception is different.

A perfect illustration of this is how the list was developed: former Phillies Nation Editor-in-Chief Pat Gallen and I spent many hours ranking, debating, re-ranking, and re-debating the Top 100. There are a few players that caused particular contention where Pat and I had to simply walk away, wait, and resume the discussion with cooler heads.

Surprisingly, one of those debates involved Von Hayes.

When discussing Hayes, Pat and I found that our ideas about baseball, while seemingly very similar, were very different at their core. Pat valued contributions to a championship or winning team while I did not mind a hired assassin having two or three career years on the Phillies. Pat took great consideration to off-the-field behavior and gave some consideration to fan interaction whereas I couldn't be bothered as much with such criteria. We even discussed consideration of known steroid users versus suspected steroid users versus perceived clean guys – one of us erred on the side of caution when considering steroid users while the other took a more liberal approach and did not use it as part of their criteria.

Yet, despite some fundamental differences, we were able to come to the proverbial "meeting of the minds." Ultimately, Pat and I came to agree on the ranking of the Top 100 Phillies players of all-time, reflecting what we believe is a delicate balance of two, sometimes philosophically different, perspectives.

In the end, each Phillie was ranked based solely on their time with the Phillies, so awards and championships won with other teams did not factor into our consideration. Pat and I made our decisions based on our own understanding or interpretation of the following: impact on the Phillies, individual achievement, team achievement, traditional stats, and analytics. Information was sourced, referenced, and cross-referenced from Baseball Reference, FanGraphs, The Baseball Cube, SABR profiles, newspaper clippings found through Google's News Search Profiles, and player interviews.

With each entry, we have provided some basic information about the player, including their franchise rank in fWAR, which is Wins Above Replacement-level as measured by the website FanGraphs, and why the player ranks where he does on the list. Finally, this list is reserved for players only – this means you won't be seeing Charlie Manuel or Paul Owens on this list. But, don't worry – there is plenty of information in these pages about those colorful characters, as well.

We hope our list of the Top 100 Phillies inspires discussion, causes debate, and brings back memories. Over time, we hope our list will serve as an interesting time capsule to share with your children and grandchildren, a snapshot of a place and a time in history where the Phillies have just concluded their most successful run in franchise history.

Thank you for reading.

Abbreviations You'll Need to Know Before Reading

AB – at-bat, a plate appearance that ends in a non-walk or non-sacrifice result.

BA – batting average, measured by dividing the number of hits a player has by at-bats.

BB – base on balls or walk.

BB/9 IP - walks per nine innings pitched, calculated by taking the number of total walks issued by a pitcher divided by the number of innings pitched and multiplied by nine to simulate expected performance over a nine-inning game. The lower a pitcher's BB/9 IP, the better.

ERA – earned run average, calculated by taking a pitcher's earned runs allowed dividing by innings pitched and multiplying by name to simulate the expected amount of earned runs a pitcher would surrender over a nine-inning game. The lower a pitcher's ERA, the better.

K – strikeouts.

K/9 IP – strikeouts per nine innings pitched, calculated by taking the number of total strikeouts pitched by a pitcher divided by the number of innings pitched and multiplied by nine to simulate expected performance over a nine-inning game. The higher a pitcher's K/9 IP, the better.

OBP – on-base percentage, calculated by adding hits plus walks and dividing by plate appearances.

OPS – on-base plus slugging, calculated by adding on-base percentage plus slugging.

PA – plate appearance, registered any time a player steps into the batter's box as a player.

SLG – slugging percentage, calculated by adding total bases and dividing by at-bats.

UZR and UZR/150 – Ultimate Zone Rating, a tool used to measure the ability of a fielder to cover ground, or range, in the field. The higher a fielder's UZR, the better.

WAR – wins above replacement-level, a quantitative counting stat that measure the value of both hitters and pitchers against the anticipated value of a replacement-level player, or a player that his reached the highest of his potential and is good enough to play in the Major Leagues but spends time at Triple-A during a given season, also.

fWAR – WAR as measured by the website FanGraphs.
rWAR – WAR as measured by the website Baseball Reference.

WHIP – walks and hits per innings pitched, calculated by adding the number of walks issued and hits against a pitcher and dividing by the number of innings a pitcher pitched. Like ERA, the lower the better.

Otto Knabe

Second Baseman

Years as a Phillie: 1907-1913
Line as a Phillie: .249/.328/.315, 5 HR, 122 SB in 4057 PA
fWAR Phillies Rank: 55th among position players, 88th overall
Signature Achievement: Led the National League in Sacrifice Hits
(1907-1908, 1910, 1913)

Knabe was a prototypical second baseman, light-hitting with great defense, and one that is looked upon more favorably with the adoption of modern statistics. Yes, Knabe finished no lower than fifth out of eight in the NL in errors among second baseman from 1908 through 1913 but his range factor rates Knabe as one of the best defensive second baseman in the early 1900s. Knabe was a durable defensive wizard, leading all second baseman in plate appearances and games played and ranking fifth in doubles from 1907 through 1913.

Making his Major League debut in 1905 as a 21-year old for the Pittsburgh Pirates, Knabe had been playing for Toledo in the American Association before the Pirates purchased him. It is relatively unknown how Knabe became a free agent but the second baseman was able to jump from Pittsburgh to Philadelphia prior to the start of the 1907 season.

Knabe was one of the cornerstone players of a group of largely mediocre teams and led all Phillies in plate appearances during his stint with the team. The best any of his teams finished was 88-63 in his last season 1913, missing the pennant by 12.5 games. The second baseman received MVP votes in three straight seasons, 1911-1913, before departing.

In 1914, Knabe jumped to the Baltimore Terrapins of the competing Federal League in 1914, narrowly missing out on an appearance in the 1915 World Series. The second baseman would play two years in Baltimore before jumping back to the National League in 1916, splitting the year between the Pittsburgh Pirates and Chicago Cubs.

Hey, have you heard of: **The 1913 Phillies**

Otto Knabe was a cornerstone on what was the Phillies best team since the introduction of the World Series ten years prior. While the eventual World Series champion would be the crosstown powerhouse Philadelphia Athletics, the Phillies displayed a moxie under manager Red Doolin not yet seen at the Baker Bowl in the World Series-era.

Led by stars Sherry Magee, Gavvy Cravath, Fred Luderus, Knabe, and aces Tom Seaton and Grover Cleveland Alexander, the 1913 Phils gave the fans in the Baker Bowl something to be proud of with an 88-63 mark. Unfortunately for them, the New York Giants were led by a well-balanced offensive attack and anchored by two aces of their own: Hall of Famers Rube Marquard and Christy Mathewson. The Giants would post a 101-51 and win the National League pennant by 12.5 games.

Woodie Fryman

Left-Handed Pitcher

Years as a Phillie: 1968 – 1972
Line as a Phillie: 42-56, 3.76 ERA, 1.312 WHIP in 838.2 IP
fWAR Phillies Rank: 34th among pitchers, 89th overall
Signature Season: All-Star in 1968 with a 2.78 ERA

Upon first glance at Fryman's statistics, he does not appear to a Phillies' Top 100 player of all time. The ERA? Above 3.75. The record? Sub-.500. Longevity? Only four and a half seasons. The pedigree of teams he was on? Yikes.

Yet, based on advanced statistics, in hindsight, Fryman checks out to be one of the top 100 Phillies, ever. Fryman ranks 24th among Phillies' starters in K/9 IP, 57th in WHIP, and 28th in FIP. Fryman faced a lot of bad luck in his career with the Phillies, having a 63-point difference between his ERA and FIP, pitching in front of the 23rd (out of 24) best fielding team in the Majors, fielders that gave up an estimated 195 runs more than a league average team.

Fryman was acquired from Pittsburgh by the Phillies on December 15, 1967, along with Bill Laxton and Don Money in exchange for future Hall of Famer Jim Bunning. The trade was a fortuitous one: Bunning, now headed into his late 30's, was slowing down while Money proved to be a solid third baseman and Fryman an above-average starting pitcher.

The pride of Fleming County HS was an All-Star in his first year with the Phillies, accruing a 12-14 record with a career-bests-as-a-starter 2.78 ERA and 151 Ks. Fryman would post a record over .500 just twice out of parts of five seasons with the Phillies, his worst mark coming in 1972 when Fryman went 4-10. Fryman was selected off waivers by the Tigers on August 2, 1972 and went on to have a turnaround for the ages, going 10-3 in 14 starts with a 2.06 ERA to help guide the Tigers into the ALCS.

Fryman would play parts of 18 years in the Majors alternating between roles of reliever and starter. The Montreal Expos inducted him into their Hall of Fame in 1995 after spending parts of eight seasons, including his All-Star 1976 campaign, there.

Despite pitching in front of one of the worst defensive alignments in Phillies history, Fryman was an above-average pitcher in the Majors for the Phillies, ranking in the upper one-third of all advanced and traditional stats among the 144 qualified starting pitchers in that time frame. Fryman did not make this list because of dominance; he made it by persevering to achieve success despite playing on weak teams.

The '68 Phils and Fryman's Hot Start

The 1968 Phils appeared to be a team of promise. With a rotation of Chris Short, Larry Jackson, Fryman, a young Rick Wise, Jeff James, and Jerry Johnson, the Fightin' Phils had enough arms to stay in the NL pennant race, and they would through early June.

Then, following a June 14 double header split with the Dodgers, the Phillies lost manager Gene Mauch just 54 games into the season despite being only 5.5 games out of first place.

The team would send just one representative to the All-Star game: Woodie Fryman. Through June 18, Fryman was a Cy Young contender, posting a 10-5 mark with a 1.61 ERA. Fryman, however, would not be immune to the team's slide, finishing with a 12-14 record and a 2.78 ERA.

#98 Brett Myers

Right-Handed Pitcher

Years as a Phillie: 2002-2009
Line as a Phillie: 73-63, 21 saves, 4.25 ERA in 1183.2 IP
fWAR Phillies Rank: 28th among pitchers, 78th overall
Signature Moments: Closing out the 2007 NL East clincher, Nine-pitch walk against C.C. Sabathia in the 2008 NLDS

If there was an initial moment of hope, a moment that led me to believe the Phillies had an opportunity to really be contenders for once with young players in the early 2000s, it was the debut of Myers. Myers was the 12th pick in the 1999 amateur draft and entered the 2002 season as the #33 prospect in baseball according to *Baseball America*. As a 21-year old, Myers earned a win at Wrigley Field by pitching eight innings of one-run ball, striking out five with the only run on his ledger coming off the bat of Sammy Sosa, out-dueling prospect darling Mark Prior.

Myers would be one of the pillars of consistency for the Phillies as they took shape from fringe contender into A-level franchise, earning 73 wins (24th in club history), striking out 986 batters (ninth in club history) posting a 4.40 ERA (30th in club history among pitchers with at least 1,000 innings pitched), and even memorably converting into a closer during the 2007 season to stabilize a bullpen that used 21 pitchers.

Though Myers was never an All-Star with the Phillies, he was part of some of the club's most memorable moments. Myers earned the win in Game 2 of the 2008 NLDS against the Brewers with a seven-inning performance, surrendering just two runs. While his pitching was good enough to hold off opposing starter C.C. Sabathia, even more impressive was his day at the plate. Myers' nine-pitch, two-out walk against the former Cy Young winner would keep the inning going for Shane Victorino two batters later to crank a two-out, grand slam into the Philadelphia twilight. Myers would see 20 pitches in three at bats, following his nine-pitch walk with a 10-pitch line out, and concluding with a single on the first pitch he saw from

Brewers' reliever Seth McClung in the bottom of the fifth. Somewhat forgotten is his stellar follow-up at the plate just a few days later in Game 2 of the NLCS against the Dodgers: a record-tying three-hit game with three RBIs in an 8-5 win over the Dodgers in Philadelphia.

Despite the late efforts of Eric Bruntlett, Myers would be out-dueled by James Shields in Game 2 of the 2008 World Series, undoubtedly on the losing end it seems because he was unable to hit in the American League park. Myers would raise the World Series trophy in 2008 and return the following year as a reliever after missing significant time with injuries. Myers is including in the Top 100 for his longevity and performance on winning Phillies' ball clubs but drops a few spots due to unfortunate off-the-field extra-curriculars.

The 1999 MLB Draft

Brett Myers was taken 12th overall in the 1999 MLB amateur draft. While Myers was a steady rotation piece, and later, a closer, for the Phillies for eight seasons, the Phillies would strike out hard through the remainder of the draft. The Phillies would draft just one other player who would crack their big league club, 10th rounder Marlon Byrd, while they missed out on signing their fifth round pick, Joe Saunders, and selected 39 other players that would never play in the big leagues.

Manny Trillo

Second Baseman

Years as a Phillie: 1979-1982
Line as a Phillie: .277/.321/.369, 19 HR, 30 SB in 2022 PA
fWAR Phillies Rank: 86th among hitters, 166th overall
Signature Series: Won NLCS MVP in 1980 after hitting .381/.364/.547

Originally signed by the Phillies in 1968 as a free agent from Venezuela, Manny Trillo would be plucked from the Phillies in the 1969 Rule 5 draft by the Oakland A's. Prior to the 1975 season, Trillo would be traded by the A's to the Chicago Cubs in a package that netted Oakland Billy Williams. At age 26, Trillo would be named an All-Star for the Cubs in 1977 before the Phillies acquired the light-hitting second baseman prior to the 1979 campaign in a trade that also netted the Phillies Greg Gross and Dave Rader.

Trillo made an immediate impact in Philadelphia, winning his first of three Gold Gloves with the Phillies at second base before winning an unexpected Silver Slugger in 1980 after hitting .292/.334/.412 with 25 doubles, 9 triples, and 7 homers.

Trillo's offensive career year carried over to the 1980 playoffs, where his clutch hitting helped push the Phillies to the World Series in 1980. Trillo nabbed 1980 NLCS MVP honors after hitting .381/.364/.574 (not a typo), including four huge RBI across Games 4 and 5. Trillo would also have go-ahead hits in the eighth innings of both Game 4 and 5 before the leads were subsequently surrendered.

Trillo's eighth inning, go-ahead, two-run triple in Game 5 off Nolan Ryan was, until recently, one of the most memorable hits in Phillies history.

Trillo managed to top that hit just a few days later in Game 4 of the 1980 World Series: with ace reliever Dan Quisenberry in the game and Del Unser on third after a game-tying double that scored Mike Schmidt, Trillo lined a ball off Quisenberry's glove that went directly to George Brett. Trillo beat out a strong throw by Brett to give the Phillies a 4-3 lead. Tug McGraw would close out Game 5 and the Phillies would take a 3-2 series lead.

Trillo would ultimately reach the NL All-Star team twice, win three Gold Gloves, and a pair of Silver Sluggers as a Phillie before being traded to Cleveland in the landmark "5-for-1" deal prior to the 1983 season. Trillo would play seven more seasons with five different teams, hitting .257/.312/.337 with 20 HR and 5 steals before retiring during the 1989 season. Trillo's postseason heroics earn him a spot in the Top 100 despite his short stay in Philadelphia.

The Phillies Venezuelan Connection

Since signing Trillo in 1968, the Phillies have committed heavily to their scouting and development in Venezuela. According to *Baseball Reference*, 2.6% of all Major Leaguers are Venezuelan born. This list includes current Phillies Freddy Galvis and Cesar Hernandez, recent Phillies Ender Inciarte and Mauricio Robles, and former players Trillo, Bobby Abreu, Miguel Cairo, Omar Daal, Freddy Garcia, and Ugueth Urbina.

While some of the above players were not signed or developed by the Phillies, the Phillies have brought a number of lesser-known or less-remembered players to the Majors as well, including Clemente Alvarez, Sergio Escalona, Yoel Hernandez, Anderson Machado, Edgar Ramos, and Danny Sandoval.

Additionally, the Phillies' prospect pipeline is currently chock full of Venezuelan-born prospects, including first baseman Willians Astudillo and outfielder Carlos Tocci.

Ryan Madson
Right-Handed Reliever

Years as a Phillie: 2003-2011
Line as a Phillie: 47-30, 59 saves, 3.59 ERA in 630 IP
fWAR Phillies Rank: 57th among pitchers, 128th overall
Signature Season: Recording 32 saves in 2011 with a 2.37 ERA

As the Phillies made strides to become competitive once more in the early 2000s, one of the pain points that thwarted them on a regular basis, and shut them out of the postseason, was the bullpen. From 2001 through 2003, the Phils pen ranked 28th in K/9 IP and 17th in xFIP. While the Vet helped suppress homers, bad defense and bad arms allowed late leads to fade away.

Enter Mad Dog.

Ryan Madson is one of just seven players to have remained a Phillie during their entire five-year run as NL East champions. Madson had a brief cameo in 2003 with the Phillies before breaking onto the scene for good under Larry Bowa in 2004. In Madson's rookie year, he put up a career-low 2.34 ERA in 77 innings pitched over 52 games. A brief experiment in the starting rotation in 2006 aside, Mad Dog was the Phillies most stable and steady relievers during their 2007-2011 run, posting a 2.89 ERA (37th among relievers) and a 1.192 WHIP, as well the 29th best FIP, and 30th best xFIP.

At various points from 2009 through 2011, Madson would fill the closer role on behalf of the injured Brad Lidge, accumulating 47 saves over those three years. Madson was also a dominant postseason pitcher, posting a 2.31 ERA in 35 innings pitched. Madson threw his last pitches as a Phillie in the 2011 NLDS against Nick Punto of the St. Louis Cardinals, where he struck him out on a 1-2 count. He had not played a game in Major League Baseball until 2015, in part because of recurring elbow issues.

Madson had attempted unsuccessful comebacks in 2012 with the Cincinnati Reds and in 2013 with the Los Angeles Angels of Anaheim before returning to baseball in 2015 with the Kansas City Royals. Madson, as of the release of this book, has been among the AL Central front-runner's top pitchers out of the bullpen.

Top 10 Leaderboard: Innings Pitched by a Phillies Reliever

1. Ron Reed	763.0 IP, 1976-1983
2. Tug McGraw	708.0 IP, 1975-1984
3. Turk Farrell	596.2 IP, 1956-1961, 1967-1969
4. Jack Baldschun	543.1 IP, 1961-1965
5. Ryan Madson	539.0 IP, 2003-2011
6. Huck Betts	530.0 IP, 1920-1925
7. Jim Konstanty	504.2 IP, 1948-1954
8. Jack Meyer	430.0 IP, 1955-1961
9. Gene Garber	392.2 IP, 1974-1978
10. Ricky Bottalico	370.0 IP, 1994-1998, 2001-2002

Top 10 Leaderboard: Strikeouts by a Phillies Reliever

1. Ron Reed	519 K, 1976-1983
2. Ryan Madson	486 K, 2003-2011
3. Tug McGraw	483 K, 1975-1984
4. Jack Baldschun	420 K, 1961-1965
5. Turk Farrell	403 K, 1956-1961, 1967-1969
6. Ricky Bottalico	361 K, 1994-1998, 2001-2002
7. Jack Meyer	357 K, 1955-1961
8. Antonio Bastardo	305 K, 2009-2014
9. Gene Garber	290 K, 1974-1978
10. Jonathan Papelbon	252 K, 2012-2015

Dave Cash

Second Baseman

Years as a Phillie: 1974-1976
Line as a Phillie: .296/.348/.371
fWAR Phillies Rank: 58th among hitters, 96th overall
Signature Achievement: NL All-Star from 1974 through 1976

The Phillies gradual move from basement dweller in the early 70's to bonafide World Series contenders in the late 70's was a result of two dynamics: great drafting and shrewd trades. The Phillies front office had a knack for making trades that made the squad better, even if they were in the smallest increments. One such trade was the acquisition of second baseman Dave Cash from Pittsburgh for pitcher Ken Brett.

While Cash and Brett would play together on the 1974 All-Star squad just a few months after being traded for one another, Cash would have the greater impact. While Cash would spend just three years in Philadelphia, he made the NL All-Star team and earned at least a Top 16 NL MVP finish each year.

During his short stay in Philly, Cash was a defensive force in Philadelphia, ranking third in baseball in FanGraphs' version of defensive runs saved from 1974 through 1976. But it was his offense that turned the heads of most Phillies' fans. Cash struck out an impressively low 3.6% while walking almost twice as frequently (7.0%). Cash was always a threat to put the ball in play, leading all second baseman in singles and triples during his stint with the Phillies while trailing only Rod Carew in hits and ranking sixth in doubles.

In 1976, Cash would be at the top of the line-up for the Phillies return to the postseason after the team's 26 year absence. Cash got the Phillies off to a great start, hitting a double off Don Gullett, later scoring a Mike Schmidt sac fly. Cash would hit .308/.286/.385 but it wouldn't be enough to spark the Phils, who went down in a 3-0 sweep to the Reds.

Following the 1976 season, Cash would leave Philadelphia as a free agent, signing with the Montreal Expos. He would spend three years with Montreal before being traded to San Diego for Bill Almon and Dan Briggs. Cash would be quietly released following Spring Training in 1981 and he retired from the game. After retirement, Cash has severed in a number of coaching roles, including as the first base coach of the 2006 Baltimore Orioles.

Perception is not reality: 1976 Phillies

There is a perceived notion that the 1976 squad, who returned the Phillies to the playoffs after 26 years, was full of home-grown talent, accumulated through shrewd drafting and signing. While their biggest stars, Mike Schmidt, Larry Bowa, and Greg Luzinski among others, were home grown talent, some of their most talented players, like Cash, were acquired from other clubs or signed as free agents.

Ollie Brown – Waivers, Houston, 1974
Steve Carlton – Trade, St. Louis, 1972
Dave Cash – Trade, Pittsburgh, 1973
Gene Garber – Purchased, Kansas City, 1974
Jay Johnstone – FA, St. Louis, 1974
Jim Kaat – Trade, Chicago (AL), 1975
Jim Lonborg – Trade, Milwaukee, 1972
Garry Maddox – Trade, San Francisco, 1975
Tim McCarver – FA, Boston, 1975
Tug McGraw – Trade, New York (NL), 1974
Ron Reed – Trade, St. Louis, 1975
Bobby Tolan – FA, San Diego, 1976

Juan Samuel
#94

Second Baseman, Center Fielder

Years as a Phillie: 1983-1989
Line as a Phillie: .263/.310/.439, 100 HR, 249 SB in 3780 PA
fWAR Phillies Rank: 57th among position players, 93rd overall
Signature Season: Finished second in Rookie of the Year voting in 1984 with 19 triples, 15 homers, 72 steals and a .272/.307/.442 line in an MLB-leading 737 PA.

Juan Samuel manned second base faithfully for the Phillies from 1984 through 1988 after a brief cup of coffee with the club in 1983, including a pair of pinch running appearances and one at-bat in the 1983 World Series against the Baltimore Orioles. For those reading this list who only know "Sammy" as a coach on Ryne Sandberg's coaching staff, Samuel was once free-swinging righty lead-off man that was regularly the Major League leader in at-bats (1984-1985, 1987), triples (1984 and 1987) as well as strikeouts (1984-1987).

From 1984 through 1988, Samuel ranked first in runs, RBIs, triples, and steals among all MLB second baseman and trailed only Sandberg in homers in that same group. While those stats are certainly as eye-popping as his 1984 line as a rookie, context and efficiency are key to assessing Samuel: Samuel was able to compile these counting stats in large part because he was able to remain healthy on teams playing largely meaningless games, aside from 1986, as a young player.

As pretty as those counting stats look during that same stretch, Samuel walked just 5.3% of the time (33rd out of 38 qualified second baseman) and posted a rather horrible .309 OBP (31st out of 38 qualified second baseman), just three points higher than the immortal Chris James and two higher than the equally-immortal Steve Jeltz in that same time span. Another factor working equally as hard against Samuel was his defensive deficiencies: Samuel ranked 37th out of 38 qualified second baseman in FanGraphs' defensive rankings from 1984-1988.

In 1989, Samuel would move to center field and be traded to the rival Mets on June 18, 1989 for Lenny Dykstra, Roger McDowell, and a player to be named later. Samuel would struggle for the contending Mets (.228/.299/.300 to finish the year), as would Dykstra for the Phillies (.222/.297/.330 in 1989), but I think we can agree that trade turned out OK. Samuel would play nine more seasons in the Majors after being traded to the Los Angeles Dodgers prior to the 1990 season. Samuel would make his second NL All Star squad in 1991 before bouncing around in part-time roles with the Royals, Reds, Tigers, Royals again, and the Blue Jays.

Samuel remains one of the most revered Phillies in their franchise history and was an inductee to their Wall of Fame in 2008.

Did You Know

Juan Samuel, one of the most popular players in recent Phillies' history, set numerous records, both good and bad. In 1987, Samuel had double-digit doubles, triples, homers, and steals for the fourth time in each of his first four seasons. Samuel was the first Major Leaguer to accomplish this feat. In that same time frame, however, Samuel tied the MLB record for most consecutive strikeout titles (four).

#93 Billy Wagner

Left-Handed Reliever

Years as a Phillie: 2004-2005
Line as a Phillie: 8-3, 59 saves, 1.86 ERA, 0.810 WHIP in 126 IP
fWAR Phillies Rank: 133rd among pitchers, 281st overall
Signature Season: All-Star in 2005, racking up 38 saves in 41 chances with a 1.51 ERA
Signature Stats: Among Phillies pitchers with at least 100 IP, ranks second in ERA, ninth in FIP, fourth in K/9 IP, and first in WHIP

For much of the ten years proceeding Billy Wagner's arrival in Philadelphia, the Phils had a lot more to worry about than their bullpen. After all, the team ranked a miserable tenth in the NL in runs scored, was the eighth easiest team to strikeout, and struggled with the twelfth best slugging percentage over that period of time.

But as the Phillies offense became proficient at scoring runs, effectively moving the team to fringe contender status, the Phils made a splash by trading for Billy Wagner, the highest paid closer in baseball at that time. The Phils sent Ezequiel Astacio, Taylor Bucholz, and Brandon Duckworth to the Astros and got Wagner in return.

Wagner was electric in his April 7, 2004 debut against the Pirates, striking out the side, and earning his first save with the Phils. Wagner would go on the disabled list following the July 21 game against the Marlins but would return better than he had been before. Wagner would follow up a pretty good 2004 with a great 2005, but he did little to build a relationship with the fans.

"Bring on Billy Boy," said then Phillies' manager Charlie Manuel to an Associated Press reporter in 2006, referring to the now-former Phillies' closer who would be facing his former club for the first time as a member of his new team the Mets. Wagner had become unpopular with Phillies fans after telling the media midway through the 2005 season "(the

Phillies) ain't got a chance" to make the playoffs. He alienated the fans even more when he gave up a 1-1 tie in the ninth inning of a September 6 game against the Houston Astros and then a three-run homer to Craig Biggio the next night, blowing the save and perhaps the season. The Phillies would finish just one game behind the Astros in 2005 for the NL Wild Card.

Despite his misdirected angst, inexplicable mid-season comments challenging the intensity of his own teammates, and his unpopular-with-former-Phillies'-teammates recollection of closed-door team meetings, Wagner threw a 100 MPH fastball and had perhaps the best two seasons in the history of the club for a relief pitcher.

Among all Phillies pitchers with at least 100 IP with the club, he ranks first WHIP, second in ERA, ninth in FIP, and fourth in K/9 IP. He was equal parts brash and dominance with a horrible sense of timing. So despite his missteps as a Phillie on the field that came after the playoff-hungry fans heard his comments about the Phils not having a chance to make the playoffs, his dominance earns him a spot in the Phillies Nation Top 100.

A Year to Remember: 2005

Billy Wagner's 1.51 ERA is the third-lowest of any qualified reliever in team history. Only Roger McDowell's 1989 1.11 mark and Tug McGraw's 1980 1.46 mark were better.

Conversely, the Phillies' record for worst single-season ERA for a qualified reliever was set by Reggie Grabowksi in 1934 when he posted a 9.23 mark in 65.1 IP.

#92 Jim Lonborg

Right-Handed Starter

Years as a Phillie: 1973-1979
Line as a Phillie: 75-60, 3.98 ERA in 1142.1 IP
fWAR Phillies Rank: 38th among pitchers, 95th overall

Jim Lonborg began his 15-year MLB odyssey in 1965 with the Boston Red Sox as a 23-year old rookie. Despite a lowly 9-17 mark with a 4.47 ERA in 31 starts, Lonborg improved in 1966 before catapulting himself to the 1967 AL Cy Young, winning the AL strikeout and wins crowns along the way. Lonborg would win two games in the 1967 World Series with the Red Sox before losing to Bob Gibson and the St. Louis Cardinals in Game 7 in Fenway Park.

Lonborg is the first of a few of what I like to call solid, "compiler" players, players who had played with the Phillies long enough to compile stats that push them into the Phillies' top 100 players of all-time. Lonborg was acquired by the Phillies from the Milwaukee Brewers along with Ken Brett (who had been traded with Lonborg from the Red Sox to the Brewers just one year earlier), Ken Sanders, and Earl Stephenson for Bill Champion, Don Money, the man Mike Schmidt replaced, and John Vukovich.

Lonborg's time as a Phillie coincides with their memorable turnaround from their historically-bad 1972 season: Lonborg would win 75 games from 1973 through the end of his career in 1979, seeing the Phillies jump from 59 to 71 wins from '72 to '73 and then to 80 wins in '74, 86 wins in '75, and, finally, 101 wins in '76. Lonborg played a major role in bringing the Phillies to their first of three straight division titles and their first playoff appearance of any kind since the Whiz Kids in 1950.

Lonborg is tied for 21st in team history in wins, ranks 18th in games started, 29th in innings pitched, and 94th in ERA. You can't tell the story of the Phillies without the story of the 1976 team that finally broke through to the playoffs. And you can't tell the story of the 1976 Phillies without telling the story of Jim Lonborg.

Lonborg would pitch his last game, both for the Phillies and as a Major Leaguer, on June 10, 1979. After retirement, Lonborg went to Tufts University and became a dentist.

So, you retired. Now what?

Jim Lonborg became a dentist after playing Major League baseball. While few Major Leaguers followed his career path, many have moved on to pursue equally ambitions professions.

Here is a list of former Major Leaguers that have made transition into the world of private citizenship, including some Phillies, with their occupations:

Jim Bunning – U.S. Senator
Robin Roberts – President, seafood company
Curt Simmons – Owner, country club
Greg Luzinski – Owner, *Bull's Barbecue*
Stan Lopata – VP of sales, concrete company
Dick Ruthven – CEO, homebuilding company

Note: Reliever Ron Reed, a two-sport star, often jokes that the MLB was his fallback career after a short stint in the NBA with the Detroit Pistons

---

#91 *Larry Jackson*

Right-Handed Starter

Years as a Phillie: 1966-1968
Line as a Phillie: 41-45, 2.95 ERA, 1.178 WHIP in 752.1 IP
fWAR Phillies Rank: 46th among pitchers, 108th overall
Signature Season: Posting a 2.77 ERA and a 1.186 WHIP as a 37 year old pitcher in 243.2 innings in 1967

Larry Jackson is one of just 28 Major Leaguers to come from the great state of Idaho. His 194 career victories not only make him the career leader in wins of anyone who was born in his hometown of Nampa but also of any player born in Idaho.

Nampa is believed have come from the Shoshoni word meaning moccasin or footprint. And for fourteen seasons, Jackson left quite a footprint in the Big Leagues. Jackson won 14 or more games in eight separate seasons before joining the Phillies, leading the 6'1" righty to four NL All-Star appearances, three with St. Louis, one with the Chicago Cubs.

On April 21, 1966, Jackson became the answer to a trivia question that hurts most Phillies fans: who did the Phillies receive in return for future Hall of Fame pitcher Fergie Jenkins in a 1966 mid-season trade? Jackson, a former four-time All-Star, was acquired to try to push the then 4-4 Phillies into the upper echelon of top NL teams just one year after finishing 85-76, 12 games behind the pennant-winning Dodgers.

For two and nine-tenths of a season, Jackson, pitching in his age 36 through 38 seasons, was pretty solid. According to WAR, Jackson, from '66 through '68, was the 16th best pitcher in baseball. In his final season with the Phillies, 1968, Jackson posted a remarkable 2.77 ERA with a 1.186 WHIP as a 38-year old, a remarkable line for a veteran pitcher in the twilight of his career.

For nearly three seasons, Jackson was a top 15 Major League pitcher for a series of Phillies teams ranging from fringe contender (1966's fourth-place, 87-75 squad) to the beginnings of the cellar dweller crews (1968's seventh place, 76-86 team). Jackson was a bright spot in three frustrating years and has become an unfortunate trivia question answer. Jackson certainly deserves more than that.

Jackson became actively involved in politics following his Major League playing days, serving four terms as the Ada County representative in the Idaho House of Representatives.

Did You Know: Phillies Taken in Expansion Drafts

After the 1968 season, Larry Jackson was selected in the October 1968 Expansion Draft by the Montreal Expos. Rather than reporting to Montreal, Jackson chose to retire. The Phillies sent shortstop Bobby Wine as compensation for Jackson retiring. Wine would lead the league in errors at shortstop in 1969 with 31.

Here is a complete list of Phillies that were selected in MLB Expansion Drafts:

1961
Choo Choo Coleman – C (NYM)   Lee Walls – UTL (NYM)
Jesse Hickman – P (HOU)   George Williams – IF (HOU)
Bobby Smith – OF (NYM)

1968
Steve Arlin – P (SDP)   Roberto Pena – SS (SDP)
Tony Gonzalez – OF (SDP)   Gary Sutherland – 2B (MON)
Larry Jackson – P (MON)   Mike Wegener – P (MON)

1992
Andy Ashby – P (COL)   Keith Shepherd – P (COL)
Braulio Castillo – OF (COL)

1997
Jason Boyd – P (ARI)   Ryan Karp – P (TAM)

#90 Lefty O'Doul
Left Fielder

Years as a Phillie: 1929-1930
Line as a Phillie: .391/.460/.614, 54 HR in 1338 PA
fWAR Phillies Rank: 56th among position players, 94th overall
Signature Stat: In his first year as a regular, at age 32, O'Doul hit
.398/.465/.622 with an OPS of 1.087 (fifth best in team history)

Imagine the story of Josh Hamilton's breakout 2008 season with the Rangers. Now make Hamilton 32 instead of 27 and instead of being someone who had battled addiction to get to the Majors, make him a former pitcher who had last seen the Majors six years earlier but stopped throwing because he had a sore arm. And make the season twice as good, one where the player breaks the National League single-season hit record, wins the batting title with a .398 average and posts an incredible 1.087 OPS. Ok, so comparing Lefty O'Doul's meteoric rise to Hamilton is almost a disservice to O'Doul but O'Doul lacks a better "out of nowhere to MVP candidate" comparable.

To put things in further context, in 1923, O'Doul broke the record for most runs given up in a relief appearance (16) although only three runs were earned. Because of soreness in his arm, he went back to the minors to become an outfielder. And what an outfielder he became. In 1928, at age 31, he reached the Majors with the Giants as part of a platoon, hitting .319/.372/.463 with eight homers and nine steals in 390 PA. He was traded to the Phillies, with cash (!), for Freddy Leach, who was pretty solid in his own right.

While Leach would continue to have a solid career (.302/.341/.429 from 1929 through 1932 as a regular), O'Doul would become one of the most feared hitters in baseball. In his first of two seasons with the Phillies, O'Doul would team up with Chuck Klein, Pinky Whitney, and Bernie Friberg to produce the National League's most dangerous offense, as the Phillies led the National League in batting average, on-base percentage, slugging percentage, doubles, and homers. Yet, despite having one of the most potent offenses in MLB history, the 1929 Phillies would finish just 71-82 and fifth in the NL due to disastrous pitching.

O'Doul would hit .383/.453/.604 with 22 homers in 606 PA for the Phils in 1930 as a 33-year old third-year player, just his second year as a regular. Despite once again having one of the best offenses in baseball, the Phillies would finish 52-112 in 1930 and O'Doul would be traded for Clise Dudley (an average starting pitcher), Jumbo Elliot (a pitcher who would lead the NL in wins in 1931 with the Phillies with 19), and Hal Lee (a left fielder who would hit .303/.343/.497 with 18 homers in 1932, his first and only full season with the Phillies).

Due to his already advanced age, O'Doul would play only five more seasons, hitting .333/.396/.502 with 51 homers in 1852 post-Phillies plate appearances. O'Doul possesses the distinction of having the highest career batting average of any player not enshrined in the Baseball Hall of Fame. O'Doul was, however, inducted into the Japanese Baseball Hall of Fame for his efforts as a baseball ambassador in Japan before and after World War II and remains an incredibly popular figure in his hometown, San Francisco, CA.

Top 10 Phillies Leaderboard: wRC+, min 500 PA

wRC+ is a stat that measures the amount of runs created while adjusting for park effects and measuring against league average. A league average player's wRC+ is 100.

1. Roger Connor	155 wRC+, 1892
2. Dick Allen	152 wRC+, 1963-1969, 1975-1976
3. Gavvy Cravath	152 wRC+, 1912-1920
4. Billy Hamilton	152 wRC+, 1890-1895
5. Lefty O'Doul	151 wRC+, 1929-1930
6. Elmer Flick	150 wRC+, 1898-1901
7. Mike Schmidt	147 wRC+, 1972-1989
8. Ed Delahanty	145 wRC+, 1888-1889, 1891-1901
9. Bobby Abreu	139 wRC+, 1998-2006
10. Sherry Magee	139 wRC+, 1904-1914

Kid Gleason

Starting Pitcher, Second Baseman

Years as a Phillie: 1888-1891, 1903-1908
Line as a Phillie: 78-70, 3.39 ERA, 1.380 WHIP in 1328.2 IP
.246/.296/.297, 2 HR in 3191 PA
fWAR Phillies Rank: 25th among pitchers, 73rd overall
Signature Achievements: Single-season franchise record holder for wins in a season, last Phillies pitcher to pitch over 500 (!) innings in a season, last Phillies pitcher to start 50 (!) games or more in a season. One of only 29 players to play a Major League game in four decades.

Gleason is the first Top 100 Phillie to have played for the franchise when the club was known as the Quakers. The turn-of-the-century second baseman holds the distinction of having the least amount of home runs of any position player to make the list. In fact, pitcher Steve Carlton (9) had more in his career and Rick Wise (6 in 1971) had more in one season than Gleason had in his entire career.

But, wait – if you said Gleason was a horrible second baseman:

A). Why did he make the list?

B). Why are his pitching statistics listed?

C). Why would you say he is a franchise-record holder in pitching categories?

Before Kid Gleason emerged as one of the MLB's least productive second baseman (aside: he produced less value at the plate than Ron Reed, the reliever, did), he was a fine pitcher. Gleason set the franchise single-season record for wins with 38 in 1890 and pitched a combined 924 innings between 1890 and 1891.

Gleason was a pitcher first, toeing the rubber during his first stint in Philly. "Kid" left Philadelphia following the 1891 season, jumping to the St. Louis Browns. Gleason would then be sold to the Baltimore Orioles during the 1894 season. It was during the 1895 season that Gleason would take the field as a full-time infielder. Gleason would join the Giants then the Tigers and then return to the Phillies for the 1903 campaign before wrapping up his career in 1912 by playing one game for the Chicago White Sox.

Aside from being a Quaker and a Phillie, Gleason has a number of other local ties: Gleason was born in Camden, New Jersey and died in Philadelphia in 1933. Nicknamed Kid for his 5'7" height and affable personality, Gleason later managed the 1918 Chicago White Sox, infamously nicknamed "The Black Sox". Gleason was cleared of any connection to the alleged throwing of the World Series and would return to coach in 1923 under Philadelphia A's manager Connie Mack, where he would help coach the team to back-to-back World Series victories in 1929 and 1930.

Top 10 Phillies Leaderboard: **Innings Pitched in a Single Season**

Gleason is just one of five Phillies to pitch over 400 innings in a season. Below are the pitchers that racked up the most innings in a single season for the Phils in club history.

1. John Coleman	538.1 IP, 1883
2. Kid Gleason	506.0 IP, 1890
3. Gus Weyhing	469.2 IP, 1892
4. Ed Daily	440.0 IP, 1885
5. Kid Gleason	418.0 IP, 1891
6. Charlie Ferguson	416.2 IP, 1884
7. Charlie Ferguson	405.0 IP, 1885
8. Charlie Buffinton	400.1 IP, 1888
9. Charlie Ferguson	395.2 IP, 1886
10. Dan Casey	390.1 IP, 1887

#88 John Denny

Right-Handed Starter

Years as a Phillie: 1982-1985
Line as a Phillie: 37-29, 2.96 ERA, 1.225 WHIP
fWAR Phillies Rank: 35th among pitchers, 91st overall
Signature Achievements: Won NL Cy Young in 1983 with 19-6 record and 2.37

Let's get this out of the way first: the mustache was very popular in the early 1980s and John Denny had a mustache that could compete with anyone, including Burt Reynolds, Tom Selleck and even Mike Schmidt. That being said, Denny was a pretty good pitcher, too. Whether or not he was powered by his mustache is still the subject of "fierce" debate.

From 1974 through 1982, Denny was a league average pitcher. Prior to the 1980 campaign, Denny was traded with Jerry Mumphrey from the St. Louis Cardinals to Cleveland for Bobby Bonds. Prior to becoming a Phillie, Denny's career highlight was winning the NL ERA crown in 1976 with the St. Louis Cardinals.

In one of the best trades in Phillies history, Denny was traded to the Phillies on September 12, 1982 for Wil Culmer, Jerry Reed, and Roy Smith. All three would reach the Major Leagues but Denny would have the biggest impact by far. When Denny was acquired, the Phillies ended the night a half-game up on the eventual NL East champion Cardinals. The trade was too little, too late for the 1982 Phillies, who were scrambling to fill the vacancy left by an injury to Marty Bystrom and avoiding using the below-average Ed Farmer as a starter. But the trade paid off in spades a year later for the 1983 Phillies.

Denny pitched a season for the ages, perhaps the best single season of any Phillie in the 1980s other than Steve Carlton's 1980 campaign, winning the Cy Young along the way and leading the Phillies into the playoffs. Denny would lose Game 2 of the NLCS against the Dodgers but rebounded to win Game 1 of the World Series against the Baltimore Orioles 2-1 after holding Baltimore to just a Jim Dwyer first-inning homer. From 1983 through 1985, Denny had the tenth best ERA and 27th best WHIP in the National League, outpacing teammate Steve Carlton in both categories.

Denny would be traded on December 11, 1985 with Jeff Gray to Cincinnati for Tom Hume and Gary Redus. Hume had a standout relief campaign for the Phillies (4-1, 2.77 ERA in 48 appearances) while Redus fizzled in left field. Denny would pitch just one more season, 1986, posting a 4.20 ERA against an 11-10 mark. Denny retired after the 1986 season, finishing his career with 123 wins and a solid 3.59 ERA.

Pitchers with Hardware

In 1983, Denny became just the second Phillie ever to win the NL Cy Young award. Here is a list of Phillies pitchers that have brought home the prestigious award:

Steve Carlton (1972, '77, '80, '82)
John Denny (1983)
Steve Bedrosian (1987)
Roy Halladay (2010)

#87 *Pinky Whitney*

Third Baseman

Years as a Phillie: 1928-1933, 1936-1939
Line as a Phillie: .307/.357/.432, 69 HR, 34 SB in 4768 PA
fWAR Phillies Rank: 53rd among position players, 83rd overall
Signature Season: Hit .327/.390/.482 with 8 HR and 7 steals in 1929

From the 1930s until the 1960s, there wasn't much debate as to who the greatest third baseman in Phillies' history was. From 1928 through 1933, Arthur "Pinky" Whitney was in a class of Pie Traynor, Woody English, and Freddie Lindstrom, the best third basemen in all of baseball. He led Phillies third basemen in almost all statistical categories until Dick Allen and Mike Schmidt took their respective places in Phillies history.

Whitney spent parts of 10 seasons with the Phillies, his first stint lasting from 1928 through 1933 before he was traded to the Boston Braves with Hal Lee for Fritz Knothe and Wes Schulmerich on June 17. In Whitney's first run with the Phils, he earned MVP votes in his first two seasons, placing 18th as a rookie and 20th in his sophomore seasons.

Even though the 1929 Philadelphia Athletics won the World Series, the 1929 Philadelphia Phillies arguably had the best offense in baseball. Ranking first in every triple slash category as well as hits and homers, Whitney was an anchor in a line-up that destroyed opposing pitching. Unfortunately for those Phillies, opposing hitters rendered their pitching ineffective, culminating in a disappointing 71-82 season.

When Whitney was traded back to the Phillies 10 games into the 1936 season for Mickey Haslin, Whitney made his first NL All Star squad, becoming the first Phillies third baseman to start for the NL at the Mid-Summer Classic. He would hit a murderous .341/.395/.446 in 1937, earning a 13th place MVP finish before quietly transitioning to first base for the 1939 campaign. Whitney would play his last game, as both a Phillie and Major Leaguer, on September 5, 1939.

The Hot Corner at the Mid-Summer Classic

Whitney was the first Phillie third baseman to not only make the National League All-Star team but to earn a starting role. He was the first in a long line of third baseman to crack the ranks of the NL's best:

Pinky Whitney (1936*)
Pinky May (1940)
Puddin' Head Jones (1950*, 1951)
Dick Allen (1965*, 1966, 1967*)
Mike Schmidt (1974, 1976, 1977, 1979*, 1980, 1981*, 1982*, 1983*, 1984*, 1986*, 1987*, 1989)
Dave Hollins (1993)
Scott Rolen (2002*)
Placido Polanco (2011*)

*indicates selection as All-Star starter

#86 Don Hurst

First Baseman

Years as a Phillie: 1928-1933, 1936-1939
Line as a Phillie: .307/.357/.432, 69 HR, 34 SB in 4768 PA
fWAR Phillies Rank: 51st among position players, 82nd overall
Signature Achievement: Ranks 15th in Phillies history in OBP, 20th in OPS, and ninth in wOBA
Signature Season: Finished seventh in the 1932 MVP voting, led the National League in RBIs

Former Ohio State Buckeye Don Hurst was acquired from the St. Louis Cardinals with Spud Davis and Homer Peel on May 11, 1928. Two days later, Hurst made his Major League debut at age 22. Hurst would have a strong rookie campaign, 19 HR with a .285/.391/.508 line for a team that won 43 games, and an even stronger sophomore campaign, 31 HR while hitting .304/.390/.525 for the improved 71-win squad.

Hurst was the primary first baseman on the historic 1929 Phillies squad that scored the fifth most runs in a single-season of any National League team but was so void of pitching that the club only won 71 games. Despite the team's general lack of success, Hurst took advantage of the Baker Bowl's short right field porch, slugging 112 homers over seven seasons, most over the 280 feet right field wall.

The Maysville, KY native was among the top NL first baseman from 1928-1934, ranking comparably to George Grantham and Jim Bottomley. In 1934, Hurst was traded for Dolph Camilli in what was a win for the Phillies. Camilli would go on to have four excellent years for the Phillies while Hurst would crawl to the finish line with the Cubs (.199 BA with just 3 homers in the last 51 games) and retire after the season ended.

The Phillies have deep roots in the state of Kentucky: 29 former Phillies were born in the Bluegrass State.

Rabbit Benton (1922, 2B)
Joe Blanton (2008-2012, SP)
Earl Browne (1937-1938, 1B)
Roy Bruner (1939-1941, RP)
Jim Bunning (1964-1967, 1970-1971, SP)
Paul Byrd (1999-2001, SP)
Howie Camnitz (1913, SP)
Bob Conley (1958, SP)
Joe Cowley (1987, SP)
Denny Doyle (1970-1973, 2B)
Woodie Fryman (1968-1972, SP)
Earl Grace (1936-1937, C)
John Grim (1888, 2B)
George Harper (1924-1926, OF)
Ed Holley (1932-1934, SP)

Rudy Hulswitt (1902-1904, 2B)
Don Hurst (1928-1934, 1B)
Irv Jeffries (1934, 2B)
Fred Koster (1931, OF)
Trever Miller (2000, RP)
Randy O'Neal (1989, RP)
John O'Neil (1946, SS)
Frank Pearce (1933-1935, RP)
Hugh Poland (1947, C)
Don Robinson (1992, SP)
Billy Sorrell (1965, SS)
Lee Tinsley (1996, LF)
Dave Watkins (1969, Util.)
Gus Weyhing (1892-1895, SP)

Dolph Camilli

First Baseman

Years as a Phillie: 1934 – 1937
Line as a Phillie: .295/.395/.510, 92 HR, 23 SB in 2322 PA
fWAR Phillies Rank: 52nd among position players, 81st overall
Signature Achievement: Ranks eighth in Phillies history in OBP, tenth in OPS, and ninth in wOBA

And directly following Don Hurst is his replacement, the man he was traded for.

Camilli was a 5'10" slugging lefty first baseman who was the shining star on four Phillies teams that were a combined 235-374. Despite the team's lack of success, Camilli was among the franchise's finest first basemen, firmly entrenched just behind Lou Gehrig, Jimmie Foxx, and Hank Greenberg among the best first basemen in baseball.

Camilli was a late bloomer, spending eight seasons in the minor leagues before the Cubs finally called up the then-26 year old near the conclusion of the 1933 season. On June 11, 1934 Camilli was sent to Philadelphia in an even swap of first baseman.

During his time with the Phillies, Camilli trailed only Ripper Collins in FanGraphs' version of WAR among National League first basemen and would receive MVP votes in 1935 and 1936 despite the teams' disappointing records. Camilli, for a long time, was the standard against which other Phillies' first baseman were judged and he still ranks eighth in Phillies history in OBP, tenth in OPS, ninth in wOBA, and tenth in ISO.

Camilli usually ranked middle of the road in range at first base but posted the highest fielding percentage in 1937, his last year with the Phillies. He would be traded to the Brooklyn Dodgers for Eddie Morgan on March 6, 1938. Camilli would drive in 100 or more runs four out of his first five seasons, including an NL-best 120 in 1941. Camilli would be selected to two All-Star teams with the Brooklyn Dodgers, win the 1941 NL MVP, and retire with the most strikeouts in NL history.

Camilli made such an impression in Brooklyn that he was inducted into their Hall of Fame in 1984. After the slugger's playing days were over, he became a scout first for the Yankees and, later, the Angels.

Phillies' Top 10: OPS or On-Base Plus Slugging, Career

An increasingly popular stat to measure the ability to get on base and hit for power is On-Base Plus Slugging. The measurement is simple: add the player's on-base percentage and slugging. The Phillies' Top 10 is filled with familiar names. Camilli retired with the fifth-highest mark in team history and now sits ninth.

1. Lefty O'Doul   1.074, 1929-1930
2. Chuck Klein   .935, 1928-1933, 1936-1939, 1940-1944
3. Bobby Abreu   .928, 1998-2006
4. Billy Hamilton   .928, 1890-1895
5. Jim Thome   .925, 2003-2005
6. Ed Delahanty   .923, 1888-1889, 1891-1901
7. Mike Schmidt   .907, 1972-1989
8. Elmer Flick   .907, 1898-1901
9. Dolph Camilli   .905, 1934-1937
10. George Harper   .904, 1924-1926

#84 Jim Thome

First Baseman

Years as a Phillie: 2003-2005, 2012
Line as a Phillie: .260/.384/.541, 101 HR in 1629 PA
fWAR Phillies Rank: 70th among position players, 127th overall
Signature Stats: Ranks first in ISO in franchise history, 13th in OBP, fourth in slugging, fifth in OPS, and 12th in wRC+
Signature Season: Tied for MLB lead in homers in 2003, finishing fourth in NL MVP voting

If the original Yankee Stadium was "the House that Ruth Built," Citizens Bank Park might as well be the "House That Jim Built." Sure, the affable Thome had arrived one year prior to the park's opening and the plans had already been unveiled by designer Stanley Cole at a ceremony on June 28, 2001. Nevertheless, Thome's free agency signing marked the Phillies' biggest free agent signing since perhaps the arrival of Pete Rose in 1979 and he came just in time for the closing of the Vet.

Thome came to Philadelphia after spending parts of 12 seasons in Cleveland where "Gentleman Jim" was a three time All-Star and a recipient of MVP votes five times. In addition to his power stroke, Thome twice led the American League in walks.

Thome tied Alex Rodriguez for the Major League lead in homers in his first season, smashing 47 homers, falling one short of Mike Schmidt's club record. Thome would raise his triple-slash line across the board while striking out 38 times less, earning a 2004 All-Star birth in the Phillies first season in CBP. A mid-season elbow injury cost Thome over half of 2005 and he was traded after the season in favor of then-Rookie of the Year Ryan Howard starting at first base.

Thome would return as a free agent in 2012, memorably hitting a walk-off homer off of Jake McGee on June 23 to win the game. In 2012, Thome became the fourth Major Leaguer to hit 100 homers with three different teams.

Though Thome had one of the shorter stays among players to make this list and never reached the playoffs as a member of the Phillies, he was instrumental in jump-starting a fan base that was slowly reawakening from the dreck of the late 1990s. "Gentleman Jim's" power numbers are comparable to anyone in Phillies history, including Schmidt, Chuck Klein, and Ed Delahanty.

The Park That Jim Built

Jim Thome hit his 400th career home run on June 14, 2004, an 0-2 blast to left-center off of Cincinnati Reds pitcher Jose Acevedo. It wasn't the first home run in CBP; no, that belonged to Bobby Abreu. Here are some important firsts:

First Pitch: Randy Wolf
First Hit: D'Angelo Jimenez, Reds
First Phillies' Hit: Bobby Abreu
First Homer: Bobby Abreu
First Phillies' Win: April 15, 2004 v. Reds
First Playoff Game: October 3, 2007 v. Rockies
First Playoff Win: October 1, 2008 v. Brewers
First NLCS Game: October 9, 2008 v. Dodgers
First World Series Series Win: October 27, 2008 v. Rays

Schoolboy Rowe

Right-Handed Starter

Years as a Phillie: 1943, 1946-1949
Line as a Phillie: 52-39, 3.54 ERA, 1.234 WHIP in 744 IP
fWAR Phillies Rank: 30th among pitchers, 80th overall
Signature Season: 11-4 with 2.12 ERA and 0.978 WHIP in 1946, returning to the MLB after serving in the Navy in World War II

The 6'4" affable Lynwood Thomas Rowe was a nationally-known, bonafide heart-throb in the 1930s. The country knew of Rowe, his calm, Southern accent, his infatuation with his fiancé Edna, and his superstitions, which included talking to the ball and only picking up his glove with his left hand.

Rowe was twice an All-Star with the Detroit Tigers (1935, 1936), winning 62 games over a three year span (1934-1936). Rowe was durable, relying on groundball outs to retire hitters, averaging 262 innings pitched over his dominant three-year stretch while only striking out 4.6 K/9 IP. Rowe battled a number of injuries after 1936 before returning full-time in 1940, posting a 16-3 record with a 3.46 ERA.

Rowe came to the Phillies in 1943 after two All-Star appearances and a World Series win with the Tigers in 1935. He posted a 2.94 ERA with a 14-8 mark in his first year with the Phillies before leaving the club to serve in the Navy during World War II.

Rowe returned rejuvenated in 1946, posting an 11-4 record with a 2.12 ERA and a 0.978 WHIP and was an All-Star for the club in 1947. Rowe ranks 58th among Phillies pitchers in ERA but 34th in FIP. Despite being a fantastic pitcher, Rowe never dominated opponents, particularly in his time with the Phillies, posting an incredibly-low 3.0 K/9 IP. Rowe was the clear ace on the staffs of the late 1940s and, while he wasn't a particularly big strikeout artist, he posted the lowest BB/9 IP in the Majors from 1943 through 1949.

What's in a (nick) name?

Lynwood Rowe was best known by his nickname, *Schoolboy*. The Phillies have a long history of players with great nicknames. Check them out below:

Antonio Alfonseca – "El Pulpo" (The Octopus)
Larry Andersen – "LA"
Richie Ashburn – "Putt Putt" and "Whitey"
Steve Bedrosian – "Bedrock"
Larry Bowa – "Gnat"
Pat Burrell – "Pat the Bat"
Steve Carlton – "Lefty"
Clifford Cravath – "Gavvy"
Darren Daulton – "Dutch"
Lenny Dykstra – "Dude" and "Nails"
Roy Halladay – "Doc"
Cole Hamels – "Hollywood"
Ryan Howard – "The Big Piece"
Willie Jones – "Puddin' Head"
John Kruk – "Krukker"
Brad Lidge – "Lights Out"
Greg Luzinski – "The Bull"
Garry Maddox – "The Secretary of Defense"
Ryan Madson – "Mad Dog"
Bake McBride – "Shake 'n' Bake"
Frank McGraw – "Tug"
Gary Matthews – "Sarge"
Lee Meadows – "Specs"
Mickey Morandini – "Dandy Little Glove Man"
Jimmy Rollins – "J-Rol"
Lynwood Rowe – "Schoolboy"
Carlos Ruiz – "Chooch"
Mike Schmidt – "Schmidty"
Jack Taylor – "Brewery Jack"
Kent Tekulve – "Teke"
Milt Thompson – "Uncle Milty"
Chase Utley – "The Man"
Shane Victorino – "The Flyin' Hawaiian"
John Vukovich – "Vuk"
Gus Weyhing – "Rubber-Winged Gus"
Arthur Whitney – "Pinky"
Mitch Williams – "Wild Thing"

Jamie Moyer

Left-Handed Starter

Years as a Phillie: 2006-2010
Line as a Phillie: 56-40, 4.55 ERA, 1.315 WHIP in 720.2 IP
fWAR Phillies Rank: 83rd among pitchers, 175th overall
Signature Moment: Selling-out in Game Three of the 2008 World Series to try to get Carl Crawford out
Signature Game: Becoming the oldest Major Leaguer to ever throw a complete-game shutout on May 7, 2010 against the Braves

In 2006, the former Souderton Indian, Class of 1981, was traded to the Phillies on August 22. The move, at the time, was a bit of a head-scratcher: the Phillies had dealt third baseman David Bell on July 28 to the Brewers and pitcher Corey Lidle and outfielder Bobby Abreu to the New York Yankees on July 30. The Phillies, who went 15-8 after trading Bell, Lidle, and Abreu, were suddenly in the thick of the Wild Card race.

A 43-year old pitcher seemed not to be the remedy to keep their roll going. On August 23, Moyer would win his first start with the Phillies and, while the Phillies would miss the Wild Card by just three games in 2006, the addition of Moyer would become a key catalyst to their 2008 World Series win.

Moyer found ways to win 56 games with the Phillies despite striking few out (ranking 187th out of 234 eligible pitchers in K/9 IP from 2006 through 2010), giving up a lot of homers (19th out of 234 in HR/9 IP), and allowing a fair amount of earned runs scored (153rd in ERA). Despite a somewhat unimpressive record, Moyer earned his place on this list because he was a starter on four of the best Phillies teams, a World Series-winning 2008 squad, and defied age night after night in red pinstripes.

There was no more goose-bump-inducing moment in my Phillies-watching lifetime than seeing Jamie Moyer, toe the rubber for a pivotal Game 3 of the 2008 World Series. Taking the mound just a few days after giving up six earned runs in less than two innings in Los Angeles for the NLCS, Moyer held the hot-hitting Rays in check, giving up only three earned, earning a no decision in a 5-4 Phillies win.

While with the Phillies, Moyer became the oldest player to throw a complete game, a complete game shutout, to earn a winning decision, and to hit an RBI. He would break his own records, and more, in 2012 in a stint with the Rockies. The kid from Souderton making it big in his hometown on the biggest possible stage makes Moyer a consensus Top 100 Phillie of All-Time.

Age is Only a Number

Jamie Moyer was the oldest player ever to suit up for the Phillies. Moyer, who broke Kaiser Wilhelm's mark in 2010, is part of a select group of players who have contributed to the Phillies after age 40.

Jamie Moyer, P – 47, 2010
Kaiser Wilhelm, P – 47, 1921
Jerry Koosman, P – 44, 1985
Grover Cleveland, P – 43, 1930
Pete Rose, 1B – 42, 1983
Larry Andersen, P – 41, 1994
Steve Carlton, P – 41, 1986
Jose Mesa, P – 41, 2007

Dan Plesac, P – 41, 2003
Kent Tekulve, P – 41, 1988
Tom Gordon, P – 40, 2008
Oscar Judd, P – 40, 1948
Jim Kaat, P – 40, 1979
Ron Reed, P – 40, 1983
Tom Zachary, P – 40, 1936

#81 Lee Meadows

Right-Handed Starter

Years as a Phillie: 1919-1923
Line as a Phillie: 48-61, 3.65 ERA, 1.394 WHIP in 856.1 IP
fWAR Phillies Rank: 27th among pitchers, 77th overall
Signature Stat: Pitched 68 complete games in four full seasons

Lee Meadows was signed by the St. Louis Cardinals as a free agent in 1913 and quickly dominated Class D ball with the Durham Bulls. After going 21-14 with a 1.85 ERA as an 18-year old and 19-12 with a 1.86 ERA as a 19-year old, Meadows would reach the Majors as a 20-year old with the Red Birds, posting a 13-11 mark with a 2.99 ERA with 14 complete games as a rookie.

Meadows was frequently a hard-luck loser with the Cardinals, going 52-67 with a 3.00 ERA in 134 starts, 58 of them, complete games. In fact, Meadows had such bad luck with the Cardinals that he led the NL in losses in 1916 despite posting a 2.58 ERA.

Meadows, known as "Specs" for his Teddy Roosevelt-like glasses, arrived in Philadelphia on July 14, 1919 in a fortuitous trade for the Fightin' Phillis. While in Philadelphia, Meadows was a complete game machine, averaging 17 complete games per season. The durable Meadows pitched the 19th most innings in the Majors from 1919 through 1924 with the 44th best ERA, and 24th most wins.

Meadows was traded to Pittsburgh on May 23, 1923 for Whitey Glazer and Cotton Tierney. In a slight reversal of fortune, Meadows would lead the National League in wins with 20 in 1925 with a 3.97 ERA for the Pirates en route to a National League pennant and a World Series victory. Meadows would go 19-10 for the 1927 Pirates, leading the NL in complete games with 25 while leading the Pirates to another pennant. The Pirates, however, would fall to New York Yankees in four games.

Despite his early bad luck with the Cardinals and the Phillies, Meadows would finish his career with a record of 188-180 and a 3.37 ERA.

Bottom 10: Most Losses in a Season

Meadows often found himself a hard-luck loser even after pitching solid complete game outings. Here are the Phillies who posted the most losses in single-seasons, perhaps victims of the same bad luck that seemed to plague Meadows.

1. John Coleman   48, 1883
2. Charlie Ferguson   25, 1884
3. Chick Fraser   24, 1904
4. Ed Daily   23, 1885
5T. Eppa Rixey   22, 1920
5T. Hugh Mulcahy   22, 1940
5T. Tom Vickery   22, 1890
5T. Kid Gleason   22, 1891
5T. Robin Roberts   22, 1957
10. Five tied with 21

#80 Jim Fogarty
Outfielder

Years as a Phillie: 1884-1889
Line as a Phillie: .247/.331/.341, 16 HR, 289 SB in 2849 PA
fWAR Phillies Rank: 39th among position players, 56th among Phillies
Signature Accomplishment: Retired as the All-Time Phillies steals leader (currently fifth)
Signature Season: Hit 12 triples, 8 homers, stole 102 bases with .261/.376/.410 line while leading NL in plate appearances and outfield assists, and second in put outs.

Outfielder Jim Fogarty may have only played six seasons with the then-Philadelphia Quakers but he certainly left his mark. Fogarty made his debut with the club at age 20 in 1884 and hit a poor .212/.251/.283 but would become one of the early stars of the Quakers. In his signature season, 1887, Fogarty would lead the National League in plate appearances with 587, hitting 12 triples, eight homers, and stealing 102 bases with a .261/.376/.410 line.

From 1884 through 1889, Fogarty ranked sixth in baseball in steals, 22nd in BB%, and fifth in FanGraphs' version of base running value. According to FanGraphs' defensive metrics, Fogarty was the most valuable defender from 1884-1889, leading the National League in assists in 1887 and 1889, put outs in 1885 and 1889, range factor in 1884 and 1885, and fielding % in 1889. Fogarty was a speedy outfielder whose quickness was eventually lost to the hands of time but was one of the club's best defensive outfielders and one of the best on the base paths.

As quickly as Fogarty's star burst on to the scene, it faded nearly as quickly. Fogarty became a player-manager of the Philadelphia Athletics of the Players League in 1890 after leaving the Phillies following the 1889 season. Fogarty became ill in 1891 and died from tuberculosis at age 27 on May 20, 1891.

Phillies' Top 10: Most Steals in a Season

Jim Fogarty was one of two Phillies to steal over 100 bases in a season. Here are the Phillies with the Top 10 most steals in a single season.

1. Billy Hamilton   111, 1891
2. Jim Fogarty   102, 1887
3. Billy Hamilton   102, 1890
4. Jim Fogarty   99, 1889
5. Billy Hamilton   98, 1894
6. Billy Hamilton   97, 1895
7. Juan Samuel   72, 1984
8. Ed Delahanty   58, 1898
9. Jim Fogarty   58, 1888
10. Tie: Hamilton (1892), Ed Andrews (1887) - 57

#79 Tony Taylor

Second Baseman, Third Baseman

Years as a Phillie: 1960-1971, 1974-1976
Line as a Phillie: .261/.322/.346, 51 HR, 169 SB
fWAR Phillies Rank: 49th among position players, 74th overall
Signature Season: Hit .287/.330/.370 with 4 HR in 1960 All-Star campaign
Signature Moment: Made signature defensive play that preserved Jim Bunning's 1964 perfect game

Tony Taylor was signed by the New York Giants as an amateur free agent from Cuba in 1954. The Chicago Cubs plucked Taylor from the Giants farm system on December 2, 1957 in the Rule 5 draft. While Taylor came up through the Giants' ranks as third baseman, Taylor found a home in the Majors with the Cubs as their everyday second baseman.

After the first 19 games of 1960, the Phillies traded Ed Bouchee and Don Cardwell to Chicago for Taylor. Taylor's speed was his biggest asset in his first run with the Phillies, ranking Top 10 in the NL in steals seven out of his first 12 seasons with the club and Top 10 in SB success rate in five out of his first 12 years with the Phils.

Taylor was traded by the Phillies on June 12, 1971 to the Detroit Tigers in exchange for Carl Cavanaugh and Michael Fremuth, neither of whom would reach the Majors. Taylor would reach the postseason for the first time in his career in 1972 with the Tigers, hitting just .133 in 15 PA in a 3-2 series loss to the Oakland A's.

Taylor returned to the Fightins prior to the 1974 season as a free agent. In parts of 15 seasons with the Fightins, Taylor was on a number of mediocre teams before finally breaking through into the playoffs with the club as a reserve during his second stint with the club in 1976. At age 40, Taylor played his final game with the Phillies on September 29, 1976. He did not make an appearance in the playoffs.

Taylor was inducted onto the Phillies Wall of Fame in 2002, having, at that time, played the most games at second base in Phillies' history. While Taylor ranks fourth among Phillies second baseman in homers and second in steals, he makes this list based on his connection with the fans and longevity.

Taylor would go on to be on Phillies' coaching staffs from 1977 through 1979 and again from 1988 through 1989. He would be a minor league manager in the Phillies system from 1982 through 1987, managing a variety of teams including the Oklahoma City 89ers in 1982 and the Reading Phillies in 1985. Taylor found little success as a manager (285-416, .407 winning percentage) before retiring from the role after the 1987 season where he managed the Utica Blue Sox of the New York-Penn League.

Phillies' Top 10: Most Steals by a Second Baseman, Career

Taylor torched teams on the basepaths. Here's how he stacked up among Phillies second basemen in steals.

1. Juan Samuel — 249, 1983-1989
2. Tony Taylor — 169, 1960-1971, 1974-1976
3. Bill Hallman — 155, 1888-1889, 1892-1897, 1901-1903
4. Chase Utley — 142, 2003-2015
5. Otto Knabe — 122, 1907-1913
6. Mickey Morandini — 103, 1990-1997, 2000
7. Kid Gleason — 88, 1888-1891, 1903-1908
8. Nap Lajoie — 87, 1896-1900
9. Fresco Thompson — 61, 1927-1930
10. Al Myers — 60, 1885, 1889-1891

Mickey Doolan

Shortstop

Years as a Phillie: 1905-1913
Line as a Phillie: .236/.282/.313, 11 HR, 119 SB
fWAR Phillies Rank: 46th among position players, 69th overall
Signature Accomplishment: Led MLB in assists and double-plays turned five times

"Doc" Doolan was drafted from the Jersey City Baseball Club by the Phillies in September 1904 in the original version of the Rule 5 Draft. A defensive wizard from Ashland, PA and an alumnus of Villanova University, Doolan (frequently, and seemingly interchangeably-spelled Doolin) led the MLB in assists and double plays in five seasons with the Phillies, receiving MVP votes in 1911 and 1913.

Doolan's .236 batting average wasn't particularly impressive, nor was his .282 on-base percentage or his .313 slugging. In fact, his .595 OPS ranks just nine points ahead of perennial Phillies punching bag Steve Jeltz. Doolan's strengths, however, were not found in his bat: instead, he was a speedy defensive wizard who patrolled the Phillies infield for nine seasons.

Doolan ranks third among Phillies' shortstops in stolen bases and was one of the premier shortstops in the National League in his time with the Phils, a clear step below Honus Wagner and Joe Tinker, but above the rest.

Doolan makes the list based on a few factors, the primary of which are his time with the Phillies and defensive consistency. Doolan has the fourth most games and plate appearances at shortstop in Phillies history.

Phillies' Top 10: Highest Defensive Value, Career

Doolan was one of the best defenders in club history. According to *FanGraphs*, he provided the fifth-most defensive value in team history among non-pitchers.

1. Mike Schmidt	3B
2. Larry Bowa	SS
3. Jimmy Rollins	SS
4. Chase Utley	2B
5. Mickey Doolan	SS
6. Clay Dalrymple	C
7. Carlos Ruiz	C
8. Garry Maddox	CF
9. Granny Hamner	SS
10. Richie Ashburn	CF

Phillies' Bottom 10: Lowest OPS in Club History

Mickey Doolan struggled to get on base and hit for power, producing the 13th worst OPS in team history. Here are 10 of the players that were even worse:

1. Mike Ryan	.534, 1968-1973
2. Charlie Bastian	.539, 1885-1888, 1891
3. Del Young	.545, 1937-1940
4. Bill Killefer	.557, 1911-1917
5. Bobby Wine	.559, 1960-1968
6. Ted Kazanski	.568, 1953-1958
7. George Scharein	.571, 1937-1940
8. Red Dooin	.572, 1902-1914
9. Bobby Bragan	.576, 1940-1942
10. Steve Jeltz	.586, 1983-1989

John Titus

Right Fielder

Years as a Phillie: 1903-1912
Line as a Phillie: .278/.368/.379, 31 HR, 131 SB in 5818 PA
fWAR Phillies Rank: 18th among position players, 26th overall
Signature Accomplishment: Seven top-10 finishes in HBP

"Silent John" Titus did not play professional baseball until age 27, starting his career with the Class B Concord Marines. The St. Clair, PA native would play just 30 games with the Marines, hitting .407 with 2 homers and 8 triples before being purchased by the Phillies on June 3, 1903.

Titus was a veritable power-house at the turn of the century, hitting 31 homers as a Phillie from 1903-1912, retiring sixth all-time on the club leader board in that category, with the seventh-best on-base percentage, and ninth-best slugging percentage. Titus, a 5'9", 156 lbs. lefty in right field was not afraid of walking. In fact, he walked 10.6% of the time when with the Phillies, third best among right fielders in the Majors from 1903 through 1912.

Modern advanced stats look very favorably on Titus due, in no small part, to his .372 OBP, fifth best among right fielders from 1903 through 1912, but his defensive numbers and the lack of team success during his time with the Phillies holds Titus further down the list. Titus was traded on June 21, 1912 by the Phillies to the Boston Braves for Doc Miller, playing just one more season. He would retire from patrolling the outfield at the conclusion of the 1913 season.

Hey, have you heard of: The 1905 Phillies

John Titus was a cornerstone outfielder for the second Phillies squad of the 20th century to crack a .500+ winning percentage. The 1905 Phils were led by 20-year old outfielder Sherry Magee, who hit 24 2B, 17 3B, 5 HR, and drove in 98 runs while scoring 100. The team also had career offensive years from long-time catcher Red Dooin and veteran third baseman Ernie Courtney.

The success of the club would not be sustainable, however, as surprise staff ace Togie Pittinger, who won 23 games in 1905 at age 33, would revert to his career norms, winning just 8 the following year, Kid Gleason and Mickey Doolin up the middle would also regress, and the stellar outfield of Titus, Magee, and Roy Thomas would all see declines in production.

Top 10: Hit By Pitch, Career

One of Titus's calling cards was his ability to get on base via being hit by pitch. Titus still ranks sixth in club history in this category over 100 years after retiring.

1. Chase Utley	173, 2003-2015
2. Mike Lieberthal	88, 1994-2006
3. Ed Delahanty	80, 1888-1889, 1891-1901
4. Mike Schmidt	79, 1972-1989
5T. Sherry Magee	78, 1904-1914
5T. John Titus	78, 1903-1912
7. Carlos Ruiz	68, 2006-Present
8. Roy Thomas	66, 1899-1908, 1910-1911
9. Greg Luzinski	61, 1971-1980
10. Tony Taylor	60, 1960-1971, 1974-1976

Jimmy Ring

Right-Handed Starter

Years as a Phillie: 1921-1925, 1928
Line as a Phillie: 68-98, 4.47 ERA, 1.576 WHIP in 1461 IP
fWAR Phillies Rank: 13th among pitchers, 43rd among Phillies
Signature Stat: Led the Phillies in the following categories in the 1920s: wins, games, games started, Ks, K/9 IP, and innings pitched

In the 1920s, there was exactly one highlight on the Phillies rather putrid pitching staffs and his name was Jimmy Ring. Through the 1920s, the Phillies went a combined 566-962 (37.04%), winning 62 games or less eight times in ten seasons, including just 50 games in 1923. Ring was acquired on November 22, 1920 for pitcher Eppa Rixey, a name you will see later in this countdown. Ring was the best player on a set of incredibly bad teams while Rixey would go on to have a Hall of Fame career. You win some trades, you lose some: the Phillies of the 1920s lost just about all of them.

Ring would be Steve Carlton in 1972 before Steve Carlton in 1972 happened: in 1923, despite his team posting a .325 winning percentage, Ring won 18 games, earning 6.0 fWAR for the season, fifth in baseball, with the eighth most innings pitched. Despite a 3.87 ERA, he was borderline dominant with the 19th highest K/9 IP in baseball. In his first stint with the Phillies, Ring was frequently above-average in terms of ERA, with the NL league average fluctuating between 3.78 and 4.26 and well above-average in K/9 IP.

Of any of the players in the Top 100, Ring likely had the most working against him during his stay on the Phillies. From 1921 through 1925, the Phillies were, by almost literally every measure, including Total Zone rating (16th out of 16 MLB teams) and fielding percentage (14th out of 16 MLB teams), the worst fielding team in all of baseball. Ring pitched in front of a team could rarely physically get to balls but a team that, when they would get to a ball, was highly likely to commit an error. Combine that with the ridiculously short right-field porch at the Baker Bowl and it was a recipe for disaster for any pitcher.

Yet, somehow, some way, Ring surpassed all expectations. His 64-81 (44.14%) mark from 1921 through 1925 while seemingly horrible but yet still outpaced the success of his team (36.71%) by a decent margin. In decisions that Ring was not involved in, the Phillies fell to a remarkably horrible 217-403. Ring was the poor-man's 1972 Steve Carlton and quite literally the only bright spot on a set of teams that were among the worst in baseball for the entire decade when offense was exploding in an offense-friendly ballpark.

Hey, have you heard of: **The 1928 Phillies**

The 1928 Phillies had the 13th worst winning percentage of all-time. With a record of 43-109, the 1928 club finished 51 games back of the pennant-winning St. Louis Cardinals. While the Fightins ranked fourth in the NL in homers, the club ranked only sixth in runs, seventh in batting average, seventh in OBP, and fifth in slugging offensively while ranking dead-last in ERA, hits, runs, earned runs, and walks allowed as a pitching staff.

Ray Benge

Right-Handed Pitcher

Years as a Phillie: 1928-1932, 1936
Line as a Phillie: 58-82, 4.69 ERA, 1.517 WHIP in 1141.1 IP
fWAR Phillies Rank: 22nd among pitchers, 62nd overall
Signature Season: Posted a 3.17 ERA with a 1.263 WHIP, leading all National League pitchers in fWAR but received no MVP votes in 1931.

Ray Benge's career started promising enough: Benge was called up to the big leagues at age 23 to pitch for Cleveland. After two cups of coffee, one in 1925 and one in 1926, Benge reappeared, this time in the National League in 1928 after the 5'9" Texan was drafted by the Phillies from Waco in the 1927 Rule 5 Draft.

Despite Benge pitching respectably, and frequently better, the Phillies were going through a cataclysmic slide into the darkest depths of the National League cellar.

How, exactly, does a pitcher that is 24 games under .500 and has a 4.69 ERA and was never on a playoff team or pennant winner make the Phillies Nation Top 100? Well, Benge would become one of the first pitchers in Phillies' history to solidify the swingman role, starting 26 games or more five times while appearing as a reliever in 12 games or more in four of those seasons.

Benge makes the list for durability and staying around long enough to climb the ladder on some of the Phillies all-time leader boards: 30th all-time in innings pitched, 38th in games pitched, 27th in games started, and 29th in complete games. It is also very important to remember context: Benge's best season came in 1931, posting a 3.17 ERA with a 1.263 ERA, numbers that probably won't get you into the All-Star game in 2015 but in 1931, those numbers put Benge far and away the fWAR leader in the National League among starting pitchers.

Benge would be traded by the Phillies in 1932 to the Brooklyn Dodgers for Neal Finn, Cy Moore, and Jack Warner. Benge would win 33 games for the Dodgers with a 4.00 ERA before being traded prior to the 1936 season to the Boston Braves. The Phillies would select Benge off waivers in 1936 on July 27 for a return engagement. He would win 1 more game with the Phillies before being purchased by the White Sox in the offseason. After a series of moves that included Benge being a temporary St. Louis Cardinal but missing the entire 1937 season, Benge finished his career in 1938 with the Cincinnati Reds and 99 career wins.

Hey, have you heard of: The 1931 Phillies

A sixth-place finish usually isn't something to get too excited about but for the 1931 Phillies, sixth place meant jumping ahead of the Cincinnati Reds and Boston Braves in the standings and a 14-win improvement.

Much of the improvement came via the addition of starting pitcher Jumbo Elliot, who went 19-14 with a 4.27 ERA. Elliot joined Benge and Phil Collins, no, not *that* Phil Collins, in a rotation that improved the Phillies team ERA by over two runs and helped jump the team from seventh to fifth in the NL in strikeouts.

#74 Dave Bancroft

Shortstop

Years as a Phillie: 1915-1920
Line as a Phillie: .251/.330/.319, 14 HR, 64 SB in 2903 PA
fWAR Phillies Rank: 47th among position players, 70th overall
Signature Season: Leading all shortstops in homers as a rookie on the pennant-winning 1915 club

Bancroft, the first person on the list who is currently in the Hall of Fame as of press time, was a cornerstone on the 1915 pennant-winning squad at shortstop. Nicknamed "Beauty," Bancroft spent six years in the minors, playing in Duluth, Superior, and finally Portland of the Pacific Coast League before his contract was purchased by the Phillies prior to the 1915 season.

Bancroft was a light-hitting shortstop in the minor leagues with a great defensive reputation, something that didn't change when he reached the Majors.

Yet, as with anything, context is everything: Bancroft's career stat-line with the Phillies may not look that impressive on the surface (.251/.330/.319 with 14 HR and 64 SB) but it stood up pretty well against other shortstops of the era. He ranked fifth in homers, tenth in steals, fifth in BB%, and fourth in defensive runs saved among shortstops from 1915 through 1920. Bancroft was one of the few Phillies to perform well in their first World Series, hitting .294/.368/.294

Bancroft would be traded to the New York Giants on June 7, 1920 for Art Fletcher, who would play only parts of 1920 and 1922 before retiring. The trade would be one of the worst in team history as Bancroft would play in parts of ten seasons with two Top-10 MVP finishes. On the winning side of the 1921 and 1922 World Series with the Giants, retired with the third-most games played in baseball history at shortstop, he was inducted into the Hall of Fame by the Veterans' Committee in 1971.

Phillies' Top 10: Most Homers by a Shortstop, Career

When Bancroft was traded during the 1920 season, he was the all-time Phillies leader in homer runs for a shortstop with a whopping 14! Amazingly, Bancroft is among the top of the list 95+ years later.

1. Jimmy Rollins	216, 2000-2014
2. Granny Hamner	103, 1944-1959
3. Dickie Thon	32, 1989-1991
4. Bobby Wine	23, 1960-1968
5. Freddy Galvis	19, 2012-Present
6. Heinie Sand	18, 1923-1928
7T. Dave Bancroft	14, 1915-1920
7T. Eddie Miller	14, 1948-1949
7T. Kevin Stocker	14, 1993-1997
10T. Bob Allen	13, 1890-1894
10T. Bobby Bragan	13, 1940-1942
10T. Larry Bowa	13, 1970-1981

#73 Spud Davis

Catcher

Years as a Phillie: 1928-1933, 1938-1939
Line as a Phillie: .321/.374/.449, 53 HR in 2712 PA
fWAR Phillies Rank: 48th among position players, 71st overall
Signature Stat: Leads all Phillies catchers with .321 batting average as a Phillie

Virgil "Spud" Davis was a 6'1" catcher who some would say was a product of the Baker Bowl's friendly dimensions. A closer inspection reveals that Davis was a righty and had to deal with the challenging 341 ft. left field wall. Davis would likely be remembered more fondly had his teams done better: one of the best hitting catchers in Phillies history, Davis' teams finished dead last in eighth place in the National League four out of the eight seasons he was with the team.

Davis arrived in Philadelphia with Don Hurst and Homer Peel in exchange for Art Decatur, Bill Kelly, and Jimmie Wilson of the St. Louis Cardinals on May 11, 1928. He wasted no time establishing himself as a top-hitting catcher, posting an OBP of .374 during his time in Philadelphia.

Davis never had the fortune of being an All-Star with the Phillies, largely because the All-Star game was not yet invented for most of his tenure, but he was among the best catchers in all of baseball during his first run with the Phillies. From 1928 through 1933, Davis led all catchers in batting average and ranked third in OBP, fourth in SLG, and third in OPS. Davis is one of the most underrated players in Phillies history, stuffed away on bad teams, and often overshadowed by the man who ranked first in the offensive categories that Davis didn't, crosstown superstar backstop Mickey Cochrane.

The Phillies would trade Davis back to the St. Louis Cardinals, this time with Eddie Delker, on November 15, 1933 for Jimmie Wilson in a rare trade involving two players who had previously been traded for one another. Davis would move into a part-time role for the rest of his career, spending time with Cincinnati before being traded once again to Philadelphia in 1938 and later purchased by the Pirates prior to the 1940 season. Davis not only remains one of the games' most underrated backstops, he is also ranked by Baseball Reference's JAWS measurement as the 46th best catcher ever.

Phillies' Top 10: Batting Average, Career, Among Catchers

Davis hit .321 for his career as a Phillie, leading all other Phillie backstops.

1. Spud Davis	.321, 1928-1932, 1938-1939
2. Smoky Burgess	.316, 1952-1955
3. Butch Henline	.304, 1921-1925
4. Ed McFarland	.294, 1897-1901
5. Jack Clements	.289, 1884-1897
6. Jimmie Wilson	.288, 1923-1928, 1934-1938
7. Mike Lieberthal	.275, 1994-2006
8. Tim McCarver	.272, 1970-1972, 1975-1980
9. Carlos Ruiz	.267, 2006-Present
10. Klondike Douglass	.261, 1898-1904

#72 Gus Weyhing

Right-Handed Starter

Years as a Phillie: 1892-1895
Line as a Phillie: 71-53, 4.23 ERA, 1.503 WHIP in 1103 IP
fWAR Phillies Rank: 31st among pitchers, 84th overall
Signature Stat: Threw 105 complete games in 127 games started (82.68%) with the Phillies in just over three seasons

Weyhing, the All-Time Leader in hit batsmen was famous, or infamous, in American culture long before he appeared on any lists of all-time great Phillies. Weyhing was allegedly charged, and likely acquitted, of $100 in pigeon theft just before jumping from the Philadelphia A's to the Philadelphia Phillies in January 1892

Aside from that, there are two other things that immediately stand out about Gus Weyhing:

1.) His mustache that puts him in a class of Phillies that includes Mike Schmidt and John Denny

2.) The complete games: 105 complete games in 127 starts in three years and two starts, or, about 35 complete games a year

Sure, the game of baseball was much different in the 1890's, but "Rubber-Winged Gus" was durable even for his time, tying for eighth in complete games from 1892 through 1894 and ranking second in shutouts, only behind Cy Young, with ten. Weyhing finished his career as the all-time leader in hit batsmen and he holds that distinction to this day.

Weyhing led a long and distinguished professional baseball career that spanned 14 years and included stops in the American Association and the Player's League. Weyhing was originally signed by the then-Quakers in 1887 but was purchased from the club by the Philadelphia Athletics prior to the start of the 1887 season. Weyhing would win 84 games in three seasons for the Athletics before jumping to Brooklyn Ward's Wonders of the Player's League for the 1890 season. In 1891, he'd jump back to the A's before joining the Phillies for the 1892 campaign.

Most of Weyhing's best years were already behind him when he joined the Phillies but he did put together one of the few 30+ win seasons in Phillies history when he went 32-21 with a 2.66 ERA for the 1892 Phillies, a run that included 46 complete games and 10 games finished as a reliever.

"Cannonball" Weyhing would be traded to Pittsburgh after two starts in the 1895 campaign before being traded to Louisville after his first start with Pittsburgh. He would play 14 years in professional baseball, rounding out his career with stints with the Washington Senators, St. Louis Cardinals, Brooklyn Superbas, Cleveland Blues, and Cincinnati Reds, finishing his career with 264 wins and the all-time hit batsmen record. Weyhing is one of only a handful of pitchers to win 100 games in both the National League and the American Association.

Bottom 10: Most Hit Batsmen in Club History

While Weyhing is baseball's all-time leader in hit batsmen, he doesn't even crack the club's top ten!

1. Chris Short	71, 1959-1972
2. Charlie Ferguson	65, 1884-1887
3. Jimmy Ring	63, 1921-1925, 1928
4. Ed Daily	60, 1885-1887
5. Eppa Rixey	58, 1912-1917, 1919-1920
6T. Dan Casey	57, 1886-1889
6T. Kyle Kendrick	57, 2007-2014
8. Charlie Buffinton	55, 1887-1889
9. Kid Carsey	54, 1892-1897
10. Kid Gleason	53, 1888-1891, 1903-1908

Lave Cross

Third Baseman, Catcher

Years as a Phillie: 1890, 1892-1897
Line as a Phillie: .295/.339/.398, 21 HR, 98 SB in 3026 PA
fWAR Phillies Rank: 50th among position players, 76th overall
Signature Stat: Set NL record with 15 assists in an 1897 game
Signature Gear: Through the late 1890's, used a catcher's mitt while playing the infield

Cross is an entry in the list that even the most ardent and dedicated Phillies fans had likely never heard of, even in passing. Born Lafayette Napoleon Cross in Milwaukee, WI in 1866, Cross would jump from the Philadelphia A's of the American Association in 1889 to the Philadelphia Quakers of the Players League for 1890. Cross would jump back to the A's for 1891 before spending 1892 through 1897 with the Phillies.

Cross was firmly a top-tier third baseman in this primitive baseball world, ranking seventh in batting average and slugging percentage while saving the most runs among any third baseman in that time period according to FanGraphs. In fact, to this day according to Baseball-Reference, Cross ranks as the 93rd best overall defender in baseball history.

Cross is a notable player in Phillies lure for playing a number of positions before settling on third base. One of those positions was catcher – he was so fond of the mitt that he frequently played second and third bases, as well as shortstop, with the catcher's mitt on before rules prohibited him from doing so.

Cross retired with a plethora of records after his 21-year career came to its conclusion. He retired second in hits among right-handed batters behind Hall of Famer Cap Anson, the career leader in assists, chances, putouts, and most games played at third base. While Cross accumulated most of those numbers outside of a Phillies uniform, his time as a Phillie should not be forgotten.

Top 10: Best Fielding Percentage Among Phils' Third Baseman

Cross accumulated many plate appearances because of his position versatility but it does not necessarily mean he was particularly good at fielding his position. Among Phillies third baseman with 1,000 innings or more at third base, Cross ranks only 28th in fielding percentage. Here are the top 10.

1. Placido Polanco		.983
2. Pedro Feliz		.969
3. Tony Taylor		.969
4. Don Money		.967
5. Scott Rolen		.965
6. Puddin' Head Jones		.963
7. Pinky May		.962
8. Bernie Friberg		.961
9. Pinky Whitney		.960
10. Abraham Nunez		.960

Phillies Cyclists

Cross was the first Phillie ever to hit for the cycle on April 24, 1894. Since Cross, just six other Phillies have completed the feat.

Lave Cross	April 24, 1894
Sam Thompson	August 17, 1894
Cy Williams	August 5, 1927
Chuck Klein	July 1, 1931 and May 26, 1933
Johnny Callison	June 27, 1963
Gregg Jefferies	August 25, 1995
David Bell	June 28, 2004

Bake McBride

Right Fielder

Years as a Phillie: 1977-1981
Line as a Phillie: .292/.335/.435, 44 HR, 98 SB in 2289 PA
fWAR Phillies Rank: 54th among position players, 87th overall
Signature Series: Hit .304/.360/.478 in the 1980 World Series, including a Game One homer that erased a 4-2 Royals lead.

Anthony "Bake" McBride, and his signature afro, burst onto the Major League scene in 1974, winning the National League Rookie of the Year award for the St. Louis Cardinals with a .309/.369/.394 line which included six homers in addition to 30 stolen bases. McBride was a terrific defender with a knack for hitting for average and getting on base. He would make his only All-Star team in 1976 with the Cardinals.

McBride's athletic ability should have shocked no-one; a three-sport athlete at Westminster College, McBride played basketball and track in addition to baseball.

"Shake 'n' Bake" came to the Phillies on June 15, 1977 in a deal with St. Louis. McBride was one of the premier offensive threats on the 1977, 1978, 1980 and 1981 Phillies playoff teams. The former Rookie of the Year came to Philadelphia and hit .339/.392/.564 with 11 HRs and 27 steals in 31 attempts (87.1%) in 314 PA, leading the team on a 12-game winning streak from August 3 through August 16, hitting an impressive .333/.375/.643 during that stretch.

From 1977 through 1981, McBride ranked 25th among Major League outfielders in batting and 48th in slugging, providing the perfect defensive compliment to Gary Maddox and speed to spare to make up for what Greg Luzinski lacked. It is no surprise that, according to Total Zone rating, the McBride, Maddox, and Luzinski outfield ranked as the second best defensive outfield from 1977 through 1980 and McBride was as big a part of that as anyone.

In addition to his defensive contributions, McBride regularly came up big for the Phillies in the postseason. He hit .304/.360/.478 in the 1980 World Series, including a Game One homer that erased a 4-2 Royals lead. McBride, not particularly known as a power threat, hit three postseason homers for the Phillies.

McBride was traded to Cleveland following the 1981 season for former All-Star reliever Sid Monge. Monge would post a 7-1 mark as a reliever with 3.75 ERA in 47 appearances in 1982 for the Phillies while McBride would struggle with injuries in 1982 before becoming a part-time player, full-time, in 1983. McBride would attempt a comeback with Texas' Triple-A Oklahoma City affiliate in 1984 before calling it a career.

Rookies of the Year

The 1980 Phillies won the World Series with three former Rookie of the Year winners: Bake McBride took home the 1974 Rookie of the Year award just one year after future teammate Gary Matthews won the award and 11 years after their future teammate Pete Rose took home the award.

There have been four Phils to win the award as Phillies. They are listed below:

1957 - Jack Sanford, P
1964 – Dick Allen, 3B
1997 – Scott Rolen, 3B
2005 – Ryan Howard, 1B

#69 Tully Sparks

Right-Handed Starter

Years as a Phillie: 1897, 1903-1910
Line as a Phillie: 95-95, 2.48 ERA, 1.133 WHIP in 1698 IP
fWAR Phillies Rank: 12th among pitchers, 42nd overall
Signature Season: 22-8 with 2.00 ERA in 1907

Sparks was an above-average to very-good workhorse for a series of teams from 1903 through 1910 that finished no higher than third place. Sparks' teams were above .500 in four of the nine seasons he played for the Phillies; quite frankly, a rarity in the early days. There is no doubt Sparks' contributions to the Phillies were among the key reasons.

Sparks made one start for the Phillies in 1897 at age 22 shortly after finishing college ball at the University of Georgia and Beloit College in Wisconsin. Sparks would jump to the Pittsburgh Pirates for the 1899 season, posting an 8-6 record with a 3.86 ERA in 28 appearances, 17 of which were starts.

In 1901, Sparks would go 7-17 with a 3.51 ERA for the Milwaukee Brewers of the American League before splitting 1902 between the New York Giants and the Boston Red Sox. Prior to the 1903 season, Sparks returned to the Phillies, this time lasting for eight seasons instead of just the one start.

From 1903 through 1910, Sparks was a slightly above average pitcher, ranking 22nd in MLB among starting pitchers according to FanGraphs' version of WAR despite ranking 110th in K/9 IP, 29th in BB/9 IP, and 64th in FIP out of 157 qualifying pitchers. Sparks became, out of necessity, an early pioneer in the swing-man role and retroactively became among the leaders in saves from 1903 through 1910 with a whopping seven. In sort of a quirky stat, when Sparks retired, he was among the game's most efficient at hitting batters and now ranks 124th all-time.

Hey, have you heard of: The 1903 Phillies

1903 was the first year the World Series was decided between the winners of the American and National League pennants. The Phillies of 1903? They were nowhere near that pennant race.

In fact, the Phillies of 1903 were so bad that they had no pitchers, starters or relievers, post a record over .500. Sparks was the standout of the team, posting a 2.72 ERA, a performance was in sharp contrast to that of Jack McFetridge, who posted a 1-11 record with a 4.89.

The Phillies would post a 49-86 record, finishing 7th out of 8 teams in the NL. Their leading home run hitter? Outfielder Bill Keister, who hit a whopping 3.

#68 *Ron Reed*

Right-Handed Reliever

Years as a Phillie: 1976-1983
Line as a Phillie: 57-38, 90 saves, 3.06 ERA in 809.1 IP
fWAR Phillies Rank: 48th among pitchers, 109th overall
Signature Moment: Earning the save in Game 2 of the 1980 World Series
Signature Stats: Compiling the most fWAR among any Phillies reliever, compiled the most wins of any Phillies reliever. One of five pitchers in MLB history to have 100 wins, 100 saves, and 50 complete games.

From LaPorte, IN, a town that boasts just over 22,000 residents, Ron Reed was a standout in both baseball and basketball. Lettering in both baseball and basketball for Notre Dame, Reed would be drafted in the third round of the 1965 NBA draft by the Pistons but actually remain undrafted in the MLB draft.

Reed played for the Pistons during the '65-'66 and '66-'67 campaigns and was signed as an undrafted free agent in 1965 by the then-Milwaukee Braves. Reed's baseball and basketball campaigns would overlap in 1966 and 1967 as Reed would see cameos in both seasons for the Braves. Reed chose to focus on baseball in 1968 and it was absolutely the correct choice: Reed would earn the first All-Star selection of his career that season and win 18 games in 1969, leading the Braves to the NL West title.

Reed ended up playing for the Cardinals before being traded to the Phillies for average outfielder Mike Anderson prior to the 1976 campaign. The Phillies certainly came out on the winning end of this deal.

Reed was a sixth, seventh, eighth, and sometimes ninth inning man for the Phillies from 1976 through 1983 and was responsible for four of the 42 100+ innings-pitched seasons in Phillies' relief history. In that time period, Reed accumulated 10 more saves than Tug McGraw, ranking ninth in baseball in those eight seasons in saves, fourth in innings pitched by a reliever, 46th in ERA but 18th in FIP. Reed was not just among the best pitchers in the Phillies bullpen during this time, he was a top 25 reliever in baseball for the duration of his run.

For advanced stat gurus, Reed holds a pretty unique distinction: Reed accumulated the most fWAR out of any relievers in Phillies history. For traditional stat gurus, Reed holds an equally unique distinction: Reed earned the most career wins with the Phillies (54) than any other reliever and his 13 wins in 1979 is the second among relievers in a Phillies single season, only trailing Jim Konstanty's 16 wins in 1950.

While Reed was very good in the regular season, he struggled in the postseason for the Phils, posting a 5.06 ERA in 32 postseason innings pitched. Three of those earned runs came in Game Three of the 1976 NLCS, when Reed blew a 6-3 lead against the Big Red Machine. However, Reed would get his playoff moment of redemption in 1980, earning a save in Game 2 of the 1980 World Series and pitching a scoreless sixth in Game 5 in Kansas City.

Hey, have you heard of: Ron Reed's Basketball Career

Ron Reed was drafted 20th overall in the 1965 NBA Draft by the Detroit Pistons, ahead of future NBA stalwarts Bob Weiss, John McGlocklin, Toby Kimball, Hank Finkel, and Bob Love.

Reed saw action in 119 NBA games across the 1965-1966 and 1966-1967 seasons, shooting poorly from the free throw line (57.1%) while averaging 8 points and 6.4 rebounds per game.

#67 Randy Wolf

Left-Handed Starter

Years as a Phillie: 1999-2006
Line as a Phillie: 69-60, 4.21 ERA, 1.333 WHIP in 1175 IP
fWAR Phillies Rank: 23rd among pitchers, 65th among Phillies
Signature Seasons: 3.20 ERA with 1.116 WHIP in 2002, All-Star in 2003

A six foot lefty, Randy Wolf was a second round draft pick out of Pepperdine University. The namesake of the lefty who got the 700 Level to their feet as the infamous Wolf Pack, Wolf had four seasons of double-digit wins and was a large part of the Phillies' turnaround in the early 2000s. Wolf was a durable workhorse from 1999 through 2004, averaging 28 starts and 144 strikeouts per season.

Wolf's standout season came in 2003. A year after posting a 11-9 mark with a 3.20 ERA, Wolf went 16-10 with a 4.23 ERA with 177 Ks in the last season at the Vet, earning a spot as the only Phillie on the 2003 All-Star team. Wolf would leave Philadelphia after the 2006 season, signing as a free agent with the Los Angeles Dodgers, narrowly missing the Phillies' first playoff berth since 1993 in 2007.

Wolf ranks 14th in Phillies history in games started, 26th in innings pitched, and seventh among starters in K/9 IP. His time with the Phillies concluded with two seasons where Wolf struggled to stay healthy. Wolf narrowly missed being on the 2007 NL East-winning team but gets credit for being on the staff of the teams that helped turn the fortunes of the Phillies.

Wolf would post a career 133-119 mark with a 4.20 ERA, reaching the playoffs twice, once with the Dodgers and once with the Brewers. At press time, Wolf is still active, having just completed a run on the Miami Marlins.

Phillies' Top 10: Highest K/9 IP Among Starters

Randy Wolf flirted with dominance as a starting pitcher for the Phillies and showed glimpses of becoming a masterful strikeout artist. Wolf ranks seventh among Phillies starters in K/9 IP.

1. Cliff Lee   8.84, 2009, 2011-2015
2. Cole Hamels   8.61, 2006-2015
3. Curt Schilling   8.42, 1992-1999
4. Roy Halladay   7.97, 2010-2013
5. Robert Person   7.94, 1999-2002
6. Brandon Duckworth   7.54, 2001-2003
7. Randy Wolf   7.40, 1999-2006
8. Steve Carlton   7.38, 1972-1986
9. Brett Myers   7.35, 2002-2009
10. Kevin Millwood   7.29, 2003-2004

#66 Clay Dalrymple

Catcher

Years as a Phillie: 1960-1968
Line as a Phillie: .234/.319/.334 with 50 HR, 3 SB in 3532 PA
fWAR Phillies Rank: 45th among position players, 68th overall
Signature Stat: 25th all-time in MLB history in caught stealing percentage
Signature Streak: Was one-time National League record holder for most consecutive games at catcher without an error (99)
Signature Moments: Broke up no-hit bid by Juan Marichal in Marichal's MLB debut in 8th inning

"Dimples" cracks the Top 70 based largely on his defensive successes. Dalrymple was worth 104.8 runs defensively in his career according to FanGraphs, far and away the most in Phillies history for a catcher and ranked no lower than fifth in the NL in caught stealing percentage from 1961 through 1967, including two first-in-the-NL finishes in 1961 and 1967.

Dalrymple came to the Phillies via the 1959 Rule 5 Draft from the Milwaukee Braves who had obtained him from Sacramento of the Pacific Coast League. Dalrymple was particularly good at getting on base, as evident by his .393 OBP in 1962 and his .365 in 1966. Dalrymple, however, was one of the Phillies that disappeared down the stretch in 1964, hitting only .190/.310/.259 from September 1, 1964 on.

While Dalrymple was firmly in the second tier of NL catchers in the 60's in terms of offensive performance he was the premier defensive catcher of his era. According to FanGraphs, Dalrymple provided the most defensive value to his team out of any catcher in the 1960's, ranking 12th all-time in Baseball Reference's Total Zone Runs measurement for catchers, and 134th of all time among all players in Baseball Reference's version of Defensive WAR.

Dalrymple's final season with the Phillies came in 1968. The defensive wizard was traded for outfielder Ron Stone on January 20, 1969. Stone would turn out to be an average to a below average outfielder for the Phils while Dalrymple would find himself on the roster of three-straight pennant winning Baltimore Orioles teams. Dalyrmple won a World Series ring as the back-up catcher on the 108-win 1970 Orioles squad.

Top 10: Homers by a Catcher

Clay Dalrymple had a .233 career batting average but was an occasional power threat behind the dish. He ranks ninth on the Phillies' all-time list for homers by a catcher.

1. Mike Lieberthal	150, 1994-2006
2. Darren Daulton	134, 1983-1997
3. Andy Seminick	123, 1943-1951, 1955-1957
4. Stan Lopata	116, 1948-1958
5. Jack Clements	70, 1884-1897
6. Bob Boone	65, 1972-1981
6. Carlos Ruiz	65, 2006-Present
8. Spud Davis	53, 1928-1933, 1938-1939
9. Clay Dalrymple	50, 1960-1968
10. Ozzie Virgil	46, 1980-1985

#65 *Kid Carsey*
Right-Handed Starter

Years as a Phillie: 1892-1897
Line as a Phillie: 94-71, 4.72 ERA, 1.596 WHIP in 1482 IP
fWAR Phillies Rank: 32nd among pitchers, 85th among Phillies
Signature Season: Going 19-16 with a 3.12 ERA and 30 complete games in 1892.

Wilfred "Kid" Carsey came to the Phillies in 1892 after losing an American Association-leading 37 games the year prior. In one of the most surprising bounce backs in professional baseball history, Carsey jumped to the National League, joined the Phillies and went 19-16 with a 3.12 ERA in 36 starts, 30 of which were complete games.

Despite pitching to a pretty poor 4.92 ERA, Carsey would win 24 games in 1895, pitching an MLB career-high 342.1 IP. Carsey battled injuries in 1896, going 11-11 with a 5.62 ERA in 21 starts. Carsey would be traded on June 1, 1897 to the St. Louis Browns with Mike Grady for Ed McFarland.

Winning 94 games in six years with the Phillies, Carsey ranked 12th in the Majors in wins, 13th in appearances and 14th in starts. While the ERA is a bit high (60th), Carsey's dependability made him a staple of the early Phillies teams, ranking him 22nd in Phillies history in games started, 15th in innings pitched, and ninth in complete games with 141.

Carsey would bounce around the Major Leagues through 1901, with stints in St. Louis, Cleveland, Washington, and Brooklyn before retiring after the 1901 season.

Hey, have you heard of: The 1892 Phillies

Just three years after changing their name from the Philadelphia Quakers, the 1892 Phillies seemed to be a team headed in the right direction. Roger Connor hit a team-leading 12 homers at first base and the outfield featured a trio of Hall of Famers: Ed Delahanty, Sam Thompson, and Billy Hamilton.

Carsey was one of three Phillies pitchers to win 19 games or more, joining 35-year old Tim Keefe (19-16) and 25-year old Gus Weyhing (32-21) at the top of the rotation.

The 1892 Phillies would win 87 games and lose 66, posting a record 21 games over .500 but still finishing in fourth place, 16.5 games behind the Boston Braves.

#64 Granny Hamner
Shortstop

Years as a Phillie: 1944-1959
Line as a Phillie: .263/.305/.385, 103 HR, 13 SB in 6222 PA
fWAR Phillies Rank: 44th among position players, 67th among Phillies
Signature Season: Hit .299/.351/.466 with 13 HR in 660 PA in 1954, the third of three straight All-Star seasons
Signature Series: Hit .429/.467/.714 with two doubles and a triple in the 1950 World Series

Granville "Granny" Hamner was a Phillie for parts of 16 seasons, including his 1944 debut at age 17 for the then-Philadelphia Blue Jays. Until Larry Bowa, and Jimmy Rollins after Bowa, Hamner was the standard at shortstop for the Phillies. Hamner, the six hitter on the 1950 Whiz Kids, made three straight All-Star squads from 1952-1954 and retired as the club's leader in doubles and homers among shortstops. Hamner played 568 games at second base for the Phillies and became the first player ever at two different positions to be voted by fans to the All-Star team.

Hamner's peak years, 1952 through 1954, coincided with his power surge: he hit 17, 21, and 13 homers in each year. Hamner posted a SLG% of .400 or more in those three years, as well.

One of the longest tenured Phillies on the list, Hamner had six of the Phillies' 16 hits in the 1950 World Series against the Yankees and was the captain of the Phillies from 1952 until he was traded in 1959 to Cleveland for Humberto Robinson. Hamner finished 1959 with Cleveland before spending 1960 and 1961 in the minors. He made one final run in the Majors, this time, as a pitcher, in 1962 with the Kansas City Athletics.

Hamner would go on to manage in the Phillies system and became a special advisor to the club in the 1980s. He was inducted onto the Phillies Wall of Fame in 1987 before passing in 1993.

Remember that time... Position Players Pitching in a Game

While Hamner never pitched for the Phillies, a few position players have. Most recently, outfielder Jeff Francoeur pitched two innings on June 16, 2015 in a 19-3 loss to the Baltimore Orioles. On August 24, 2013, outfielder Casper Wells took the hill for the Phillies in the 18th inning before being relieved by infielder John McDonald. Infielder Wilson Valdez, famously, had favorable results.

Valdez entered the May 25, 2011 4-4 game in the 19th inning, switching from second base to pitcher. With the clock striking midnight, and the calendar at May 26, Valdez threw a scoreless inning and the Phillies wrapped the game up on a Raul Ibanez sacrifice fly that scored Jimmy Rollins. Surprisingly, as good as Valdez's performance as a position player was, there was at least one that was even better.

Hall of Famer Jimmie Foxx was on the last legs of his career as a first baseman when he was asked to take the mound for the second half of a doubleheader. Foxx would pitch 6.2 innings, earning the first and only win of his career against the Cincinnati Reds.

Charlie Ferguson

Right-Handed Starter, Outfielder

#63

Years as a Phillie: 1884-1887
Line as a Phillie: 99-64, 2.67 ERA, 1.120 WHIP in 1514.2 IP
.288/.364/.372, 6 HR, 22 SB in 1078 PA
fWAR Phillies Rank: 16th among pitchers, 50th overall
Signature Season: Had one of the most dominant seasons in the history of Philadelphia baseball in 1886 (30-9, 1.98 ERA, 0.976 WHIP in 395.2 IP)
Signature Game: Pitched a No Hitter on August 29, 1885
Oddball Stat: Once drove in 85 runs in just 264 at-bats (1887)

If you look up rubber arm in the dictionary, there is a chance you might find Charlie Ferguson's photo in the dictionary.

Ferguson's story is one of great promise that ended in great tragedy. A graduate of the University of Pennsylvania, Ferguson made his debut with the then-Philadelphia Quakers in 1884. Ferguson was one of the early two-way play players and one of the best to be able to do both. Ferguson made an early impact with the Quakers by throwing the club's first no hitter on August 29, 1885 against the Providence Grays.

In 1886, Ferguson would put together one of the finest seasons in professional Philadelphia sports, posting a 30-9 record with a 1.98 ERA and a 0.976 WHIP. Ferguson would also play second base and the outfield, managing to put up one of the great statistical oddities, ever: 85 RBIs in just 264 at-bats in 1887.

Ferguson, who was quickly becoming one of the best players in the young National League, would pass away tragically in 1888 after contracting Typhoid Fever. His career ended just short of 100 wins in four seasons and Ferguson sits at tenth all-time in ERA among qualified Phillies pitchers.

30 Wins in a Season

Only four pitchers in Phillies history have won 30 games or more in a single season and no one since Grover Cleveland Alexander has accomplished this feat.

1. Kid Gleason, 1890 – 38-17, 2.63 ERA, 222 Ks
2. Grover Cleveland Alexander, 1916 – 33-12, 1.55 ERA, 167 Ks
3. Gus Weyhing, 1892 – 32-21, 2.66 ERA, 202 Ks
4. Grover Cleveland Alexander, 1915 – 31-10, 1.22 ERA, 241 Ks
5. Grover Cleveland Alexander, 1917 – 30-13, 1.83 ERA, 200 Ks
6. Charlie Ferguson, 1886 – 30-9, 1.98 ERA, 212 Ks

No Hitters as Phillies

There have been thirteen no-hitters thrown in Phillies history, beginning with Ferguson's on August 29, 1885 against the Providence Grays. Ferguson's game was not only the first Phillies no hitter, but the first at Recreation Park.

Charlie Ferguson	August 29, 1885 v. Providence Grays
Red Donahue	July 8, 1898 v. Boston Beaneaters
Chick Fraser	September 18, 1903 v. Chicago Cubs
Johnny Lush	May 1, 1906 v. Brooklyn Dodgers
Jim Bunning*	June 21, 1964 v. New York Mets
Rick Wise	June 23, 1971 v. Cincinnati Reds
Terry Mulholland	August 15, 1990 v. San Francisco Giants
Tommy Greene	May 23, 1991 v. Montreal Expos
Kevin Millwood	April 27, 2003 v. San Francisco Giants
Roy Halladay*	May 29, 2010 v. Florida Marlins
Roy Halladay**	October 6, 2010 v. Cincinnati Reds
Hamels, Diekman, Giles, Papelbon	September 1, 2014 v. Atlanta Braves
Cole Hamels	July 25, 2015 v. Chicago Cubs

* indicates Perfect Game   ** indicates thrown in postseason

#62 Brad Lidge

Closer

Years as a Phillie: 2008-2011
Line as a Phillie: 3-11, 100 saves, 3.54 ERA, 1.430 WHIP in 193.0 IP
fWAR Phillies Rank: 188th among pitchers, 367th among Phillies
Signature Season: 48 for 48 in save opportunities in the regular and postseason with a 1.95 regular season ERA and a 0.96 ERA with 13 K in 9.1 postseason innings
Signature Environment: Big-game postseason pitcher (1-1, 12 saves, 24 K with a 1.77 ERA and .203 BAA in 20.1 postseason innings with the Phillies)

Brad Lidge... stretches. The 0-2 pitch. SWING AND A MISS, STRUCK. HIM. OUT. The Philadelphia Phillies are 2008 world champions of baseball!

- Harry Kalas' call of Lidge's strikeout of Eric Hinske to end the 2008 World Series

You can't tell the story of the Philadelphia Phillies without the story of Brad Lidge. Lidge was acquired from the Houston Astros in between the 2007 and 2008 seasons for Michael Bourn, Mike Costanzo, and Geoff Geary in a trade that Keith Law said was a coup for Phillies at the time. Lidge had been one of the most effective relievers in the Majors but had fallen out of favor after a shaky 2005 postseason with the Astros, finding himself in a closer-by-committee situation by 2007.

Lidge, entering a pivotal age-31 2008 season, one where he would become a free agent after his final year of arbitration, became a Phillie sort of behind the 8-ball. While he was still a top reliever in baseball some questioned not only his dominance but whether the Phillies were really a playoff team in 2008. In fact, some folks who questioned whether the Mets collapsed or the Phillies won the division heading into the season. How much would adding a closer help?

As Lidge's numbers in 2008 would indicate, he was still every bit as dominant as advertised and he helped them a lot. "A lot" as in closed out the World Series with 48 saves in 48 attempts through the regular and postseasons. Lidge had perhaps the greatest relief season in Phillies history culminating in a World Series win.

Lidge couldn't quite replicate the dominance of 2008 but would have two additional very good seasons in 2010 and 2011, albeit not entirely in the closer's role. Lidge's dominance would carry over, however, in the playoffs with the Phillies, posting a 1.77 ERA with 12 saves in 20.1 IP.

Phillies' Top 10: Saves

Brad Lidge's dominant 2008 had many believing he had a chance to become the all-time saves leader for the franchise. Lidge would fall 12 short of then-record holder Jose Mesa.

1. Jonathan Papelbon	123, 2012-2015
2. Jose Mesa	112, 2001-2003, 2007
3. Steve Bedrosian	103, 1986-1989
4. Mitch Williams	102, 1991-1993
5. Brad Lidge	100, 2008-2011
6. Tug McGraw	94, 1975-1984
7. Ron Reed	90, 1975-1983
8. Ricky Bottalico	78, 1994-1998, 2001-2002
9. Turk Farrell	65, 1956-1961, 1967-1969
10. Billy Wagner	59, 2004-2005

Bonus
In Their Own Words:
Brad Lidge

It is hard to tell the story of the greatest Phillies of All-Time without going to the source: the players themselves! Throughout the book, there are excerpts of interviews I conducted for use on Phillies Nation and *Phillies Nation TV*, inserted and edited when appropriate. Some questions and answers may have been omitted but answers from players are presented in full.

Ian Riccaboni: How does it feel to have won a World Series in Philadelphia and being recognized as a returning hero each time you come back to the ballpark?

Brad Lidge: Every time I come back to Philly I feel so blessed and fortunate to be back in the city and to have won that World Series here of all places because this town is such an amazing sports town.

IR: What do the fans ask you the most when you come back to Philadelphia?

BL: The fans here have been amazing! After I retired, it has been just a real joy every time I come in here. They tell me a lot of times "You have no idea what an incredible moment it was!" for them winning the World Series but I think they forget that it was probably the most remarkable moment I've had also. It's fun for us to go back and forth and talk about it also.

Bonus

Transactions That Shaped the Phillies: Gillick Acquires Lidge

Jimmy Rollins proclaimed the 2007 Philadelphia Phillies as the team to beat in the NL East. After a remarkable late season surge, erasing a 7 ½ game lead with just 17 to play, the Phillies found themselves NL East champions for the first time since 1993. The man on the mound to close out the clincher? Starter-turned-closer Brett Myers.

Myers was one of 21 pitchers to appear out of the bullpen that season for the Phillies, joining more memorable Phils like J.C. Romero, Jose Mesa, and Clay Condrey and blink-and-you'll-miss-'em Phils like John Ennis, Joe Bisenius, and Anderson Garcia in a bullpen that ranked 24th in MLB in ERA, 26th in K/9 IP, and 24th in HR/9 IP. Looking for bullpen stability after their first-round sweep at the hands of the Colorado Rockies, General Manager Pat Gillick was looking to make a splash to upgrade the bullpen of a team with the best offense in the Majors per fWAR.

There were two players that allowed Gillick to make such a move. The development of "The Flyin' Hawai'ian" Shane Victorino into an above-average everyday regular outfielder at age 26 (.281/.347/.423 with 12 HR and 37 SB in 510 PA in 2007) and the emergence of Jayson Werth at age 28 (.298/.404/.459 with 8 HR and 7 SB in 304 PA in 2007) gave the Phillies a pair of cheap, controllable. A robust outfield free agent market helped make the Phils decision easier as well: even if Gillick wasn't sold on Werth as an everyday option in right, which he wasn't, there were a number of players available. These included Geoff Jenkins, who the Phillies would ink to a two-year deal, which could give the Phillies insurance in the outfield.

With the Phillies comfortable in their outfield situation with Victorino, Werth, and Pat Burrell all locked up through 2008, Gillick decided that he could use one of his biggest trade chips, outfield prospect Michael Bourn to lure an opposing GM's ace reliever. Bourn was a fast-rising outfielder, a fourth-round selection from the University of Houston in 2003, who made his debut with the Phillies in 2006. After earning time as Charlie Manuel's preferred pinch-runner and defensive replacement through much of the season, Bourn would miss all of August and some of September after hurting himself on a diving catch attempt at Wrigley Field in the seventh inning.

Gillick took a calculated risk, sending Bourn, reliever Geoff Geary, and 2005 second-round pick, Springfield, PA native infielder Mike Costanzo, to Houston for closer Brad Lidge and utility man Eric Bruntlett. The initial reaction to the trade was a lot of head scratching: yes, the Phillies needed bullpen help, and a utility infielder wouldn't hurt either, but Lidge was coming off the two worst seasons of his career.

In 2005, Lidge seemingly had his psyche shaken by an Albert Pujols homer that may not yet have landed. Lidge would also take two losses in the '05 Fall Classic, allowing a walk-off homer to Scott Podsednik in Game Two and the eventual game-winning Jermaine Dye single in the eighth inning of Game 4. In 2006, while Lidge's ERA skyrocketed to 5.28 and in 2007, it came back down to earth at 3.36 but he had been removed from Houston's closer role for much of the season with his K/9 IP dwindling and his BB/9 IP increasing.

Yet, the risk paid off for Gillick and the Phillies, even if just for one or two years. Lidge would appear in 72 games for the Phillies, posting a 1.95 ERA, saving 41 in 41 chances in 2008. With a career-low HR/9 IP in his back pocket, Lidge carried his success into the postseason, converting seven of seven save opportunities in the playoffs out of eleven Phillie wins, including the save in Game 5 of the World Series which clinched the Fall Classic for the Phils. In the middle of the 2008 season, Gillick signed Lidge to a three-year, $36 million pact that would keep Lidge in Philly through the 2011 season. For his 2008 performance, Lidge earned an All-Star birth, finished fourth in Cy Young voting, and helped the Phillies lead the NL in bullpen ERA.

While battling injuries, Lidge would disappoint in 2009, posting a 0-8 record with 31 saves and a 7.21 ERA. Regardless, he was a solid player for the rest of his tenure, going 1-3 with a 2.49 ERA in 75 games with 28 saves across 2010 and 2011. Lidge is one of the Phillies' best postseason relievers in club history, as well, posting a 1.77 ERA with a .203 BAA with a 1-1 record and 12 saves, effectively eviscerating the ghosts of his postseason past.

Bruntlett would do little for the Phillies offensively in 2008 and 2009 but did provide defensive relief at every position but catcher. Bruntlett would hit just .202/.273/.278 with only two homers and eleven steals but did manage to create a few memorable moments for Phils fans to remember him by: Bruntlett would score the game-winning runs as a pinch-runner in Games Three and Five of the 2008 World Series, hit a homer in Game Two of the same World Series, and turned an unassisted triple play on August 23, 2009.

As for Bourn, he would become a pretty solid ballplayer in his own right, winning three-straight NL stolen base titles from 2009 through 2011. Bourn would be named to the NL All-Star squad in 2010 with Houston, and 2012 with Atlanta after being dealt in a 2011 deadline deal. Following a career year in 2012, worth 6.1 wins according to FanGraphs, Bourn inked a four-year, $48 million deal with a vesting option for a fifth year at $12 million in 2017.

Geary would have a career-year in 2008, posting a career-low 2.53 ERA in 64 IP but would be out of the Majors following an 8.10 ERA in 16 games for the 2009 Astros. Geary would last play organized ball for the Albuquerque Isotopes in 2010 before wrapping up in 2011 in the independent Atlantic League with York. Costanzo finally earned a cup of coffee in the Majors at age 28 in 2012 but hit just .056/.095/.056. From a value perspective, the Phillies gave up more long-term in Bourn than they received short-term in Lidge. But, Bourn had nowhere to play and the Phillies won a World Series. Can you put a value on a World Series win? For the 2008 perfect season, and Lidge's postseason success, the Phillies acquiring Brad Lidge is the one of the best trades in Phillies' history.

Charlie Buffinton

Right-Handed Starter

Years as a Phillie: 1887-1889
Line as a Phillie: 77-50, 2.89 ERA, 1.203 WHIP in 1112.1 IP
fWAR Phillies Rank: 17th among pitchers, 54th among Phillies
Signature Season: Went 28-17 with 1.91 ERA, 0.957 WHIP in 400.1 IP
in 1888

A pioneer of the sinker, Buffinton was sold to the then-Philadelphia Quakers just two seasons removed from winning a third-best-in-the-NL 48 games with the Boston Beaneaters between the 1886 and 1887 seasons. Buffinton would make the most of the opportunity offered by his new surroundings, winning 21, 28, and 28 games with the Quakers in 1887, 1888, and 1889 respectively. His signature season came in 1888, winning 28 games with a 1.91 ERA and a 0.957 WHIP.

During Buffinton's time in Philadelphia, he was among the best pitchers in the young National League. Buffinton had the tenth most appearances, 11th most innings pitched, the ninth-best ERA, and eighth-best FIP. Buffinton used his sinker to accumulate the ninth-most strikeouts in the NL with the 12th best strikeout rate.

Buffinton would jump to the Philadelphia Quakers of the Players' League from the Philadelphia Quakers (Phillies) of the National League in between the 1889 and 1890 seasons. Buffinton won 19 games before jumping to the Boston Reds of the American Association for the 1891 season, where he would win 29 games. Buffinton played his final season in 1892 with the Baltimore Orioles, where he posted a 4-8 record with a 4.92 ERA.

Buffinton is one of a handful of folks on this list who are curious omissions from the Baseball Hall of Fame. He stacks up as the 56th best pitcher in the history of baseball by Baseball Reference's version of WAR and 136th by

FanGraphs' version, which does not give Buffinton as much credit for his amazing run with the Phillies.

The Sub-2 ERA Club

Only ten pitchers in Phillies history have posted a sub-2 ERA over a full season. Buffinton was the second Phillie to accomplish this feat in 188.

1. Grove Cleveland Alexander, 1915 – 31-10, 1.22 ERA
2. George McQuillan, 1908 – 23-17, 1.53 ERA
3. Grove Cleveland Alexander, 1916 – 33-12, 1.55 ERA
4. Lew Richie, 1908 – 7-10, 1.83 ERA
5. Grover Cleveland Alexander, 1917 – 30-13, 1.83 ERA
6. Eppa Rixey, 1916 – 22-10, 1.85 ERA
7. Ben Sanders, 1888 – 19-10, 1.90 ERA
8. Charlie Buffinton, 1888 – 28-17, 1.91 ERA
9. Steve Carlton, 1972 – 27-10, 1.97 ERA
10. Charlie Ferguson, 1886 – 30-9, 1.98 ERA

#60 Bob Boone

Catcher

Years as a Phillie: 1972-1981
Line as a Phillie: .259/.325/.370, 65 HR in 4152 PA
fWAR Phillies Rank: 42nd among position players, 64th among Phillies
Awards as Phillie: Three Gold Gloves
Signature Season: Hit .412/.500/.529 in 22 PA in the 1980 World Series

A Stanford graduate, Boone was part of the strong core of Phillies that came through the Phillies system together in the early 1970s to form the late-1970s juggernaut that would win the 1980 World Series. Boone gained a stellar defensive reputation, winning three Gold Gloves as a Phillie, a total of seven for his career, all after the age of 30.

Boone was no slouch as a hitter, either, particularly from 1976 through 1979. In those four seasons, Boone was fifth in batting among catchers, which was higher than Johnny Bench and Gary Carter, eighth in on-base percentage, higher than Bench, Carter, and Thurmon Munson, and tenth in slugging, higher than Munson.

Boone was selected in the sixth round of the 1969 draft by the Phillies out of Stanford and quickly made his way through the Phillies system. He made his debut on September 10, 1972 at age 24, coming in to the game as Mike Ryan's replacement to catch veteran reliever Bucky Brandon.

Boone would make three All-Star teams (1976, 1978-1979) and hit .412/.500/.529 in 22 PA in the 1980 World Series for the Phillies. Upon entering his age 34 season, Boone was purchased by the Angels on December 6, 1981 where he served as the primary catcher for the Angels from 1982 through 1988, winning two division titles. Those two division titles, combined with his five division titles with the Phillies, would mark seven trips for Boone to the playoffs where he was a particularly strong player (.311/.353/.387, 2 HR, 13 RBI in 121 PA).

Rounding out his career with the Kansas City Royals, culminating with his final season coming in 1990 at age 42, Boone finished his career with seven total Gold Gloves, four All-Star selections, and two top 25 MVP finishes.

Boone's staffs from 1976 through 1980 ranked fourth in the NL in ERA over those five seasons, third in K/9 IP, and first in BB/9 IP. Always exerting a strong impact on the field and in the line-up, Boone was the 2005 inductee on to the Phillies Walk of Fame.

Phillies' Top 10: Games Caught

Bob Boone retired as the Major League's all-time leader in games caught. Today, he ranks third in baseball history, behind only Ivan Rodriguez and Carlton Fisk. In Phillies' history, Boone also ranks third.

1. Red Dooin   1219, 1902-1914
2. Mike Lieberthal 1174, 1994-2006
3. Bob Boone   1125, 1972-1982
4. Darren Daulton   1109, 1983-1997
5. Clay Dalrymple   1006, 1960-1968
6. Jack Clements   997,   1884-1897
7. Carlos Ruiz   993,   2006-2015
8. Andy Seminick   985,   1943-1951, 1955-1957
9. Jimmie Wilson   838   1923-1928, 1934-1938
10. Stan Lopata   821   1948-1958

Placido Polanco

Third Baseman, Second Baseman

Years as a Phillie: 2002-2005, 2010-2012
Line as a Phillie: .289/.341/.398, 51 HR, 31 SB in 2963 PA
fWAR Phillies Rank: 43rd among position players, 66th among Phillies
Signature Season: Won Gold Glove and made All-Star team in 2011
Signature Stat: From 2002-2005 and 2010-2012, Polanco was the toughest third baseman to strike out in baseball. Was third-most difficult to strikeout active player at retirement.

On July 29, 2002, the Phillies acquired Polly, along with Bud Smith and Mike Timlin, for Scott Rolen and Doug Nickle. Polanco would play second and third, and a little bit of left field and short, before being traded for Ramon Martinez and Ugueth Urbina on June 8, 2005. Despite outplaying David Bell at third (38 HR, 23 SB, .297/.352/.439 in 1510 PA v. Bell's 32 HR, 1 SB, .253/.327/.381 in 1568 PA), Polanco was thought to be an expendable super-sub thanks to the presence of Bell at third and Chase Utley at second base. Well, at least one worked out.

The trade was a shame and would hurt the team in more ways than one. Urbina would face jail time in his home country Venezuela on murder charges and miss the 2006 season and beyond, Bell would be traded to the Brewers in 2006, and, despite winning the World Series in 2008, the Phillies struggled to find an offensive force at third base until Polanco returned as a free agent for the 2010 season. The move is still a curious one: Polanco led all third baseman from 2002 through 2005 in batting average, was 12th in OBP, and was the hardest third baseman to strike out in the Majors.

Polanco returned with fanfare in 2010, joining a team that had reached the World Series the previous two years. He had a strong 2010 and a very strong first half of the 2011 season that saw him elected to the NL All-Star team. For a year and a half, Polly was as advertised – a fine offensive third baseman who would get a lot of base hits, who wouldn't strike out, and would play a fine third base. Perception was reality: from 2010-2012, Polly ranked ninth in batting average among third baseman, was the most difficult to strikeout third baseman, and, according to FanGraphs, saved the most runs defensively.

Polly may have ranked higher on this list had he stayed healthy through the end of 2011 and through more of 2012. Unfortunately, health issues forced him to miss a chunk of 2011 and a significant chunk of 2012. Polanco also struggled in the playoffs for the Phillies, hitting just .167/.226/.208 in 53 PA across 2010 and 2011. But because of his consistent hitting and top notch defense, Polly cracks the Phillies Top 60.

Phillies' Top 10: Batting Average, Third Basemen

In 2005, Polanco hit .338 between time with the Phillies and Tigers, leading the Major Leagues in batting average, but did not have enough plate appearances to win either batting title.

Polanco ranks seventh among Phillies' third basemen in batting average.

1. Pinky Whitney	.307,	1928-1933, 1936-1939
2. Russ Wrightstone	.298,	1920-1928
3. Lave Cross	.294,	1892-1897
4. Hans Lobert	.293,	1911-1914
5. Harry Wolverton	.292,	1900-1904
6. Dick Allen	.290,	1963-1969, 1975-1976
7. Placido Polanco	.289,	2002-2005, 2010-2012
8. Scott Rolen	.282,	1996-2002
9. Don Demeter	.276,	1961-1963
10. Pinky May	.275,	1939-1943

Dick Ruthven

Right-Handed Starter

Years as a Phillie: 1973-1975, 1978-1983
Line as a Phillie: 78-65, 4.00 ERA, 1.357 WHIP in 1262.2 IP
fWAR Phillies Rank: 20th among pitchers, 61st among Phillies
Signature Moment: Pitching two perfect innings in relief to hold off the Houston Astros in the deciding Game 5 of the 1980 NLCS only four days after starting and pitching seven innings in Game 2

In 1973, Ruthven was taken first overall in the January Secondary MLB draft (a draft held from 1965 through 1986 to accommodate college and high school players who graduated in the winter). Ruthven would make his Major League debut just three months later on April 17, earning a no-decision after getting chased off in the second inning of an eventual 9-6 win against the Expos.

On December 10, 1975, Ruthven would be packaged with Alan Bannister and Roy Thomas and sent to the Chicago White Sox for a package that included Jim Kaat. Less than three years later, Ruthven would be reacquired by the Phillies, who sent Gene Garber to Atlanta to complete the deal. Ruthven returned to Philadelphia a former All-Star and would go 13-5 with a 2.99 ERA to finish the 1978 season for the Phillies.

Ruthven had arguably the best year of his career in 1980, going 17-10 with a 3.55 ERA in 33 games started. Ruthven emerged as an unexpected hero in relief for the Phillies in the NLCS, pitching a perfect ninth and tenth to finish the Houston Astros in the deciding Game 5. Ruthven would pitch very well in Game 3 of the World Series, taking a 3-3 stalemate through nine, earning a no decision in the eventual 4-3 loss.

Ruthven made the 1981 All-Star team as a Phillie before being traded on May 22, 1983 with Bill Johnson to the Chicago Cubs for Willie Hernandez.

Ruthven would remain in the Majors with the Cubs through 1986 before retiring, wrapping up an impressive 14-year career.

The January Secondary Draft

From 1966 through 1986, Major League Baseball hosted a "January Secondary" draft to accommodate winter college graduates. Just a two-round draft, the Phillies were able to turn 42 total picks into 7 Major Leaguers.

1966 First Round – RHP Lowell Palmer (1969-1971), 3-10, 5.39 ERA

1973 First Round – RHP Dick Ruthven (1973-1975, 1978-1983), 78-65, 4.00 ERA

1975 First Round – OF Bobby Bonnell (Did not play for Phillies, traded for Dick Allen and Johnny Oates in 1975)

1979 First Round – LHP Mark Davis (1980-1981, 1993), 2-6, 6.31 ERA

1981 First Round – RHP Kevin Gross (1983-1988), 60-66, 3.87 ERA

1984 Second Round - RHP Mike Jackson (1986-1987), 3-10, 4.11 ERA

1986 First Round – RHP Blas Minor (Did not sign with Phillies, would reach Majors with Pirates)

#57 *Terry Mulholland*

Left-Handed Starter

Years as a Phillie: 1989-1993, 1996
Line as a Phillie: 62-57, 3.81 ERA, 1.230 WHIP in 1070.1 IP
fWAR Phillies Rank: 21st among pitchers, 63rd among Phillies
Signature Moment: Pitched a no-hitter, facing the minimum 27 batters, on August 15, 1990 against the San Francisco Giants
Signature Season: Started the All-Star Game in Camden Yards in 1993 for the Phillies
Signature Record: Picked off 15 base runners in 1992

The pride of Uniontown, PA, Mulholland joined the Phillies on June 18, 1989 in a fortuitous trade that sent Mulholland, Charlie Hayes, and Dennis Cook from San Francisco to Philadelphia for Steve Bedrosian. Mulholland, a former first round pick, would pay dividends instantly for the slowly improving Phils. Mulholland would win 54 games in his first four-plus seasons with the Phillies. Those 54 wins included a very special win: a 1990 no-hitter against the San Francisco Giants where Mulholland faced the minimum 27 hitters. The only base runner reached on a Charlie Hayes error was retired in a double play.

Mulholland would be a key pitcher on the 1993 pennant-winning squad, winning 12 games with a then-career low 3.25 ERA and 1.132 WHIP. His performance earned him the nod as the starting pitcher for the National League in the All-Star game. Although Mulholland would earn the winning decision in Game 2 of the 1993 World Series, Mulholland struggled in the postseason, posting a 6.89 ERA and .375 OBP-against in 15.2 IP across three starts. Mulholland exited Game 6 down 5-1. The Phillies would pull ahead 6-5 but ultimately lose the game and the series.

While Mulholland returned for a cup of coffee in 1996, he was later dealt to Seattle for Desi Relaford. Mulholland's ability to keep runners of the basepaths has him ranked 25th among Phillies starters all-time in WHIP and 13th among qualified/applicable starters in BB%. Mulholland left

Philly with its single-season record for most runners picked off in a season (15 in 1992) and he allowed only 14 steals across 1718 innings from 1992 through 2006.

Mulholland would spend parts of twenty years in the Major Leagues, pitching every year from 1986 through 2006 with the exception of 1987. He played for 11 teams, including the Phillies, Giants, Cubs, Twins, Braves, Dodgers, Indians, Diamondbacks, Pirates, Mariners, and Yankees but spent the most time (6 years) with the Phillies.

Hey, have you heard of: **The 1993 Phillies Starting Rotation**

Mulholland made 28 starts in 1993 and was part of the incredibly healthy, and lucky, run the entire starting rotation was a part of. The five starters, Curt Schilling, Danny Jackson, Tommy Greene, Mulholland, and Ben Rivera made an astounding 152 out of 162 (93.83%) starts for the Phillies and kept the bullpen well-rested by pitching 24 complete games.

It is hard to tell the story of the greatest Phillies of All-Time without going to the source: the players themselves! Throughout the book, there are excerpts of interviews I conducted for use on Phillies Nation and *Phillies Nation TV*, inserted and edited when appropriate. Some questions and answers may have been omitted but answers from players are presented in full.

Ian Riccaboni: When you were traded to the Phillies, they weren't quite a contender yet. What were the expectations of the team at that point?

Terry Mulholland: Well, that was in July of '89 and it was Charlie Hayes, Dennis Cook, and myself in exchange for Steve Bedrosian and I believe Rick Parker, who later on, I believe was a player to be named later. Obviously, at that time, the Phillies were struggling a little bit. Ya know, Bedrosian was one of the finest relievers in the game and the Giants were in the pennant race that year so a deal was made. Young guys from the Giants came over to the Phillies and I think it turned out really well for all three of us involved in the trade because we were given the opportunity to take the ball and run on a regular basis for the next few years. Charlie got to play third base, Dennis went on to have a very nice career; I had the opportunity to make my contributions to the Phillies organization for a few years, too.

IR: Was there a year where you sensed things were changing or turning around for the Phillies? (The Phillies) acquired you, John Kruk from the Padres, Lenny Dykstra from the Mets...

TM: Yeah, Lee Thomas did a great job assembling a group of guys. We weren't big named ball players leading the league in anything but we came together as a very good team in terms of playing baseball the way you are supposed to play it. It was a hardnosed group of guys and I take my hat off to Lee Thomas and, later, Jim Fregosi, for putting up with us and getting us to win ballgames.

IR: How important was Jim Fregosi? There was a lot of different personalities of folks like Dykstra who seemed fiery to the public and Dutch who seemed laid back.

TM: Jim was a player's manager. He wasn't going to treat you like a kid. We were all men in his eyes and our biggest responsibility was to go out between the foul lines and give him everything he asked for from us and it turn, he let us do whatever we wanted outside those lines.

IR: Who would you say was your favorite battery mate? I know you were caught by Dutch, Todd Pratt...

TM: And Steve Lake earlier on. They were all great and they all handled the game how they saw I could best utilize what I had that day. I didn't always have the best stuff every time out but Dutch and Steve and Todd were always really good about communicating and we were always honest. Nobody was blowing smoke up anyone's ass. If you didn't have it that day, they would tell you. But then the days when you had the good stuff, it was a lot of fun.

IR: What was it like in '93 to finally break through and get to the NLCS against the Braves and then the World Series against the Blue Jays?

TM: It was something that whole group of guys worked awfully hard for. It wasn't just the guys who showed up in '89, '90, or '91. It was also the young players that stepped in and made large contributions. Kim Batiste is a guy who comes to mind. Batty, it seems like, that year came up with clutch hits and clutch plays in the field. You can look across the whole roster and find someone who contributed in a big game at any point in the season. To me, it was really rewarding seeing us as a group of guys to see hard work paying off and to see some success out of it. We came up short in Toronto but we had a great time getting there.

IR: You still hold the club record for pickoffs in a season and in a career. What was your secret?

TM: Well, my secret was when I was a little boy my parents always told me it was wrong to steal so I took that literally. So, as a lefthander, I was able to come up with a rather quick step-off pick move to first. I was also rather diligent in recognizing when guys were taking their leads, ya know, and looking for little nuances to see if they were going, like if they were turning their toe out toward second base or if they were getting a little further out, where their weight was shifted. Having a good snap throw to first, I was really able to screw with them a lot. I had guys diving back to first more than they were taking off to second.

IR: I guess Otis Nixon was a guy who was on base a lot. You probably didn't see Rickey (Henderson) too much in your Phillies days?

TM: No, I didn't see Rickey with the Phillies. I used to see him a lot in Spring Training when I was with the Giants in my younger days. I saw him a little later on, too, with some American League clubs. Otis was a challenge, Vince Coleman was a challenge, he was very fast, Tim Raines was another. That's one of the things I cherish about my career: there were speed demons on the bags and they didn't succeed very much against me. I kind of liken it to not giving up home runs in the steroid era.

#56 Tug McGraw

Closer

Years as a Phillie: 1975-1984
Line as a Phillie: 49-37, 3.10 ERA, 1.198 WHIP in 722 IP
fWAR Phillies Rank: 61st among pitchers, 133rd overall
Signature Moment: Closing out the 1980 World Series
Signature Season: Posted a 1.46 ERA in 92.1 IP with 20 saves in 1980

"Ya gotta believe!"

Sure, Tug's phrase had been coined seven years earlier as a member of the hated Mets and would be played out to the point that it later appeared in ads for hot dogs. But the phrase was indicative of McGraw's infectious energy and his moxy, a key ingredient in the Phillies' first World Series championship.

There may have been some that were better: some would argue that Ryan Madson and Ron Reed were better relievers. There may have been some who had better strikeout rates, like Antonio Bastardo, Ricky Bottalico, and Steve Bedrosian. But for ten seasons, Tug was one of the best relievers in baseball for the Phillies and the man on the mound at the end of the longest drought among professional sports teams at that time, striking out Willie Wilson in Game Six of the 1980 World Series.

In 1980, McGraw, celebrating the World Series win amongst a frenzied crowd at JFK Stadium, uttered a similarly famous quote:

All through baseball history, Philadelphia has had to take a back seat to New York City. Well, New York City can take this world championship and stick it! Cuz we're number one!

McGraw was inducted to the Phillies Wall of Fame in 1999 and would serve as a roving Spring Training instructor for the club through 2003.

Diagnosed with a brain tumor in 2003, McGraw was still able to close out Veteran's Stadium, recreating the final out of the 1980 World Series.

Tug passed away in 2004. His son, country music superstar son Tim, would spread a handful of his ashes on Citizens Bank Park in tribute before Game 3 of the 2008 World Series. Perhaps it is no coincidence that the Phillies would win that game 5-4 and the series in five games.

Phillies and Mets – Rivals or *Greatest Talent Sharers?*

As of press time, Tug McGraw is one of 110 players to play at least one Major League game as a Phillie and one as a Met. Despite being rivals, the two squads have had huge levels of roster similarity, sharing All-Stars and even Hall of Famers. In fact, seven of the *Phillies Nation 100* have been Mets!

Bobby Abreu
Richie Ashburn
Wally Backman
Ricky Bottalico
Larry Bowa
Marlon Byrd
Lenny Dykstra
Julio Franco
Dallas Green
Bud Harrelson
Tom Herr

Tug McGraw
Chan Ho Park
Gregg Jefferies
Ricky Ledee
Pedro Martinez
Willie Montanez
Juan Samuel
Del Unser
Billy Wagner
David West

Bonus

Transactions That Shaped the Phillies: Owens Brings Believer Into Fold

Most modern Major League general managers will tell you that one of the keys to staying under budget while fielding a competitive team is spending wisely on relief pitching. These days, Jonathan Papelbon's four-year, $62 million pact gets a lot of deserved flack for perhaps being too long, too expensive, or both for a reliever while young players like Greg Holland and Ernesto Frieri seemingly turn up every year or reclamation projects like Joe Nathan or Jason Grilli become success stories.

The rationale behind these long commitments is that good, and more importantly consistently repeatable, relief pitching is incredibly difficult to find. While Holland has continued his excellence in 2014, Frieri has not, posting a 6.39 ERA in 2014. And while Grilli and Nathan were great stories of value relief pick-ups for 2013, 2014 has been disastrous to say the least for either.

As you may imagine, the struggle to find reliable, consistent relief pitching being difficult to obtain existed even during a time when relief pitching was first becoming specialized. Tug McGraw was one of the original stewards of this expansion of roles on a baseball team. According to the SABR Baseball Biography Project, a then-swingman McGraw was told in 1969 by Mets manager Gil Hodges "Tug, I have three pieces of advice for you. One, I think you should think about staying in the bullpen permanently. You could be a great reliever and at best an average starter. Two, this team needs a late-inning stopper, and I want you to be my stopper. Three, I think you'll make a lot more money as a reliever than as a starter. Now it's up to you."

McGraw took Hodges' advice and became one of the premier relievers in baseball. From 1969 through 1974, McGraw posted a 2.79 ERA with 85 saves in pretty stellar 615.1 IP with a K/9 of 7.44 which ranked fifth among Major League pitchers with 600 or more innings pitched in that span. The wheels, seemingly, were coming off the wagon in 1974 for McGraw, however. McGraw battled through injuries in May, which limited him to just three appearances. His 41 appearances would be the lowest since he became a permanent Major Leaguer in 1969 and his 4.16 ERA the highest in the same time frame. McGraw would even earn the dubious record of giving up the most grand slams in a season, four, in 1974.

McGraw was battling shoulder issues throughout 1974 and the stretch run did no favors to help McGraw heal. The Mets, rather inexplicably, choose to start McGraw in September despite hovering no closer than 10 games out of first place. McGraw would earn the only complete game shutout of his career in that time but went 6-11 with a 4.16 ERA and just three saves. It is the belief of some, including McGraw himself per his book, *Ya Gotta Believe!*, that the Mets made him a starter to demonstrate that McGraw wasn't hurt. It worked: the Phillies, unaware of his medical condition, took the bait and his, comparatively-massive $90,000 per year deal, in a deal with the Mets that moved he, Don Hahn and Dave Schneck for Mac Scarce, John Stearns, and Del Unser on December 3, 1974.

The Phillies, breaking a yet-unestablished, unwritten rule, seemingly overpaid for a broken reliever. Scarce was 25 at the time of the trade and posted a solid 3.65 ERA in 141 relief appearances with the Phillies from 1972 through 1974. Stearns was a high-profile catching prospect taken second overall in the 1973 draft by the Phillies who was just 22 at the time of the trade. Finally, Unser had become a slightly above-average veteran outfielder for the Phillies in 1973 and 1974.

If the Phillies were to "win" this trade, they were hoping to get something out of then-25-year old center fielder Don Hahn. Hahn had shown promise as a Montreal farmhand and was coming off his best season as a Major Leaguer with the Mets (.251/.328/.337, 4 HR in 366 PA). Schneck was a 26-year old outfielder who had served in Vietnam in 1969 and 1970 and had a 1972 in the minors that put him squarely on the map (.304/.373/.595 with 24 HR and 7 steals across AA and AAA ball). Yet, despite Hahn playing just nine games as a Phillie, Schneck, a native of Allentown, never reaching the Majors with his hometown club, Unser growing as a player in 1975, and "Bad Dude" Stearns becoming a four-time NL All-Star, the Phillies won a trade where what they received was a player labeled as an aging, injured, loose cannon, free-spirited, overpaid reliever.

How many times has a team won a trade with a player fitting that description?

McGraw combined great performance with a strong element of "right place, right time". His personal success was aided by the successful removal of a cyst that was causing McGraw's pain in Spring Training 1975. As with all of the entries on the list, context is key. The Brad Lidge trade, for instance, was actually a pretty solid win for a rebuilding Houston Astros squad that was looking to reduce payroll and acquire assets. But would the Phillies have won the 2008 World Series had they not acquired Lidge? I will let you imagine for a moment Geoff Geary trying to close out 48 out of 48 games.

The 1975 Phillies were a team finally recovering from several years of dismal baseball. Great scouting had gotten them Bob Boone, Larry Bowa, Mike Schmidt, and Larry Christenson. Great trading had gotten them Jim Lonborg, Jay Johnstone, Dave Cash, McGraw, and, midseason, Garry Maddox. After seven consecutive seasons of sub-.500 baseball, the Phillies were poised to turn the corner. And in one fell swoop, they almost did, finishing just 6.5 games back of the division-winning Pirates.

The success of the Phillies was tied, in large part, to the arrival of McGraw. McGraw was one of four Phillies to earn a trip to the NL All-Star game in 1975 and go back to his familiar role as closer. From 1975 through 1984, his age 30 through 39 (!) seasons, McGraw posted a 3.10 ERA with a 1.198 WHIP in 722 IP. Among players with at least 600 IP in that span, McGraw ranked 28th in K/9 IP, 17th in ERA, and 21st out of 199 in WHIP.

Even though McGraw's impact was seen immediately, as evident by the Phillies three consecutive division wins from 1976 through 1978 due in no small part to having the lowest bullpen ERA in baseball over those three years, McGraw's finest season would come in 1980.

Posting career-lows (1.46 ERA, 0.921 WHIP) with his first 20 save season since 1973, McGraw had a 1980 season for the ages, finishing fifth in the NL Cy Young voting and a 16th place finish in the NL MVP voting. McGraw would take the hill for nine postseason games in 1980, including earning the save in Game 6 of the Fall Classic in front of a raucous Veteran's Stadium crowd to clinch the World Series.

General Manager Paul Owens followed a blueprint of developing young talent and acquiring solid veterans after assuming the role of General Manager in 1973. Owens built a team that earned six playoff appearances and acquired a quirky, rowdy, overpaid, possibly burnt out reliever early in the run who became the heart and soul of the first Phillies World Series championship squad. Sometimes, ya just gotta believe.

#55 Pat Burrell

Left Fielder, First Baseman

Years as a Phillie: 2000-2008
Line as a Phillie: .257/.367/.485, 251 HR in 5388 PA
fWAR Phillies Rank: 41st among position players, 59th among Phillies
Signature Seasons: Hit .282/.376/.544 with 37 HR and 116 RBI in 2002 and .281/.389/.504 with 32 HR and 117 RBI in 2005
Signature Moments: Leading off the bottom of the seventh in Game 5 of the 2008 World Series with a double. Being Grand Marshall of the 2008 World Series victory parade.

"Pat the Bat" was the Phillies' number one pick, and the number one pick overall, in the 1998 amateur draft out of the University of Miami. The former Hurricane would reach the Majors after just a season and a half in the minors, finishing fourth in the 2000 Rookie of the Year voting. By his third season, Burrell had received MVP votes after hitting 37 HR and racking up 116 RBIs.

Inconsistency, though, would plague Burrell during his time as a Phillie and no bigger evidence was his 2002 through 2005 seasons. The span was bookended by two of the finer offensive campaigns by a Phillies outfielder but also featured a 2003 that saw Burrell follow up a 37 HR campaign with just 21 HR and a .404 SLG%. Toward the end of his run, Burrell had found consistency somewhere in the middle, reliably averaging .254 with 31 HR per season across 2006 through 2008.

While Burrell was never one of the baseball's premier players, hamstrung by poor defense and a penchant for striking out, he holds up quite well against other Phillies left fielders. Burrell played the fourth most games in left field out of any Phillie, hit the second most homers, and drove in the fourth most runs. In 2008, Burrell got his day in the sun with the franchise he helped turn around: with rain tapering off, Burrell would lace a double to right field off of submariner Chad Bradford to lead off the seventh inning of Game 5 of the 2008 World Series. Burrell would be replaced by pinch runner Eric Bruntlett who would score the go ahead, and series' clinching, run for the Phillies on a Pedro Feliz single two batters later.

Burrell would be the Grand Marshall of the 2008 World Series parade, the last remaining player from the dark days of the 2000 Phillies. Burrell trusted the Phillies to compete and was a cornerstone in their turnaround from cellar-dweller to contender. On May 19, 2012, Burrell would sign a one-day contract to retire a Phillie.

First Round Success

As the number one pick of the 1998 draft, Pat Burrell was part of quite an amazing run of scouting and drafting by the Phillies: from 1993 through 2007, every first round and supplemental first round draft pick the Phillies selected reached the Majors, including a pretty fantastic run from 1998 through 2002.

2002 – Cole Hamels, 17th overall
2001 – Gavin Floyd, 4th overall
2000 – Chase Utley, 15th overall
1999 – Brett Myers, 12th overall
1998 – Pat Burrell, 1st overall

#54 *Larry Bowa*
Shortstop

Years as a Phillie: 1970-1981
Line as a Phillie: .264/.301/.324, 13 HR, 288 SB in 7358 PA
fWAR Phillies Rank: 40th among position players, 58th among Phillies
Signature Season: Hit .305/.334/.377 with 2 HR and 24 SB in 1975

"Bo" has become one of the more polarizing figures in recent Phillies history but nobody can take away the 12 seasons he had manning shortstop for a series of winning ball clubs. Bowa ranks as one of the best defensive shortstops in history, leading the Majors in fielding percentage as a Phillie in 1971, 1972, 1974, 1978, and 1979. He also lead the Majors in total zone runs saved as a shortstop in 1978, ranking 57th in baseball history in defensive WAR, ninth in assists among shortstops, sixth in games played at shortstop, and eleventh in double plays turned as a shortstop.

Bowa would win Gold Gloves in 1972 and 1978 with the Phillies, making the NL All-Star squad five times (1974-1976, 1978-1979).

Bowa's defensive abilities helped overshadow below-average offensive output. While Bowa ranked ninth in batting average among shortstops from 1970 through 1981, he ranked 35th in on-base percentage, 29th in slugging, and 34th in wOBA. Bowa did excel, however, on the base paths, ending his Phillies tenure after the 1981 campaign with 288 steals, good enough for sixth in Phillies history.

Despite Bowa's offensive shortcomings, Bowa would come up huge for the Phillies in the 1980 postseason. Bowa would hit .349/.391/.372 in the 11 games of the 1980 postseason, including leading off the eighth inning of Game 5 of the 1980 NLCS with a single off of Nolan Ryan with the team down 5-2.

On January 27, 1982, Bowa would be traded to the Cubs with Ryne Sandberg for Ivan DeJesus. The trade would favor the Phillies immediately following the 1982 season, however, we all know the eventual ramifications of that trade. Bowa would play three and a half seasons as the Cubs' starting shortstop, helping them win the 1984 NL East crown before being traded midway through the 1985 season to the Mets, where he ended his career.

Bowa would return to the Phillies organization as its manager for the 2001 season, winning NL Manager of the Year after taking the last place Phillies to within two games of first place in 2001. While Bowa managed the club to a 337-308 record during his tenure as manager, he would be fired with two games left in the 2004 season after clashing with general manager Ed Wade. Bowa was named a bench coach for Phillies manager Ryne Sandberg's staff for 2014.

Phillies' Top 10: **On-Base Percentage, Shortstops**

While a defensive wizard, Bowa struggled to get on base for large stretches as a Phillie. His .301 OBP with the Phillies ranks 20th out of 30 qualified shortstops, behind Steve Jeltz (.314) at 11 and these ten men.

1. Dick Bartell	.358,	1931-1934
2. Kevin Stocker	.347,	1993-1997
3. Bobby Morgan	.344,	1954-1957
4. Heinie Sand	.343,	1923-1928
5. Bob Allen	.331,	1890-1894
6. Dave Bancroft	.330,	1915-1920
7. Jimmy Rollins	.327,	2000-2014
8. Ivan DeJesus	.319,	1982-1984
9. Ruben Amaro Sr.	.315,	1960-1965
10. Desi Relaford	.315,	1996-2000

#53 *Pete Rose*

First Baseman

Years as a Phillie: 1979-1983
Line as a Phillie: .291/.365/.361, 8 HR, 51 SB in 3232 PA
fWAR Phillies Rank: 146th among position players, 273rd among Phillies
Signature Series: Hit .400/.520/.400 in the 1980 NLCS
Signature Moment: *The Catch* – Rose snags a foul ball fumbled by Bob Boone in Game 5 of the 1980 World Series

The straw that stirred the drink, Rose joined the Phillies for the 1979 season, signing a four year, $3.225 million deal. Rose was the veteran mercenary, turning 38 just a few games into the 1979 season, jumping to the Phillies as the missing piece, the first baseman to put the Phillies firmly from playoff disappointment over the Dodgers and into their first World Series since 1950.

It didn't work. At least in 1979, that is.

It certainly wasn't Rose's fault: Rose, at 38, had one of the best seasons of his career, hitting .331/.418/.430, leading the league in OBP. The Phillies, however, struggled to find consistent starting pitching and Tug McGraw, Ron Reed, and Rawly Eastwick had some of their worst seasons of their careers out of the bullpen. The Phillies fired Danny Ozark with 30 games left in the season and finished 84-78, a fourth place finish after three straight years of winning the NL East.

The stars would align in 1980: Rose would lead the league in doubles, playing all 162 games, and despite having a low triple-slash line as a 39-year old (.282/.352/.354), Rose would make his second All-Star team in as many seasons with the Phillies, helping the Phillies win 91 games, just one more than the 90-win, second-place Expos had.

Still proudly known as Charlie Hustle into the twilight of his career, Rose would hit .400/.520/.400 in the 1980 NLCS against the Houston Astros and would hit .326/.431/.349 in 51 PA in the 1980 postseason. And of course, there was the Phillies version of The Catch in Game 6 of the World Series:

Rose would return to the World Series with the Phillies in 1983 with his Big Red Machine teammates Tony Perez and Joe Morgan, hitting .344/.382/.375 in the 1983 postseason. Charlie Hustle ended his time with the Phillies with a final line of .291/.365/.361 with 8 HR in five seasons. While Rose made four consecutive All-Star teams, he compared poorly to his contemporary first baseman. Rose ranked just 33rd out of 44 qualified first baseman in fWAR from 1979 through 1983, his batting average ranking 12th and OBP ninth, but his 8 HR ranking 42nd, slugging 41st, wOBA 33rd, wRC+ 34th, and his defense 44th.

But that, in a way, says why Rose definitively deserves to be on this list: as one of baseball's elder statesman, Rose's presence alone on a championship-caliber was perceived to be enough to put them over the top. And whether it was perception, reality, or if perception became reality, Rose was one of the greatest Phillies of all time.

Phillies' Bottom 10: **Slugging Percentage, First Basemen**

Pete Rose, while an on-base machine, was not known as a particularly powerful hitter. While Rose ranks tenth among Phillies in OBP, he ranks 26th out of 32 qualified first basemen in SLG.

32. Klondike Douglass	.320,	1898-1904
31. Sid Farrar	.342,	1883-1889
30. Tom Hutton	.349,	1972-1977
29. Kitty Bransfield	.349,	1905-1911
28. Jack Boyle	.356,	1893-1898
27. Eddie Waitkus	.359,	1949-1955
26. Pete Rose	.361,	1979-1983
25. Kevin Jordan	.363,	1995-2001
24. Jimmy Wasdell	.371,	1943-1946
23. Walter Holke	.401,	1923-1925

Bonus

The Top Five Managers in Phillies' History

The Phillies have won two World Series, seven pennants, and twelve NL East championships. To compete at the highest level and achieve these accomplishments, a professional baseball manager has an incredible task on his hands: balancing the talent, concerns, egos, and emotions of 25 players at a time, and up to 40 in September, through the longest schedule in professional sports. Here are the five men who did this best for the Phillies since their inception in 1883.

5. Gene Mauch, 1960-1968, 645-684 record

Gene Mauch guided the Phils through most of the 1960s and was charged with rebuilding the Phillies who had enjoyed a solid run through the fifties. Mauch responded with six seasons over .500 out of nine and helped the Phillies improve from 47 wins to 81 from 1961 to 1962.

4. Danny Ozark, 1973-1979, 594-510 record, three division titles (1976-1978)

In 1973, Danny Ozark piloted a team that had won just 59 games the year before to 71 victories. Ozark guided generational talents Mike Schmidt and Steve Carlton, along with a cast of developing All-Stars to three-straight division titles from 1976-1978 before being fired with just 30 games left in 1979 because, in large part, he failed to repeat his success with the best Phillies to date.

3. Eddie Sawyer, 1948-1952, 1958-1960, 390-424 record, one pennant (1950)

Some teams rebuild with young talent. Good managers lead those teams to a pennant when expectations are the lowest. With an average age of 26.4, Eddie Sawyer led the 1950 Whiz Kids to a 91-63 and their first NL Pennant since 1915.

2. Dallas Green, 1979 – 1981, 169-130 record, one World Series (1980), one pennant (1980)

Dallas Green was a 6'5" right-handed pitcher from Newport, DE that was signed as an amateur free agent in 1955 by the Phillies. In two stints with the Phillies, Green would post a 20-22 record and a 4.28 ERA. After his playing days faded away, Green would emerge as a late season replacement for the fired Ozark in 1979, ending the season 19-11.

Green was able to do the one thing Ozark was unable to do: win a National League pennant and guide his team to a World Series appearance. And with stellar starting pitching by Lefty and an amazing Fall Classic by Series MVP Schmidt, Green took the team's growing success one step further: he had won the franchise's first World Series. Green would step down following a playoff exit in 1981 to the Montreal Expos.

1. Charlie Manuel, 2005 – 2013, 780-636 record, one World Series (2008), two pennants (2008, 2009)

Manuel's easy going, soft-spoken personality was in stark contrast to the man who had last led the Phillies through a full season, the fiery Larry Bowa. Manuel narrowly missed the playoffs in 2005 and 2006 before leading the Phillies to the first of five-straight NL East titles.

In 2008, "Chuck" was able to guide one of the youngest teams in baseball, led by ace Cole Hamels and MVPs Ryan Howard and Jimmy Rollins to a World Series. Manuel set the franchise record for wins with 102 in 2011, owns the record for most playoff wins among Phillies' managers, and set the franchise record for most wins for a Phillies' manager before being replaced during the 2013 season, the only season where the team finished under .500.

#52 Jayson Werth

Right Fielder

Years as a Phillie: 2007-2010
Line as a Phillie: .282/.380/.506, 95 HR, 60 SB in 2114 PA
fWAR Phillies Rank: 36th among position players, 53rd among Phillies
Signature Season: Led the league in doubles, hitting .296/.388/.532 with 27 HR and 13 SB in 2010
Signature Accomplishment: Leads Phillies with 11 HR in postseason, including a 2-run homer in Game 4 of 2008 World Series

Pat Gillick's greatest gambling reward, and one of Ruben Amaro's finest extensions, Werth came to the Phillies on December 19, 2006 as an outfield depth piece. Werth had been the 22nd overall pick in the 1997 MLB amateur draft by the Baltimore Orioles. Their GM? Gillick. Other teams were scared away by the fact that the 6'5" Werth had missed the entirety of 2006 with a broken left wrist. But the Hall of Fame general manager was not deterred. Said Gillick:

"Jayson is a young outfielder with a combination of power and speed. He's had some injuries over the past couple years, but we think he has tremendous athleticism and we're very happy to have him in a Phillies uniform. He's a great addition to the club."

Werth entered camp as the fourth outfielder on the Phillies, penciled in behind Pat Burrell, Aaron Rowand, and Shane Victorino. In 304 plate appearances, Werth played about as well as a part-time player could have played, hitting .298/.404/.459 with 8 HR and 7 SB, contributing to the Phillies reaching the postseason for the first time in 14 years. Entering 2008, Werth entered camp competing with Geoff Jenkins for the starting right fielder role. The veteran Jenkins won the job out of camp but Werth would end the season the starter, hitting 24 HR with 20 SB, becoming one of four Phillies to hit at least 10 homers and steal 10 bags that season.

In Werth's second postseason, he delivered in a huge way. Werth would hit .444/.583/.778 in the 2008 World Series en route to the Phillies' second World Championship. 2009 would be Werth's breakout campaign, hitting 36 HR with 20 SB, making, to this date, his only All-Star team. The Phillies may have fallen short in the 2009 World Series but it was not due to Werth: Werth would hit seven homers in the 2009 postseason, including a two-homer game in the pennant-clinching Game 5 of the 2009 NLCS and a two-homer Game 3 of the 2009 World Series.

Werth would have an even-better 2010, hitting .296/.388/.532 with 27 HR and 13 SB, cementing himself in Phillies lore. Werth wound up 15th all-time among Phillies' outfielders in OBP, seventh in slugging, 15th in wOBA, and ninth in OPS.

Werth was an elite outfielder in his brief four-year stay in Philadelphia, ranking as the second best NL outfielder according to FanGraphs' version of Wins Above Replacement level, ranking third in OBP, sixth in slugging, and fourth in OPS. Because of his elite postseason performance and Werth's stay near the top of the advanced statistic food chain, Werth is listed among the 100 greatest Phillies of all-time.

Phillies' Top 10: Isolated Power, Right Fielders

Jayson Werth's long, sweet swing lead to many extra-base hits. Werth was one of the Phillies most powerful right fielders of all-time as evident in his place among ISO leaders.

1. Chuck Klein   .228, 1928-1933, 1936, 1939-1944
2. Jayson Werth   .224, 2007-2010
3. Bobby Abreu   .209, 1998-2006
4. George Harper   .205, 1924-1926
5. Gavvy Cravath   .198, 1912-1920
6. Cy Williams   .194, 1918-1930
7. Del Ennis   .192, 1946-1956
8. Bill Robinson   .191, 1972-1974, 1982-1983
9. Johnny Callison   .186, 1960-1969
10. Wally Post   .185, 1958-1960

Bonus
The Top Ten Free Agent Signings in Phillies' History

Prior to the landmark 1972 United States Supreme court decision ruling *Flood v. Kuhn* which eliminated baseball's reserve clause and allowed for a less-restricted free agent market place, it was difficult for Major League teams to acquire measurable talent by any means other than signing amateur players and, later, drafting amateur talent.

The decision was in response to outfielder Curt Flood refusing to report to Philadelphia after being traded in a package that would send Dick Allen to the St. Louis Cardinals on October 7, 1969. Flood, an All-Star and Gold Glove-winning centerfielder, refused to report to Philadelphia citing the Phillies position in the standings, Connie Mack Stadium's condition, and a contingent of the team's belligerent, racist fans.

Players' Union leader Marvin Miller assisted Flood with a lawsuit effectively creating free agency in Major League Baseball. While Flood never reported to Philadelphia, and was ostensibly blacklisted after spending 1971 with the Washington Senators, the Phillies would quickly benefit from the new free agency rules, stocking up on role players that would help them return to the postseason and beyond.

10. Jay Johnstone – signed April 3, 1974

After winning a World Series ring with the A's in 1973, Johnstone became one of the Phillies most dangerous players, whether it was off the bench or in the starting line-up. Johnstone would hit .303/.368/.455 for the Phillies from 1974 through 1978 and .778/.800/1.111 against the Reds in the 1976 NLCS before being traded to the Yankees on June 14, 1978 for reliever Rawly Eastwick. Johnstone would later win two more World Series, one in 1978 with the Yankees and another in 1981 with the Dodgers.

9. Del Unser – signed March 29, 1979

In his second go-round with the Phils, Unser was a pinch-hitting specialist whose big moments of glory came in the 1980 postseason. Unser was smack dab in the middle of the eighth inning rally in Game 5 of the NLCS, driving in Greg Gross via single en route to a 7-5 lead. In the tenth inning with the game knotted at seven, Unser hit a one-out double and scored the pennant-winning run on a Garry Maddox double to center field.

Unser became a postseason hero twice more in 1980, hitting a pinch-hit, RBI double that split the gap in left-center off of Dan Quisenberry and helped the Phillies take a 6-4 win in Game 2. Later he hit an RBI double in Game 5 in the top of the ninth that knotted the game at three before scoring the winning run on a Manny Trillo dribbler.

8. Cliff Lee – signed December 15, 2010

Since being reacquired by the Phillies, all Lee has done is put up ace caliber numbers. Lee was 41-29 with a 2.83 ERA in his second go-round with the Phillies from 2011-2014, ranking behind only Clayton Kershaw among NL pitchers in FanGraphs' version of WAR and xFIP. While Lee only has one playoff appearance in his second turn in Philly, the lefty from Arkansas has been one of the biggest factors in keeping games competitive at Citizens Bank Park.

7. J.C. Romero – signed June 22, 2007

It's difficult to see how Romero became a free agent in 2007. After all, he had a 3.15 ERA for the first-place Red Sox. Not bad. But for whatever reason, Romero wasn't a good fit in Boston and he was let loose, midseason to the open market. General Manager Pat Gillick swooped in, picked Romero up, and the rest is history.

Romero led all Phillies relievers in ERA (1.24 in 36.1 IP) in 2007, helping to stabilize one of the worst bullpens in the Major Leagues en route to an NL East division crown. Romero would post a 2.73 ERA while with the Phillies in 165 regular season IP, earning two wins in the 2008 World Series as the Phillies marched to a Fall Classic victory.

6. Jim Thome – signed December 6, 2002

"Gentleman Jim" came to the Phillies a year removed from a promising, yet disappointing, 80-81 finish in 2002. A clear upgrade over incumbent first baseman Travis Lee, Thome would lead MLB in homers with 47 in 2003 and help the Phillies improve to an 86-76 mark. The following season, Thome would earn an All-Star birth, hitting 42 homers and leading the Phillies to an identical 86-76 mark.

Injuries limited Thome's first stay in Philadelphia and the slugging lefty was dealt away midway through 2005 to make room for Ryan Howard but not before creating some lasting memories in Citizens Bank Park, including hitting his 400th home run there on June 14, 2004.

5. Eppa Rixey - signed June 6, 1912

Rixey was a rare, straight-from-college signee in 1912, who wasted no time establishing himself in the Majors, winning ten games in his rookie season with a 2.50 ERA. Rixey would be a key pitcher on the staff that took the 1915 club to the World Series but lost his only decision, the series-ending Game 5, to the Red Sox. Rixey would have his finest season in 1916, going 22-10 with a 1.85 ERA.

4. Jim Eisenreich – signed January 20, 1993

A man who narrowly missed our 100 greatest countdown, Eisenreich was a right fielder on a mission to prove that he was a Major League caliber player. And did he ever. Eisenreich hit .324/.381/.453 for the Phillies with 24 HR and 32 steals from 1993 through 1996. Eisenreich's .318/.363/.445 line in 1993 was a huge upgrade from Ruben Amaro's .219/.303/.348 line there in 1992 and was a major factor in the Phillies winning the NL Pennant.

3. Jayson Werth – signed December 19, 2006

A shot in the dark by then-GM Pat Gillick turned into a goldmine for the Phillies. The Phillies' postseason home run leader, the shaggy haired and bearded Werth was an All-Star in 2009 for the Phillies while garnering MVP votes in 2009 and 2010. Werth hit 95 homers for the Phillies in just four seasons while hitting .266/.376/.590 with 11 homers and five steals in the postseason.

2. Gavvy Cravath – signed September 1911

A clerical error helped the Phillies land "Cactus Gavvy" shortly after the completion of the 1911 season. The definition of a late bloomer, Cravath was signed as a 31-year old outfielder and proceeded to hit .291/.381/.489 with 117 homers and 80 steals for the Phillies from 1912 through 1920. Cravath was the NL MVP runner up in 1913 and helped power the Phillies to their first pennant in 1915.

1. Pete Rose – signed December 5, 1978

For three straight seasons, the Phillies were eliminated from the postseason. In 1979, they sensed an opportunity to upgrade first base. Enter Pete Rose. Rose would make his first of four-straight All-Star appearances with the Phillies in 1979 but the club would fall short of the NL East.

1980 was a different story.

With the then-39 year old Rose at the top of the line-up, the Phillies went 91-71, winning the NL East, defeating the Houston Astros in the NLCS, and beating the Kansas City Royals in the World Series. Rose would become one of the Phillies' all-time great postseason hitters, hitting .326/.402/.358 in 25 games in 1980, 1981, and 1983.

Nap Lajoie

Second Baseman

Years as a Phillie: 1896-1900
Line as a Phillie: .345/.374/.520, 32 HR, 87 SB in 2204 PA
fWAR Phillies Rank: 38th among position players, 55th among Phillies
Signature Season: Hit .361/.392/.569 with 9 HR, 20 SB, and 127 RBIs in 1897.

Another Hall of Famer on this list, Napoleon Lajoie, the pride of Woonsocket, RI, made his debut with the Phillies as a 21-year old on the 1896 squad. Lajoie is one of the best second baseman of all-time and his early seasons with the Phillies definitely were an indication of things to come: Lajoie ranks fourth among Phillies in batting average and eighth in slugging, leading all second baseman from 1896 through 1900 in FanGraphs' version of WAR, homers, RBIs, batting average, and slugging, and third in OBP and fifth in steals.

Lajoie would leave the Phillies because of a salary dispute following the 1900 season. Frustrated that Ed Delahanty was making more money than he was, Lajoie asked notoriously frugal owner John Rogers to make the same amount as Delahanty, a jump from $2,600 to $3,000 per season. When Rogers only offered an additional $200, Lajoie jumped to the Philadelphia A's for 1901, setting a still-unbroken single-season record for batting average of .426, winning the triple-crown, setting the then-single-season record of 232 hits.

Lajoie would end his career with 3243 hits and a .338/.380/.466 line and was inducted into the Hall of Fame's second class in 1937. And to think, just an extra $200 may have kept Lajoie in a Phillies uniform. And who knows: Lajoie may have been able to help some of the early 1900s Phillies teams to a pennant.

Lajoie would play one game for the A's in 1902 before being granted free agency and signing with the Cleveland Bronchos (note: not a typo). Lajoie was so talented, and so popular that the team was renamed the Cleveland Naps in 1903. Lajoie would become player/manager of Cleveland in 1905 after leading the AL in all three triple-slash categories in 1904.

Lajoie would return to Philly, this time, to the A's in 1915 after spending 13 years with Cleveland. Lajoie ended his career with 3243 hits and a .338/.380/.466 line. Lajoie ranks 12th in singles, seventh in doubles, 33rd in triples, 33rd in RBI, and 14th in career hits.

Oh, what might have been.

Hey, have you heard of: The 1901 Phillies

Fresh off a 75-63 season with two of the best outfielders in baseball still on their roster, the 1901 Phillies were determined to finally win the pennant despite the loss of Nap Lajoie. The team, led by the outfield trio of Roy Thomas, Elmer Flick, and Delahanty and a trio of 20-game winners in Red Donahue, Bill Duggleby, and Al Orth, would overachieve without Lajoie, winning 83 games and finishing in second place.

According to FanGraphs, Lajoie was worth an astounding 8.9 wins in 1901. The Phils finished just 7.5 games behind the Pirates for the NL Pennant.

Oops.

Bonus

Top Five Devastating Losses to Free Agency

Equipped with a payroll of over $180 million headed into the 2014 season, the Phillies had notoriously been frugal spenders for much of their 130+ year history. Some of these decisions have cost the Phillies dearly. Here are the Top Five most devastating Phillies losses to free agency.

5. Willie Hernandez becomes a free agent following the 1983 season.

Acquired mid-way through the 1983 season, Hernandez became one of the most stable pieces of the Phillies bullpen en route to the 1983 pennant. The Phillies let him walk following their World Series loss and Hernandez would sign with the Detroit Tigers. Hernandez returned to the World Series in 1984, this time with the Tigers, and would not only win a World Series ring but become one of the few relief pitchers ever to win a Cy Young Award.

4. Elmer Flick jumps to Philadelphia A's after pay dispute following 1901 season, becomes Hall of Famer.

Elmer Flick was a lot like a turn-of-the-century Ken Griffey Jr.: he could hit for average, power, draw walks, could steal bases, play good defense, and had a strong arm. As a Phillie, through age 26, Flick had hit .338/.419/.487 with 29 homers and 119 steals, when he jumped to the crosstown A's for more money. The Phillies should have ponied up: Flick put up video game numbers, even by today's standards, and played his way into the Hall of Fame.

3. Ed Delahanty jumps to the Washington Senators after the 1901 season.

For a short time, "Big Ed" was the premier player in baseball, leading the NL in almost every statistical category in one season or more throughout his career. At 33 years old, Delahanty, coming off a .354/.427/.528 season, jumped to Washington for the 1902 season, where he would lead the American League in all three triple-slash categories. Following his departure, the Phillies win total from 1901 to 1902 dropped 27 games. This one could have been worse had Delahanty not died mysteriously at Niagara Falls in 1903.

2. Phillies release Curt Simmons on May 17, 1960.

The Phillies pulled a diamond out of the rough finding the All-Star pitcher in Allentown, PA suburb Egypt, PA in 1947. Thinking Simmons was running on fumes, the Phillies released the lefty on May 17, 1960. Three days later, Simmons signed with the Cardinals. In 1964, as the Phillies overused the combination of Jim Bunning and Rick Wise down the stretch, Simmons pitched 224 with a 3.43 ERA to lead the Cardinals beyond the Phillies in the standings in one of the most improbable comebacks ever for a team chasing a pennant.

1. Nap Lajoie leaves, becomes one of the greatest players ever.

Even though it has been over 100 years, this one is still tough to swallow. Nap Lajoie left the Phillies because frugal owner John Rogers offered him a raise of only $200 instead of the $400 he asked for. Lajoie's 102.2 career fWAR ranks third all-time among second baseman and 19th among all position players.

#50 Dode Paskert

Center Fielder

Years as a Phillie: 1911-1917
Line as a Phillie: .272/.357/.374, 28 HR, 158 SB in 4020 PA
fWAR Phillies Rank: 37th among position players, 52nd among Phillies
Signature Season: Hit .315/.420/.413 with 36 steals and two homers in 1912, finishing 14th in MVP voting.

Paskert may be the highest ranked player many fans have never heard of. Paskert was one of the offensive hinge pins of the first successful era in Phillies history, hitting primarily third and playing center field for a set of seven teams that went a combined 582-484 (54.60%) behind the big arms of Grover Cleveland Alexander and Erskine Mayer.

Paskert was acquired by the Phillies on November 12, 1910 along with Fred Beebe, Hans Lobert, and Jack Rowan in an eight player deal that sent Johnny Bates, Eddie Grant, George McQuillan, and Lew Moren to the Cincinnati Reds. Paskert was a speed and power threat for the Phils, averaging 25 doubles and 21 steals a season.

Paskert and Pirates' center fielder Max Carey were the two marquee center fielders in the National League, playing the second-most games among NL center fielders in that time, scoring the second-most runs, driving in the fourth-most RBIs, and stealing the third most bags.

Despite Paskert having some of his best years surrounding the Phillies' first pennant, Paskert fought through an injury-plagued 1915 campaign and stumbled in the 1915 World Series (.158/.200/.158 in 20 PA). Paskert's name is littered throughout the MLB history books, with the 52nd-most outfield assists of all-time from center field and 95th among outfielders in putouts.

Paskert would be traded to the Chicago Cubs for Cy Williams following the 1917 season. He would be the Cubs starting center fielder for three seasons before being selected off of waivers by the Cincinnati Reds in December 1920. He ended his career where it began, as a Cincinnati Red.

The 1915 World Series and the Curious Case of the Disappearing Offense

The 1915 Phillies, historically, generally aren't considered an offensive powerhouse. Even though Gavvy Cravath smashed an almost-unthinkable 24 homers and their leading hitter, first baseman Fred Luderus, hit .315, the club ranked just fifth in the NL in batting and third in OBP.

What they did do well, however, was smash the baseball. The club ranked third in doubles, first in homers, second in SLG, and first in OPS. In the 1915 World Series, that power just about disappeared in two hitters' parks, the Baker Bowl and Fenway Park.

The Phillies lost the 1915 World Series 4-1, with every Phillies loss decided by one run. The Phillies would hit just .182/.244/.243 with only one home run. They would not win another World Series game for nearly 65 years.

#49 *Andy Seminick*
Catcher

Years as a Phillie: 1943-1951, 1955-1957
Line as a Phillie: .244/.351/.419, 123 HR, 20 SB in 3449 PA
fWAR Phillies Rank: 34th among position players, 49th among Phillies
Signature Season: Hit .288/.400/.524 with 24 HR, finishing 14th in MVP voting, in 1950 Whiz Kids season

"Grandpa Whiz" as Seminick was affectionately known, was the starting backstop for the 1950 pennant-winning Phillies, navigating the rotation of Robin Roberts, Curt Simmons, Bob Miller, Russ Meyer, Bubba Church, and Ken Heintzelman to a 91-win season.

Seminick was a reliable battery mate for the young rotation, seeing over 400 PA in five straight seasons (1946-1950). While Seminick was reliable, and a reasonably potent hitter, he was not very sure-handed: while a premier offensive catcher of his generation, ranking second in homers among catchers from 1943-1951, fourth in runs, seventh in OBP, sixth in SLG, and eighth in OPS, Seminick struggled defensively. Seminick led baseball in errors in 1946, 1948-1950, and 1952, while allowing the most stolen bases from 1946-1948 and in 1950. To be fair, Seminick also led baseball in runners thrown out in 1948 and 1949.

Seminick would play through a broken ankle in the 1950 World Series, which may have contributed to his .182/.250/.182 line against the Yankees. In 1952, he was traded in a seven player deal to the Reds for his first replacement, Smokey Burgess.

Seminick would return to the Phillies in a 1955 trade that sent him back to the Phillies for, among other players, Smokey Burgess. It is Seminick's rare power behind the plate that puts him into the Top 50 Phillies of all-time. Seminick retired with the seventh-most homers ever as a catcher and ranks third among Phillies catchers in homers, fourth in runs scored, fifth in RBIs, third in BB%, 11th in OBP, and ninth in slugging.

Seminick would remain with the Phillies organization after his retirement, including stints as a coach in 1958-1959 and 1967-1969, managing minor league clubs from 1959-1966 and 1970-1973, and working as a roving scout and instructor until his death in 2004. Seminick's name lived on long beyond the end of his career with the Phillies: he managed or coached 90 players in the minors that would reach the Majors, including Mike Schmidt and Greg Luzinski.

The Whiz Kid All-Stars

In 1950, the Phillies sent four players to the All-Star game, including eventual NL MVP Jim Konstanty, future Hall of Famer Robin Roberts, third baseman Puddin' Head Jones, and outfielder Dick Sisler.

In addition to these four players, the 1950 squad had seven other players that had either been All-Stars or would go on to become an All-Star, including Andy Seminick.

OF – Richie Ashburn (1948, 1951, 1953, 1958)
OF - Del Ennis (1946, 1951, 1955)
SS – Granny Hamner (1952-1954)
3B – Puddin' Head Jones (1950, 1951)
P – Jim Konstanty (1950)
C – Stan Lopata (1955-1956)
P – Robin Roberts (1950-1956)
C – Andy Seminick (1949)
P – Curt Simmons (1952-1953, 1957)
OF – Dick Sisler (1950)
1B – Eddie Waitkus (1949)

#48 Stan Lopata
Catcher

Years as a Phillie: 1948-1958
Line as a Phillie: .257/.355/.459, 116 HR, 18 SB in 2545 PA
fWAR Phillies Rank: 35th among position players, 51st among Phillies
Signature Season: Hit 32 HR with .267/.353/.535 in 625 PA in All-Star 1956 season

"Stash" was one of the most unlikely stars in Phillies history. Tabbed the starting catcher over veteran Andy Seminick prior to the start of the 1949 season, Lopata ended up starting less games than Seminick but put up a solid .271/.330/.425 line with 8 HR in 261 PA as a 24-year old rookie. Lopata would remain the back-up catcher for the 1950 Whiz Kids and reach the World Series.

By 1951, Lopata was fighting injuries and was being shuttled back and forth between Philadelphia and the Triple-A Baltimore Orioles. Lopata would return to the Phillies full-time in 1952, becoming one of the league's most productive back-ups, hitting 14 homers with a .290/.369/.544 line in 298 PA.

It was during the 1954 campaign that Lopata adapted a batting stance so low that Jeff Bagwell would be envious. In 1955, Lopata would split time with the returning Seminick and a June hot streak (.339/.382/.613, 5 HR) would push Lopata on to the All-Star team. He would return to the All-Star team in his only year with the Phillies where he accumulated over 450 plate appearances, hitting 32 HR.

Despite his limited playing time, Lopata ranked fifth in homers among catchers, had the sixth best walk-rate among catchers, was ninth in OBP, and fourth in slugging among catchers between 1948 and 1958. Despite rarely being a starter, Lopata, with his signature glasses, was one of the very best catchers the Phillies had and was one of the best catchers in baseball for eleven seasons.

On March 31, 1959, Lopata would be traded to the Milwaukee Braves with Ted Kazanski and Johnny O'Brien for Gene Conley, Harry Hanebrink, and Joe Koppe. He would play just 32 more Major League games in his career, hitting .107 for the Braves before calling it quits following the 1960 season.

Phillies' Top 10: Homers in a Season by a Phillies Catcher

In his second of two consecutive All-Star seasons, Stan Lopata set the Phillies club record for home runs by a catcher with 32, a record that still stands today.

1. Stan Lopata	32, 1956
2. Mike Lieberthal	31, 1999
3. Benito Santiago	30, 1996
4. Darren Daulton	27, 1992
5. Darren Daulton	24, 1993
6. Andy Seminick	24, 1950
7. Andy Seminick	24, 1949
8. Stan Lopata	22, 1955
9. Mike Lieberthal	20, 1997
10. Ozzie Virgil	19, 1985

John Kruk

First Baseman, Right Fielder

Years as a Phillie: 1989-1994
Line as a Phillie: .309/.400/.461, 62 HR, 33 SB in 3001 PA
fWAR Phillies Rank: 33rd among position players, 46th among Phillies
Signature Moment: At-bat in the 1993 All-Star Game against Randy Johnson

"The Krukker" arrived in Philadelphia with Randy Ready in a trade that sent Chris James to San Diego on June 2, 1989. The trade was a fortuitous one for the Phillies: Kruk would play parts of six seasons with the Phillies, making three-straight All-Star teams from 1991 through 1993, successfully splitting time between the outfield and first base while James hit .264/.314/.429 in a half season for San Diego before being traded to the Cleveland Indians, making no All-Star teams.

Kruk didn't look like a baseball player: listed at 5'10", 170 lbs on his rookie card, Kruk often took the field looking disheveled, often with stubble, unkempt hair, most notably worn in a mullet, and what looked like an increasingly large paunch. Kruk was lampooned by Saturday Night Live's Chris Farley and would write a book, *I Ain't an Athlete, Lady* in 1994. Yet despite all that Kruk had to work against, Kruk was a leader on the 1993 pennant-winning Phillies squad that would reach the World Series.

Kruk is the Phillies All-Time leader among first baseman with at-least 3,000 PA in batting average and OBP and is fifth in the same group in slugging. Among first baseman from 1989 through 1994, Kruk trailed only Frank Thomas in OBP and ranked eighth in OPS, higher than Mark McGwire, Rafael Palmeiro, and Andres Galarraga, among others. Kruk was one of the most likable players in Phillies history but also one of the most underrated: his appearances on three consecutive All-Star teams were deserved and his World Series performance (.348/.500/.391 in 30 1993 World Series PA) was one to remember.

Kruk has gone on to become a somewhat-larger-than life character outside of baseball. An errant pick-off attempt by Mitch Williams in 1994 broke Kruk's protective cup but led to a screening that helped detect testicular cancer. While Kruk was the fodder for comedians throughout the 90s, he has become quite the media personality in his own right, joining the ESPN Baseball Tonight crew in 2004 and remaining there to this day. In 2003, Kruk was elected via fan vote as the first baseman on the All-Vet Team and in 2011, Kruk was inducted on to the Phillies Wall of Fame.

Phillies All-Stars at First Base

The Phillies have sent a first baseman to the All-Star game 13 times, including three trips by John Kruk.

Babe Dahlgren (1943)
Frank McCormick (1946)
Eddie Waitkus (1949)
Pete Rose (1979-1982)
John Kruk (1991-1993)
Jim Thome (2004)
Ryan Howard (2006, 2009)

Mike Lieberthal
Catcher

Years as a Phillie: 1994-2006
Line as a Phillie: .275/.338/.450, 150 HR, 8 SB in 4613 PA
fWAR Phillies Rank: 32nd among position players, 45th among Phillies
Signature Achievement: All-time Phillies' leader in games caught, plate appearances as a catcher, and homers as a catcher

Mike Lieberthal arrived in Philadelphia with great promise and astonishingly-high expectations. The prep catcher was taken third overall in the 1990 draft out of Westlake High School in Glendale, CA and progressed rather quickly through the Phillies farm system. By 1994, "Lieby" had tasted a cup of coffee with the Phils and would become a regular by 1997, becoming just one of four catchers to hit 20 homers that year. The others? Mike Piazza, Todd Hundley, and Ivan Rodriguez. Not bad company to be in at age 25.

Lieberthal's time in Philly was seemingly defined as much by his power as it was by his injuries. In 1999, arguably his healthiest season, Lieberthal cranked 31 homers while setting the team record for slugging percentage for a catcher, making the All-Star team and earning a Gold Glove while hitting .300/.363/.551. Lieberthal would rank once more in 2000, hitting .301/.370/.529 with 13 homers through the All-Star break, earning his second All-Star nod. Injuries would derail his stellar season in July and he would miss the remainder of September, ending what was debatably the lone bright spot in a 65-97 season.

Despite playing parts of 13 seasons in Philadelphia, Lieberthal would only see the 500 PA threshold in five of those seasons. It is not uncommon for starting catchers to see significantly less time than other starting players but knee injuries kept one of the best Phillies' prospects off the field more than fans would have liked. Yet, Lieberthal remained just healthy and productive enough to be the singular bridge that lasted the entire time between playoff teams. While Lieberthal would never make the playoffs himself, he ranks seventh in Phillies history in batting average and third in slugging among catchers.

Lieberthal left the Phillies after the 2006 season to play for the Los Angeles Dodgers. The Dodgers would wind up 82-80 while the team Lieby left won 89 games and the NL East. Sorry, Mike. Lieberthal would return to Philadelphia on June 7, 2012 to be inducted on to the Phillies Wall of Fame.

Wall of Fame Inductees

Mike Lieberthal returned to Philadelphia in 2012 to join the Phillies Wall of Fame. Here is the complete list of all 36 Phillies alumni to be honored on the Wall of Fame.

1978 – Robin Roberts	1998 – Greg Luzinski
1979 – Richie Ashburn	1999 – Tug McGraw
1980 – Chuck Klein	2000 – Gavvy Cravath
1981 – G.C. Alexander	2001 – Garry Maddox
1982 – Del Ennis	2002 – Tony Taylor
1984 – Jim Bunning	2003 – Sherry Magee
1985 – Ed Delahanty	2004 – Billy Hamilton
1986 – Cy Williams	2005 – Bob Boone
1987 – Granny Hamner	2006 – Dallas Green
1988 – Paul Owens	2007 – John Vukovich
1989 – Steve Carlton	2008 – Juan Samuel
1990 – Mike Schmidt	2009 – Harry Kalas
1991 – Larry Bowa	2010 – Darren Daulton
1992 – Chris Short	2011 – John Kruk
1993 – Curt Simmons	2012 – Mike Lieberthal
1994 – Dick Allen	2013 – Curt Schilling
1995 – Puddin' Head Jones	2014 – Charlie Manuel
1996 – Sam Thompson	2015 – Pat Burrell
1997 – Johnny Callison	

#45 Fred Luderus

First Baseman

Years as a Phillie: 1910-1920
Line as a Phillie: .278/.340/.403, 83 HR, 55 SB in 5304 PA
fWAR Phillies Rank: 31st among position players, 44th among Phillies
Signature Series: Hit .438/.500/.750 with two 2B and a HR in the 1915 World Series

The pride of Three Lakes, WI, Luderus was a fixture at first base on the 1910s Phillies clubs that would be in regular contention for the pennant. Acquired in 1910 for starting pitcher Bill Foxen, Luderus would spend eleven power-filled seasons with the Fightin' Phils. The trade would end up being one of the best in Phillies history. With the aid of the short right field porch at the Baker Bowl, Luderus would appear in the Top 10 in the NL in homers from 1911 through 1919, finishing second in batting average and slugging in the pennant-winning 1915 season.

Luderus retired with several Phillies records for first baseman, including being the clubs' all-time leading home run hitter at first (82), as well as the leader in runs, RBI, and slugging, beating out such Phillies notables before him as Kitty Bransfield and Klondike Douglass. Luderus would be just about the only Phillie to show up offensively in their first appearance in the Fall Classic in 1915, hitting the club's first World Series homer as well as batting .438/.500/.750, leading the team in every triple-slash category, as well as doubles, homers, and OPS.

Some of the shine has worn off Luderus' run with the Phillies as time has moved on and offensive numbers have exploded. Luderus' .404 career slugging as a Phillie first baseman has been topped by players like Willie Montanez, Nick Etten, Ricky Jordan, Rico Brogna, and Pancho Herrera while his RBI title lasted officially until Ryan Howard blew it out of the water. Entering the 2014 season, Luderus still had two records among Phillies' first baseman: most games played and most plate appearances. Howard broke both of those in 2014 leaving Luderus a man with significant contributions to the Phillies but with little to show for it in terms of records. Still, Luderus was one of the earliest in a line of boppers at first for the Phillies and ranks among the teams' best first baseman in history.

Phillies' Top 10: Isolated Power, First Basemen

When Fred Luderus retired, he was the leader in just about every statistical category for Phillies first basemen, including isolated power or ISO. ISO is slugging minus batting average and is used as a rate statistic to measure a player's power through extra base hits.

1. Jim Thome   .282, 2003-2005, 2012
2. Ryan Howard   .270, 2004-Present
3. Dick Allen   .240, 1963-1969, 1975-1976
4. Dolph Camilli   .215, 1934-1937
5. Deron Johnson   .191, 1970-1973
6. Don Hurst   .185, 1928-1934
7. Roy Sievers   .181, 1962-1964
8. Cliff Lee   .176, 1921-1924
9. Rico Brogna   .176, 1997-2000
10. Ed Bouchee   .165, 1956-1960

#44 Jack Taylor

Right-Handed Starter

Years as a Phillie: 1892-1897
Line as a Phillie: 96-77, 4.34 ERA, 1.497 WHIP in 1505.1 IP
fWAR Phillies Rank: 18th among pitchers, 57th among Phillies
Signature Stat: Threw 150 complete games over six seasons, averaging of 25 per season

"Brewery Jack", a nickname gained through his affection for alcohol, overcame a number of roadblocks to become one of the then-Philadelphia Quaker's premier workhorse pitchers. Taylor was the son of a twice-widowed working mother but quickly grew an affinity for baseball. By age seven, Taylor had moved several times but ended up in Staten Island, playing ball in the same neighborhood as other future Major Leaguers Jack Cronin, George Sharrott, Jack Sharrott, and Tuck Turner.

Despite growing up with a deck stacked against him, Taylor became one of the strongest pitchers of the early "modern" era. Making most of his starts and appearances after the pitching rubber was moved to 60 feet, six inches, Taylor would throw 150 complete games, good enough for seventh in team history. Taylor was a three-time 20-game winner despite never posting an ERA under 4 in any of his full seasons with the Phillies. From 1892 through 1897, Taylor ranked 15th in the Majors in innings pitched and 15th in games started.

In a 24/7 news cycle, Twitter, and TMZ world, it is likely that Taylor would have become a national celebrity of interest. The 6'1" right-handed pitcher liked alcohol, a fact that frequently ended up in the newspapers and he butted heads with his manager in 1897, disciplinarian George Stallings. Taylor would be traded to the St. Louis Browns after the 1897 season. Sadly, Taylor would pass away at age 26, attributed to kidney disease. Despite pitching just six seasons for the Phillies, Taylor ranks 13th in franchise history in innings pitched, tenth in wins, and 21st in starts.

Phillies' Top 10: Complete Games by Phillies Starters

Jack Taylor pitched just over five seasons for the Phillies and managed to throw complete games in 64.1% of his starts. Even though he had a short tenure in Philadelphia, his 150 complete games is tied for sixth in team history.

1. Robin Roberts – 272
2. Grover Cleveland Alexander - 219
3. Steve Carlton – 185
4. Charlie Ferguson – 165
5. Bill Duggleby – 156
6. Tully Sparks – 150 (tie)
6. Jack Taylor – 150 (tie)
8. Al Orth – 149
9. Kid Carsey – 141
10. Chick Fraser - 133

#43 Al Orth

Right-Handed Starter

Years as a Phillie: 1895-1901
Line as a Phillie: 100-72, 3.49 ERA, 1.330 WHIP in 1504.2 IP
fWAR Phillies Rank: 15th among pitchers, 48th among Phillies
Signature Season: Went 20-12 with a 2.27 ERA and a league-leading 1.001 WHIP with a league-leading six complete-game shutouts in 1901

Throwing little other than variations on a fastball, Al Orth the "Curveless Wonder" was one of the Phillies earliest pitching stars. At age 22, Orth made quite an impression as a rookie, going 8-1 with a 3.89 ERA in 88.1 innings pitched. Orth would be the Phillies most reliable work horse from 1895 through 1901, leading the team in innings pitched and ranking 12th in the Majors in that same time frame.

Orth's 100 wins from 1895 through 1901 rank him seventh among starters, behind names like Cy Young and Kid Nichols. Orth's 3.49 ERA in that time put him at a respectable 24th while he threw the fifth-most complete game shutouts in that time frame.

While Orth was one of the overall top pitchers in the National League, he was also one of the top hitting pitchers in baseball. Orth hit .294/.311/.405 in 751 PA with the Phillies with 7 HR and 15 SB. He ranks fourth among pitchers from 1895 through 1901 in batting average, 11th in OBP, and third in slugging. Orth's bat would slow down after leaving the Phillies but his arm wouldn't.

After the 1901 season, Orth jumped to the Washington Senators and would later be traded to the then-New York Highlanders during the 1904 season. Orth would lead the American League in wins and innings pitched in 1906, finishing his career with a 204-189 record and a 1.259 WHIP, becoming an early star for the team that would become the New York Yankees.

Phillies' Top 10: Home Runs by Phillies Starting Pitchers

Al Orth hit seven home runs as a Phillie, which is tied for fifth all-time among Phillies starting pitchers.

1T.	Rick Wise	11
1T.	Larry Christenson	11
3T.	Steve Carlton	9
3T.	Schoolboy Rowe	9
5T.	Al Orth	7
5T.	Bucky Walters	7
7T.	Charlie Ferguson	6
7T.	Bill Duggleby	6
7T.	Ed Daily	6
10.	Robin Roberts	5

Phillies' Top 10: Average by Phillies Starting Pitchers

Al Orth leads all Phillies starting pitchers in batting average among those that have 500 PA or more.

1.	Al Orth	.294
2.	Charlie Ferguson	.288
3.	Johnny Lush	.268
4.	Bucky Walters	.260
5.	Jack Taylor	.256
6.	John Coleman	.238
7.	Ed Daily	.230
8.	Charlie Buffinton	.228
9.	Kid Carsey	.225
10.	Steve Carlton	.207

Tony Gonzalez

Center Fielder

Years as a Phillie: 1960-1968
Line as a Phillie: .295/.359/.433, 77 HR, 68 SB in 4194 PA
fWAR Phillies Rank: 28th among position players, 39th among Phillies
Signature Season: Hit .302/.371/.494 with 20 HR and 17 SB in 1962

The versatile, left-handed hitting outfielder, Gonzalez was acquired by the Phillies on June 15, 1960 in a trade that sent right fielder Wally Post back to Cincinnati with starting left fielder, West Chester alum Harry "The Horse" Anderson. At the time, it was a bit of a gamble: the Phillies had finished 64-90 the previous season and seemingly weren't on track to get much better in 1960, while Post and Anderson had combined for 34 HR the previous season.

The Phillies, however, still had a giant hole in center field after trading Richie Ashburn in January for a package that included Al Dark and John Buzhardt. After a 14-2 loss to Sandy Koufax and the Los Angeles Dodgers, the 1960 Phillies, at 20-34, pulled the trigger and acquired the 23-year old center fielder from the Reds.

In his second full season with the club, Gonzalez would explode with a career-best 20 HR and 17 SBs and a career-high slugging percentage. In 1963, he would top his batting average and OBP of 1962, hitting .306/.372/.436 with just four homers and 17 steals and finish 23rd in the MVP voting. Gonzalez would be one of the many Phillies to disappear, however, in September 1964, hitting an uncharacteristically-low .225/.253/.300. Aside from that minor blip, Gonzalez was one of the primary offensive leaders on a set of clubs that would exceed expectations throughout the mid-60s but ultimately fall short of reaching a pennant.

Gonzalez ranks fifth among Phillies center fielders in homers, tenth in runs, fifth in RBIs, eighth in batting average and OBP, and ninth in slugging. Among contemporary center fielders, from 1960 through 1967, Gonzalez ranked seventh in the MLB in batting average, eighth in OBP, and eleventh in slugging. When those lists are filtered for just National League players, it shortens to include only names like Willie Mays, Richie Ashburn, and Vada Pinson in front of Gonzalez. Not bad company.

Gonzalez would be selected from the Phillies by the San Diego Padres as the 37th pick in the 1969 MLB expansion draft. The Padres would trade Gonzalez on June 13, 1969 for Walt Hriniak and Van Kelly. At the end of the 1970, the California Angels would purchase Taylor from the Braves. Gonzalez would finish his career as the everyday center fielder for the Angels.

Phillies' Top 10: Slugging by Phillies Center Fielders

Gonzalez ranks fifth among Phillies center fielders in doubles, fourth in triples, and fifth in homers thus it is no surprise Gonzalez is among the leaders in SLG%.

1. Cy Williams	.500
2. Aaron Rowand	.479
3. Freddy Leach	.460
4. Billy Hamilton	.460
5. Bill Robinson	.452
6. Shane Victorino	.439
7. Ethan Allen	.434
8. Tony Gonzalez	.433
9. Lenny Dykstra	.422
10. Kiddo Davis	.416

#41 Rick Wise

Right-Handed Starter

Years as a Phillie: 1964, 1966-1971
Line as a Phillie: 75-76, 3.60 ERA, 1.302 WHIP in 1244.2 IP
fWAR Phillies Rank: 14th among pitchers, 47th among Phillies
Signature Game: Threw a no-hitter and hit two home runs against the Cincinnati Reds on June 23, 1971

Wise is frequently remembered most as the answer to the following trivia question: what Phillies pitcher was traded to the St. Louis Cardinals for Steve Carlton? But Wise was much more than a trivia answer; for parts of seven seasons, Wise was an All-Star caliber pitcher stuck in a franchise headed in a downward spiral. Wise would be dealt before the team hit rock bottom in 1972 but was far and away the staff leader from 1966 through 1971.

Wise was among the most durable starters in the pitching-heavy National League during his stay in Philly, pitching 180 innings or more in five straight seasons, pitching the sixteenth-most innings in the National League from 1966 through 1971, winning the seventeenth-most decisions, and posted an ERA on the positive side of the league average three times. Wise's 52 complete games from 1966 through 1971 ranked 13th in the National League while his 13 shutouts during that period tied him for 16th.

Wise would continue to progress as a pitcher the longer he stayed in Philadelphia. By his final season in Philadelphia, Wise had thrown a career-high 272.1 innings, had decreased his walks while increasing strikeouts, and posting a career-low 2.88 ERA. His success in 1971 earned him his first All-Star birth, his only appearance as a Phillie. Wise's defining moment as a Phillie, and perhaps one of the most memorable games in baseball history, came on June 23 of that year when Wise no-hit the Big Red Machine a year before they became the Big Red Machine, using just three strikeouts to do so.

Also memorable: he hit two homers in the same game.

Wise would have another multi-homer game in the second half of a double-header against the San Francisco Giants on August 28. While he would not achieve a no-hitter against the Giants, but would still come away with a complete game victory. To cap off his career year with the Phillies, Wise would retire 32 straight batters against the Giants on September 18 and drive in the game's winning run in the 12th. Something tells me Wise recalls 1971 fondly even though the Phillies won just 67 games.

Wise is usually an afterthought in the minds of Phillies' fans when discussing greatest Phillies ever, but shouldn't be: the 6'1" righty from Portland, OR used a repertoire of off-speed pitches to limit walks and keep the ball in Connie Mack Stadium. Wise was traded for Carlton on February 25, 1972. At the time of the trade, Wise had a better strikeout-to-walk ratio while Carlton had a better K/9 IP%. Wise even had two more victories than Carlton.

Unfortunately for Wise, and fortunately for Phillies fans, Carlton turned out to be an all-time great pitcher and Wise went on to have about six above-average seasons. Wise would reach the World Series with the 1975 Red Sox, earning the win for Game 6 after throwing a scoreless 12th just a few days after getting chased in the sixth inning of Game 3. Wise finished his career with the San Diego Padres in 1982 and was the last remaining active player that had played for the 1964 Phillies.

Larry Christenson

Right-Handed Starter

Years as a Phillie: 1973-1983
Line as a Phillie: 83-71, 3.79 ERA, 1.280 WHIP in 1402.2 IP
fWAR Phillies Rank: 10th among pitchers, 37th among Phillies
Signature Season: Went 13-14 with a 3.24 ERA, 1.123 WHIP in 1979
Oddball Fact: Was the only Phillies' starting pitcher to have the privilege of wearing the *Saturday Night Special*, all-red uniform on May 19, 1979

From the mid-1970's through the early 80's, the Phillies could count on a few things: Mike Schmidt was going to hit between 35 and 40 homers, play great defense, and be in the MVP race; Steve Carlton was going to strikeout between 200 and 250 batters and be in the Cy Young race; Larry Bowa and Garry Maddox were going to play Gold Glove defense; and Larry Christenson was going to average 25 starts a year with a mid 3's ERA and a low 1.2s WHIP.

While his contemporary teammates may have brought home individual hardware, Christenson was quietly a workhorse. Despite injuries shortening his 1979 and 1980 seasons, Christenson pitched the 17th most innings in Phillies history with the eleventh most strikeouts. While he ranks just 85th in team history in ERA among qualified pitchers, he ranks 43rd in WHIP, and 16th in wins. Among his contemporaries, Christenson ranked 17th in the NL in wins from 1973 through 1983, and 46th out of 193 in FIP.

Christenson came to the Phillies as the number 3 overall pick in the 1972 draft and made his debut with the big club at just age 19 less than one year later. At the time of his debut, he was the youngest player in baseball, and rewarded the Phillies for an early call-up by beating the Mets 7-1 in a complete game shutout.

Christenson would be a Phillie through some of their brightest moments, although he struggled to stay on the field later in his career. In 1979, he suffered elbow problems and dislocated his collarbone in a charity bicycle race. In 1980, he had elbow surgery but returned in time for the World Series. Christenson would get chased in the first inning of Game 4 of the 1980 World Series. After a 2-4 start to the 1983 campaign, Christenson had more surgery on his elbow. He did not make the 1983 playoff roster.

Despite his unfortunate accident during a charity event, Christenson is among the most charitable former Major Leaguers. In interviews, Christenson has been connected to the following charities: ALS Foundation, Phillies Charities, American Heart Association, Tug McGraw Foundation for brain cancer research, Leukemia & Lymphoma Society and Fighting Blindness with Wayne Gretzky.

Did You Know: Phillies 1st Round Whiffs

From 1965 through 2007, 33 of 43 first round and supplemental first round picks reached the Major Leagues, good for a 76.44% success rate. While Christenson (1972), Utley (2000), and Hamels (2002) were no brainers in hindsight and Lonnie Smith (1974) and JD Drew (1997) killed it with other teams, the Phillies missed hard in years when they didn't draft a future Major Leaguer.

Take a look below at some of the names the Phillies *could* have had in years where their first round pick didn't reach the Majors.

Year	Phillies Pick	Could Have Taken
1967	14 – LHP Phil Meyer	19 – SS Bobby Grich
1975	12 – RHP Sammye Welborn	28 – RHP Lee Smith
1976	17 – SS Jeff Kraus	25 – SS Alan Trammell
1978	23 – 1B Rip Rollins	48 – SS Cal Ripken Jr.
1985	16 – C Trey McCall	22 – OF Rafael Palmeiro
1990	4 – OF Jeff Jackson	7 – 1B Frank Thomas
1992	13 – OF Chad McConnell	23 – C Jason Kendall

#39 Elmer Flick

Right Fielder

Years as a Phillie: 1898-1901
Line as a Phillie: .338/.419/.487, 29 HR, 119 SB in 2346 PA
fWAR Phillies Rank: 27th among position players, 35th among Phillies
Signature Stats: Fourth in Phillies history in OBP (.419)

Ah, the age-old story of the early Phillies: develop superstar player, get into contract squabble, let player go for nothing, player goes on to be Hall of Famer. As if the Phillies didn't learn in 1901 with Nap Lajoie, the Phillies would play hardball with Flick and Ed Delahanty after the 1901 season and lose both future Hall of Famers as well. My my, what could have been?

So why was losing Elmer Flick so devastating? Well, from 1898 through 1901 Flick was second in baseball with 29 HR, sixth in runs scored, third in RBIs, eleventh in steals, sixth in isolated power, seventh in batting average, sixth in OBP, fifth in slugging, fourth in wOBA, and third in OPS. In short, Flick was essentially a turn-of-the-century Ken Griffey Jr.-in-his-prime, lefty-hitting right fielder: he could hit for average, power, steal bases, and would even lead the league in outfield assists in 1901.

Flick is an easily forgotten name from the offensively-gifted turn-of-the-century Phillies squads – just about everything he did, Delahanty did as well. And unlike Delahanty, who reportedly died by falling over Niagara Falls in 1903 just a few years after leaving the Phillies, Flick would be a Hall of Fame-caliber outfielder with the Philadelphia A's in 1902 and the Cleveland Naps from 1902-1910, joining fellow Phillies' hold-out Lajoie on a team that appreciated Lajoie so much, they eventually, yet briefly, named themselves after him.

Flick would lead a long, healthy life, becoming the oldest living inductee to the Baseball Hall of Fame in 1963 at age 87 and passing away at age 94. For four years, Flick was among the best of the best in baseball for the

Phillies, and one of a handful of painful reminders of why it is important to keep young talent.

National League Leaders in RBI

In 1900, Elmer Flick became the first Phillie in the 20th century to lead the National League in RBI. Since the league's inception, 13 Phillies have led the NL in RBI 25 times. Here are all of the Phillies that accomplished this feat:

Ryan Howard (2009, 2008, 2006)
Darren Daulton (1992)
Mike Schmidt (1986, 1984, 1981, 1980)
Greg Luzinski (1975)
Del Ennis (1950)
Chuck Klein (1933, 1931)
Don Hurst (1932)
Gavvy Cravath (1915, 1913)
Sherry Magee (1914, 1910, 1907)
Elmer Flick (1900)
Ed Delahanty (1899, 1896, 1893)
Nap Lajoie (1898)
Sam Thompson (1895, 1894)

Puddin' Head Jones

Third Baseman

Years as a Phillie: 1947-1959
Line as a Phillie: .258/.343/.413, 180 HR, 39 SB in 6241 PA
fWAR Phillies Rank: 26th among position players, 36th among Phillies
Signature Achievements: Played 34th most games at third base in Major League history, ranks tenth in putouts among third baseman, was top five in range factor from 1950 through 1959, and led the league in fielding percentage six times as a Phillie

He couldn't spell Constantinople,
Didn't know beans from bones.
Pencils and books were never made for
Wooden-head Puddin' Head Jones.

"Wooden-Head, Puddin' Head Jones" – 1930s

I'm not really sure how smart Willie Jones was or whether or not he could spell Constantinople but one thing is abundantly clear regarding the man who shared a nickname with a 1930s novelty song: he was an above-average Major League third baseman for parts of thirteen seasons with the Philadelphia Phillies.

From 1947 through 1959, Jones ranked third among National League third baseman in homers, second in runs scored, first in RBIs, fourth in steals, 12th in OBP, 11th in slugging, and fifth in fWAR. Jones was a power-threat from the right side, hitting the second-most homers for the Phillies in the 1950s behind only Del Ennis. Jones' signature seasons came in 1950 and 1951 when he made two consecutive all-star squads: in 1950, he had career highs in RBI (88), runs (100), hits (163), and homers (25), helping lead the Phillies to their improbable 1950 NL pennant.

Jones finished his career the all-time leader in plate appearances by a third baseman for a Phillie – he now sits at third place on that list behind

Tony Taylor and Mike Schmidt. Jones also retired the Phillies' leader in homers among third baseman – he is now third among Phillies who primarily played third base, behind only Dick Allen and Schmidt.

Jones currently ranks 13th among all Phillies in homers, 14th in RBI, and 17th in runs. A fine offensive third baseman, Jones ranked among the top five in defensive range factor at third base from 1950 through 1959 and led the league in fielding percentage six times as a Phillie.

Jones retired as the Phillies' all-time greatest third baseman. Because of the accomplishments of Allen and Schmidt, Jones' name is one frequently forgotten by Phillies fans that shouldn't be. An anchor on the Whiz Kids, Jones is unquestionably among the greatest Phillies of all-time.

Phillies' Top 10: Runs Scored by Phillies' Third Basemen

Jones retired as the Phillies' all-time leader in many categories including runs scored by a third baseman. These days, Jones ranks third, behind Mike Schmidt and Tony Taylor.

1. Mike Schmidt	1506, 1972-1989	
2. Tony Taylor	737, 1960-1971, 1974-1976	
3. Puddin' Head Jones	735, 1947-1959	
4. Dick Allen	697, 1963-1969, 1975-1976	
5. Pinky Whitney	554, 1928-1933, 1936-1939	
6. Scott Rolen	533, 1996-2002	
7. Lave Cross	483, 1892-1897	
8. Russ Wrightstone	424, 1920-1928	
9. Joe Mulvey	410, 1883-1889, 1892	
10. Placido Polanco	365, 2002-2005, 2010-2012	

Eppa Rixey
Left-Handed Starter

Years as a Phillie: 1912-1918, 1920
Line as a Phillie: 87-103, 2.83 ERA, 1.245 WHIP in 1604.0 IP
fWAR Phillies Rank: 9th among pitchers, 34th among Phillies
Signature Achievements: Pitched ninth-most innings in Phillies' history, 16th best ERA and ninth-best FIP among Phillies' starters
Signature Season: Went 22-10 with a 1.85 ERA with 1.091 WHIP in 1916

Easily the best pitcher in club history with a losing record, Rixey joined the Phillies at the age of 21, fresh out of the University of Virginia. Rixey skipped minor league baseball altogether, making his Major League debut on June 21, 1912. Rixey would go 10-10 with a 2.50 ERA in 20 starts, throwing 10 complete games. Rixey had a breakout campaign in the Phillies' 1915 pennant-winning season, posting a 2.39 ERA with a 1.285 WHIP in 29 games, 22 of which were starts.

Rixey would be a hidden gem on the staffs of the successful 1910's Phillies' squads. Despite leading the National League in losses in 1917 with 21, Rixey posted a 2.27 ERA and a 1.123 WHIP. From 1912 through 1920, Rixey would rank seventh in the NL in fWAR, 23rd in WHIP, and 13th in starts and appearances. Rixey would be overshadowed, however, by perhaps the best pitcher of that generation in the National League, Grover Cleveland Alexander, who won 207 games in the same span with a 2.00 ERA.

Rixey would play a big role leading the 1915 Phillies to a pennant. He would have an even better 1916, posting a 1.85 ERA and a 1.091 WHIP. Rixey would be one of many Phillies from the first quarter of the 20th century who would prove to have an even better career after he left Philadelphia. Rixey would serve in the U.S. Army's Chemical Warfare Division, missing the 1918 season. It looked like World War I may have slowed Rixey down: a rocky 6-12, 3.97 ERA 1919 and with only a slightly better 11-22, 3.48 ERA 1920 made some believe this.

The Phillies would trade Rixey to the Cincinnati Reds before the 1921 season after Rixey had butted heads with manager Gavvy Cravath. There, he was reunited with the Phillies' 1915 skipper Pat Moran. Rixey would be traded for Jimmy Ring and Greasy Neale, who would lead the Philadelphia Eagles to back-to-back NFL titles in 1948 and 1949 and became a Pro and College Football Hall of Fame coach. From 1921 through 1932, the National League average ERA was between 3.78 and 4.97, the Phillies' average ERA was between 4.47 and 6.71 (!!), and Rixey's ERA was 3.33. Oops.

Rixey would go on to win 179 games with the Cincinnati Reds in 13 seasons and retire as the all-time National League wins leader. In 1963, he was inducted into the Baseball Hall of Fame by the Veteran's Committee.

***Phillies' Top 10:* FIP by Phillies' Starters**

FIP, or Fielding Independent Pitching, estimates what a pitcher's ERA would look like if their stats were independent of the performance of their defense. It is based on a pitcher's strikeouts, walks, hit by pitches, and home runs allowed. Rixey compares quite nicely to the great Phillies' pitchers using FIP.

1. Grover Cleveland Alexander	2.33, 1911-1917, 1930
2. George McQuillan	2.37, 1907-1910, 1915-1916
3. Frank Corridon	2.43, 1904-1909
4. Doc White	2.44, 1901-1902
5. Al Demaree	2.44, 1915-1916
6. Tully Sparks	2.51, 1897, 1903-1910
7. Jim Bunning	2.69, 1964-1968, 1970-1971
8. Johnny Lush	2.70, 1904-1907
9. Lew Richie	2.72, 1906-1909
10. Eppa Rixey	2.75, 1912-1920

Shane Victorino

Center Fielder

Years as a Phillie: 2005-2012
Line as a Phillie: .279/.345/.439, 88 HR, 179 SB in 3977 PA
fWAR Phillies Rank: 25th among position players, 33rd among Phillies
Signature Moment: Grand Slam in Game 2 of the 2008 NLDS off of C.C. Sabathia

The Flyin' Hawaiian came to the Phillies prior to the 2005 season as part of the Rule 5 draft. Selected from the Dodgers by General Manager Ed Wade, Victorino would not make the Phillies out of camp and would be offered back to Los Angeles. The Dodgers would decline the return of Victorino and the rest is history: Victorino would win International League MVP honors after a birth in the International League All-Star game, being named Phillies minor league player of the year. By September 2005, he would reach the Majors and stay there for good.

Victorino quickly became a fan favorite for his excellent outfield defense and his tantalizing speed. In 2006, the switch-hitting outfielder would see time across all three outfield positions and move to right field for 2007. In 2008, Victorino would cross the 600 PA threshold for the first time in his career, starting 134 games in center field. Victorino would have a breakout campaign, turning heads with not only his speed but his emerging power: the 5'9" speedster would hit 30 2B, 8 3B, and 14 HR with a .292/.352/.447 line while also winning his first Gold Glove.

Victorino would cement his place in Phillies history in the 2008 postseason, hitting two very memorable homers. The first was a bases-loaded, two-out shot in the second inning of Game 2 of the NLDS off of C.C. Sabathia to give the Phillies a 5-2 that they wouldn't relinquish. The second, a two-run, one-out shot off of Cory Wade of the Dodgers in the Top of the 8th to knot Game 4 of the NLCS up at 5, setting the stage for Matt Stairs' moonshot three batters later.

Victorino would win three-straight Gold Gloves from 2008 through 2010, earn All-Star appearances in 2009 and 2011, win the Lou Gehrig Memorial Award in 2008, and the Branch Rickey Award in 2011. For his career, Victorino has an 82.84% stolen base success rate, the 23rd best percentage all-time, ranks second in baseball history in fielding percentage for a center fielder, and fifth in baseball history in fielding percentage among outfielders.

Victorino would rank sixth among center fielders in steals from 2005 through 2012, seventh in runs, and 18th in OPS. Among Phillies to primarily play center field, Victorino ranks third in homers, sixth in runs and RBIs, seventh in steals, and tenth in OPS.

On July 31, 2012, Victorino's tenure with the Phillies would come to an end, being dealt to the Los Angeles Dodgers for pitchers Ethan Martin and Josh Lindblom only a few hours before the trade deadline. After the 2012 season, Victorino would sign with the Boston Red Sox, winning a Gold Glove for his work in right field and earning another World Series ring.

Power and Speed in the Outfield

Victorino is one of only nine Phillies outfielders to hit at least 75 homers and steal 75 bases during his tenure as a Phillie.

Bobby Abreu	195 HR, 254 SB
Gavvy Cravath	117 HR, 80 SB
Ed Delahanty	87 HR, 411 SB
Von Hayes	124 HR, 202 SB
Garry Maddox	85 HR, 189 SB
Sherry Magee	75 HR, 387 SB
Sam Thompson	95 HR, 189 SB
Shane Victorino	88 HR, 179 SB
Cy Williams	223 HR, 77 SB

The Phillies reputation for being frugal has paid off in big ways, finding talent through any process or means. Previous Phillies regimes have left no stone unturned and have come up with some solid players through the Rule 5 Draft.

The Rule 5 draft, in a way, prevents teams from accumulating too many young, talented players and allows other teams the opportunity to draft them, under the condition that the player remains on the team he is drafted by for the full season. If the drafting team wants to send the player down to the minors, the player must be first offered back to the team he came from before being able to attempt to clear waivers.

5. Todd Pratt – Pratt was taken from the Baltimore Orioles in the 1991 Rule 5 draft. Primarily a back-up to All-Star Darren Daulton, Pratt would hit nine home runs across 259 plate appearances in his first three seasons with the Phillies with a SLG of over .426. Pratt would return to the Phillies in a 2001 trade and remain with the team through the 2005 season.

4. Jack Baldschun – Baldschun was selected as a Rule 5 pick from the Cincinnati Reds in the 1960 Rule 5 draft. Baldschun wasted no time making an impact, pitching in an MLB-best 65 games in 1961. Baldschun would become the Phillies closer in 1962, tallying 59 saves in five seasons with the club against a 3.18 ERA.

3. Dave Hollins - Hollins made his Major League debut on April 12, 1990 after the Phillies selected him in the 1989 Rule 5 draft from the San Diego

Padres. Hollins would be named to the NL All-Star team in 1993 after hitting .273/.372/.442 with 18 home runs. Hollins was one of the most successful Phillies at getting on base during the 1993 World Series, reaching base at a .414 clip.

2. Clay Dalrymple – Acquired in the 1959 Rule 5 draft, "Dimples" went on to become one of the National League's finest defensive catchers. Dalrymple spent nine seasons with the Phillies before being traded to the Baltimore Orioles in 1969 where he would reach the World Series three consecutive years, winning it all in 1970.

1. Shane Victorino – The player so nice, he was Rule 5'ed twice. Originally drafted by the Los Angeles Dodgers in 1999, Victorino was selected by the San Diego Padres in the 2003 Rule 5 draft. The Padres, presumably sensing Victorino needed more minor league seasoning, had no place to play Victorino on their Major League roster and offered him back to the Dodgers.

The Dodgers left Victorino available once more in the 2004 Rule 5 draft and this time, the Phillies took him. At one point during the 2005 season, the Phillies offered Victorino back to the Dodgers but the Dodgers let the Phillies keep him. Victorino passed through waivers and became the Phillies 2005 minor league player of the year.

Victorino, however, would do so much more. The Flyin' Hawaiian started the 2009 All-Star Game as a Phillie and was a key cog in their 2008 World Series win. Victorino would win three Gold Gloves with the Phillies, lead the NL in triples twice, and was a .269/.338/.446 hitter in the postseason with six homers and eight steals. Victorino was traded to the Dodgers in 2012 and signed with the Red Sox prior to the 2013 season. The Flyin' Hawaiian would win a Gold Glove, this time in right field, and a World Series ring in his first season there.

#35 *Jack Clements*
Catcher

Years as a Phillie: 1884-1897
Line as a Phillie: .289/.352/.426, 70 HR, 54 SB in 4105 PA
fWAR Phillies Rank: 22nd among position players, 30th among Phillies
Signature Fact: Is believed to be the last regular left-handed throwing catcher in the Major Leagues

Born in Philadelphia during the American Civil War, Jack Clements was truly one of a kind. Clements caught 1,073 games over his 17-year career, spending parts of his career as a reserve. But those 1,073 games were record-breaking: Clements was the last-remaining regular left-handed throwing catcher when he retired in 1900. Despite the inherent disadvantages of being a left-handed catcher, during his time with the Phillies Clements ranked third among his peers in defensive runs saved.

Make no mistake: Clements made the Top 100 not because of his uniqueness; he could hit. Clements ranks first among Phillies' catchers in fWAR, ranking fifth in batting average, tenth in OBP, and seventh in slugging. From 1884 through 1897, Clements led all catchers in homers, ranked fourth in batting average, third in doubles, fifth in RBI, and fourth in ISO.

Clements had a few standout seasons. For instance, in 1890, Clements would finish third in batting average, sixth in the NL in OBP, second in slugging, and second in OPS. Clements would follow his very strong 1890 season with a similarly strong 1891: Clements would finish fourth in the NL in batting, sixth in OBP, sixth in slugging, and seventh in OPS.

In 1895, Clements would hit .394, setting a still-standing single-season batting average record for catchers with 350 PA or more. Clements would retire with the single-season home run record among catchers and retire as the all-time leader in homers among catchers. Clements was an early pioneer for the then-Quakers and remains one of the best catchers in

Phillies history. A historical curiosity, Clements is undoubtedly one of the all-time great Phillies.

Hey, have you heard of: **The 1895 Phillies**

Jack Clements hit a scorching .395 for the 1895 Phillies behind the dish in 355 PA. Under manager Arthur Irwin, the team used historic offense to attract fans (highest attendance in the National League) and to stay close in the standings.

At 78-53, the 1895 Phillies mark of 25 games over .500 was the club's best win/loss difference since their 1887 season when they were 27 games above .500. With the pitching staff hovering a 5.47 ERA for most of the season, the Phils relied on a trio of Hall of Famers in the outfield (Ed Delahanty, Sam Thompson, and Billy Hamilton) as well as Clements to keep within arm's length of the eventual pennant winners, the Baltimore Orioles.

#34 Darren Daulton

Catcher

Years as a Phillie: 1983, 1985-1997
Line as a Phillie: .245/.357/.427, 134 HR, 48 SB in 3977 PA
fWAR Phillies Rank: 24th among position players, 32nd among Phillies
Signature Game: Caught Terry Mulholland's August 15, 1990 No-Hitter and hit a homer

The pride of Arkansas City, KS, Dutch was selected in the 25th round of the 1980 draft, just a few months before the Fightin Phils would bring home the first World Series crown to the Vet. By 1983, Daulton was crushing pitching at Double-A Reading to the tune of .262/.425/.486 with 19 HR and he had earned a call-up to the eventual NL pennant-winning squad. In the final game of the season, Dutch would single off Cecilio Guante in the bottom of the eighth for his first Major League hit.

With remarkable plate discipline and a powerful lefty stroke, Dutch was a one-of-a-kind catcher. Fighting through a number of injuries, Daulton would finally earn the starting gig by 1989. Daulton would get off to a slow start offensively in his early days as a starter, hitting just .228/.328/.368 from 1989 through 1991. While he displayed offensive shortcomings early in his career, Daulton would immediately guide the rotation to a lower ERA than the ERA of the staff he took over (4.16 ERA in 1988).

In 1992, Dutch would have a breakout offensive campaign, smashing 27 HR, stealing 11 SB with a .270/.385/.524 line, leading all catchers in OBP, SLG, and OPS, and winning a Silver Slugger in the process. The pinnacle of Dutch's career came in 1993, catching 147 games, hitting .257/.392/.482 with 24 HR, guiding the Phillies staff to a 3.97 ERA and a 20.4 fWAR, the highest staff WAR since 1983.

Dutch would hit a homer in Game 5 of the 1993 NLCS off of Greg McMichael and a big, two-out, bases-loaded, two-run double off of Greg

Maddux in the bottom of the third of Game 6. In the strike-shortened 1994 season, Daulton was on pace to have his best season yet, hitting 15 HR with a .300/.380/.549 line in 292 PA.

Dutch would earn his third All-Star birth in 1995 before missing most of 1996. He would round out his Phillies career in right field and first base in 1997 before being traded to Florida for Billy McMillon. Dutch would hit a scorching hot .389/.455/.667 in 22 1997 World Series PA, including a homer in Game 3, to help the Marlins win their first World Series crown. Retiring after the 1997 season, Daulton is the Phillies' all-time leader among catchers in walk rate, is second in homers, sixth in OBP, eighth in slugging, and sixth in OPS.

Dutch was among the best catchers in baseball during his prime years with the Phillies. From 1989 through 1995, only Mickey Tettleton accumulated more fWAR, leading all catchers in WAR in the six year period. Dutch was second among all catchers from 1989 to 1995 in homers, runs, RBIs, and walk rate behind only Tettleton, while ranking sixth in OBP, fifth in slugging, and fifth in OPS.

In June 2013, Dutch was diagnosed with two brain tumors. Surgery to remove the tumors was reported a success and Daulton would join the Phillies for alumni weekend in August 2013 and marry his long-time girlfriend, Amanda, in December. Dutch continues to support multiple charity efforts, including Phillies Charities, Florida Marlins Community Foundation, Lakewood Blue Claws Charitable Foundation, and MLBPAA "Kids Weekend".

His infectious spirit continues to inspire many as does his encouraging slogan "Right on, fight on".

Bonus
In Their Own Words:
Darren Daulton

It is hard to tell the story of the greatest Phillies of All-Time without going to the source: the players themselves! Throughout the book, there are excerpts of interviews I conducted for use on Phillies Nation and *Phillies Nation TV*, inserted and edited when appropriate. Some questions and answers may have been omitted but answers from players are presented in full.

Ian Riccaboni: We'll start with a tough one – what was your favorite moment as a Phillie?

Darren Daulton: The '93 season.

IR: Any particular game or moment that sticks out?

DD: Not really! It was, well, that year we had such a good team that it was every day there was something you could see. Whether it was Dude, who was the greatest lead-off hitter ever, in the game, swear to God, during '93 or (Terry) Mulholland or any of the teammates I had, it was definitely '93.

IR: You were the only player who bridged the '83 team to the '93 team. What was it like playing with (Mike) Schmidt, (Pete) Rose...

DD: Tony Perez! Joe Morgan! Garry Maddox! Lefty! It was my first year and it was a learning session. It's kind of where I broke in. These guys used to do stuff to me... *laughs* if it's going in a book, I don't want them to read about it! *laughs* But that team was a lot of fun.

IR: What was it like being an All-Star for the Phillies in an era of transition from non-contender to contender?

DD: If you make an All-Star team, ya know, that means you're an All-Star, one of the best players at your position. It was just fun!

IR: Last question: favorite battery mate?

DD: There's one of them right there! (points to Terry Mulholland). Terry Mulholland. Ya know, Schilling was very good at that time and he was still a younger player. But you know, from a catcher's standpoint, it was easy to catch those two guys.

Hey, Have You Heard Of: **The Wheeze Kids**

In 1983, General Manager Paul Owens made one last run at glory, stocking a Phillies team that had finished just three games out of the playoffs the year before with veteran players like Hall of Fame second baseman Joe Morgan (age 39) and first baseman Tony Perez (age 41).

Of the 44 players that would suit up for the Phillies in 1983, 23 were age 30 or older, with seven of eight regular starters all 30+, as well as four out of the five most-used relievers. Even the manager got older as Pat Corrales was replaced midseason by Owens after a 43-42 start.

The gamble paid off as the club went on an 11-game winning streak down the stretch, culminating in a 47-30 mark for Owens as manager and an NL East crown. The Phillies would win the NL pennant in four games over the Dodgers before losing the World Series in five games to the Orioles.

The club was not completely void of young talent, however. At age 24, Von Hayes was a starter for most of the season in right field while Marty Bystrom, Kevin Gross, and Charles Hudson were all 24 or younger and turned in fine seasons from the rotation. The team's youngest player? Darren Daulton, a late-season call-up at age 21.

#33 Scott Rolen

Third Baseman

Years as a Phillie: 1996-2002
Line as a Phillie: .282/.373/.504, 150 HR, 71 SB in 3643 PA
fWAR Phillies Rank: 16th among position players, 24th among Phillies

Is there a player that is met with more of a collective groan in Phillies history than Scott Rolen? A second round draft pick out of Jasper, IN in 1993, Rolen was a three-time *Baseball America* Top 100 prospect from 1995 through 1997, topping out at #13 prior to his official rookie year. Rolen would burst on to the scene as a 21-year-old Phillie in 1996, hitting .300/.363/.444 through his first 26 games. Rolen would cool off through the end of 1996, getting a break for much of September, but would make the team out of camp in 1997, winning the NL Rookie of the Year, hitting 21 HR, stealing 16 bags and hitting .283/.377/.469.

Rolen would be among the best third basemen in baseball for the parts of seven seasons he spent in Philadelphia. From 1997 through 2002, Rolen ranked second in baseball in fWAR among third basemen behind only Chipper Jones, ranking third in homers, second in runs, second in RBIs, second in steals, ninth in OBP, third in slugging, and third in OPS.

Despite his production, Rolen was frequently the subject of boos and cheers after he rejected a Phillies' offer prior to the 2002 season of 10 years, $140 million, including a shower of boos when Rolen refused a curtain call after hitting two homers against the Montreal Expos in a June 1, 2002 win against the Expos. Rolen's introverted personality clashed with manager Larry Bowa's extremely extroverted personality and Rolen's demand for a trade to a contender was executed on July 29, 2002. Rolen and reliever Doug Nickle were traded to St. Louis for Placido Polanco, starter Bud Smith, and reliever Mike Timlin.

Had Rolen stuck with the Phillies, he may have been a top fifteen or perhaps even a top ten player in club history. Rolen went on to win a

World Series ring in 2006 with St. Louis, making seven All-Star teams, winning eight Gold Gloves, a Silver Slugger, and ranks ninth in fWAR in baseball history among third basemen.

It can be fun to ponder what might have been for the teams that were so close to making the playoffs in 2003, 2005, and 2006 had Rolen been at the hot corner but knowing Rolen didn't want to be in Philadelphia, it makes his departure a lot easier to digest. And admittedly, it was fun watching Rolen go 1 for 11 in the 2010 NLDS against the Phillies.

Regardless, Rolen was one of the best, one of the Holy Trinity at the hot corner. Yet, his ugly exit taints his position in Phillies history among fans. Rolen would wrap up his career after the 2012 season, finishing his career with 316 HR and 118 SB.

Phillies' Top 10: **Stolen Bases by Phillies' Third Basemen**

Rolen may not be remembered as fleet of foot by Phillies fans but his 71 stolen bases while playing third stack up quite well against the others at the hot corner.

1. Mike Schmidt   174, 1972-1989
2. Tony Taylor   169, 1960-1971, 1974-1976
3. Hans Lobert   125, 1911-1914
4. Joe Mulvey   113, 1883-1889, 1892
5. Lave Cross   96, 1892-1897
6. Eddie Grant   90, 1907-1910
7. Dick Allen   86, 1963-1969, 1975-1976
8. Milt Stock   72, 1915-1918
9. Scott Rolen   71, 1996-2002
10. Harry Wolverton   48, 1900-1902, 1903-1904

Carlos Ruiz

Catcher

Years as a Phillie: 2006-Present
Line as a Phillie: .267/.352/.397, 65 HR, 20 SB in 3668 PA
fWAR Phillies Rank: 29th among position players, 41st among Phillies
Signature Moments: Dribbler up the line to score Eric Bruntlett from third to win Game 3, meeting Brad Lidge on the mound of Game 5 of the 2008 World Series
Signature Stat: Tied for MLB record for most No-Hitters caught (four)

Chooooooooooch.

The affable Panamanian catcher was a mainstay on the five-time NL East champions, establishing a reputation as one of baseball's best defensive catchers. Ruiz was a 27-year-old rookie when he was called up for a cup of coffee in May and September of 2006. Ruiz would somewhat surprisingly make the Phillies out of camp in 2007 and would win the starting catching gig over veteran free agent acquisition Rod Barajas, 34-year old, second-year catcher Chris Coste, and 29-year old veteran catcher Pete LaForest.

Ruiz would win the Phillies starting catching gig once and for all in the 2008 postseason, hitting .261/.346/.391 in the 2008 postseason, with a pivotal homer, and game winning dribbler up the third base line, in Game 3 of the 2008 World Series.

With the starting job fully in tow, Ruiz would become one of the National League's best catchers, both offensively and defensively. From 2010 through 2014, Chooch ranked fifth among all catchers in batting average, third in OBP, 11th in SLG, fifth in defensive runs saved, and sixth in fWAR.

Chooch's signature offensive campaign came in 2012 when he trailed only Buster Posey among catchers in batting average, was third in OBP, and second in SLG. He would make his first and only All-Star appearance in 2012.

Defensively, Chooch has been the receiver for four Phillies no hitters, including Roy Halladay's May 29, 2010 Perfect Game against the Marlins, Halladay's postseason no-no against the Reds on October 6, 2010, a combined Phillies' no hitter assembled by Cole Hamels, Jake Diekman, Ken Giles, and Jonathan Papelbon on September 1, 2010 against the Braves, and Hamels' solo effort against the Chicago Cubs on July 25, 2015.

Phillies' Top 10: **Career OBP Among Phillies Catchers**

Chooch has been like a fine wine – getting better as he ages. One of his best skills has been getting on base. He ranks ninth among catchers in club history in this category.

1. Smoky Burgess   .393, 1952-1955
2. Spud Davis   .374, 1928-1933, 1938-1939
3. Butch Henline   .372, 1921-1926
4. Tim McCarver   .359, 1970-1972, 1975-1980
5. Ed McFarland   .357, 1897-1901
6. Todd Pratt   .357, 1992-1994, 2001-2005
7. Darren Daulton   .357, 1983-1997
8. Stan Lopata   .355, 1948-1958
9. Carlos Ruiz   .352, 2006 - Present
10. Jack Clements   .351, 1884-1897

It is hard to tell the story of the greatest Phillies of All-Time without going to the source: the players themselves! Throughout the book, there are excerpts of interviews I conducted for use on Phillies Nation and *Phillies Nation TV*, inserted and edited when appropriate. Some questions and answers may have been omitted but answers from players are presented in full.

Ian Riccaboni: What was your favorite moment as a Phillie?

Carlos Ruiz: The final out of the World Series. Definitely when we won the World Series. It was one of those things you'll never forget, it was real special.

IR: What was it like to have a game-winning hit in the World Series?

CR: Oh, it was huge, you know. I knew I had to put the ball in play and I was lucky that I hit the ball. I did not hit the ball real hard *laughs* but it was a big moment in my career.

IR: What has it been being in an organization with players like Chase Utley, Jimmy Rollins, Roy Halladay, Cliff Lee, and Cole Hamels? Guys like yourself who play at a very high talent level?

CR: You know, when you come in from nowhere and you are working real hard, there's a chance you can end up in a place like this and play with superstars. It's great to be able to go to the ballpark every day and spend time with them and try to learn everything you can from them. I have a lot of good memories from when we have all of those guys on the field.

IR: If you had to pick, who was your favorite pitcher to catch?

CR: Oh, you know, every guy and every guy is special. Me and Roy (Halladay) had something special and so do me and Cole (Hamels), (and Brad) Lidge. There has been a lot of good pitching and it makes it really difficult to pick!

Bonus

Top 5 International Free Agent Signings in Phillies' History

The Phillies have extensive scouting around the globe and currently have a roster that is represented by players from six different countries. Over the years, the Phils have found a number of hidden gems from foreign lands.

Unfortunately for them, these same foreign hidden gems were either left unprotected and selected in Rule 5 drafts, as was the case for 1987 AL MVP George Bell of the Dominican Republic, 1984 AL MVP Willie Hernandez of Puerto Rico, and Manny Trillo of Venezuela, or traded too quickly, like Hall of Fame pitcher Fergie Jenkins of Canada.

Below is a list of the top five talents that the Phillies signed as amateur free agents from foreign countries that had the best careers with the Phillies.

5. Robinson Tejeda – signed November 24, 1998

While only with the Phillies for one season, a 23-year-old Tejada put together a strong season as a swing-man, going 4-3 with a 3.57 ERA in 26 games, 13 starts. Tejeda would be traded on April 1, 2006 for outfielder David Dellucci.

4. Pancho Herrera – signed October 15, 1954

Herrera was technically signed away from the Kansas City Monarchs of the Negro League in 1954 but was extensively scouted as a player in Cuba.

Herrera's stop in Philadelphia was brief but sweet, hitting .271/.349/.430 with 31 homers in 300 games with a Rookie of the Year runner-up finish to his credit.

3. Antonio Bastardo – signed February 17, 2005

Bastardo was signed out of the Dominican Republic in 2005. The lefty specialist often fooled hitters with a fastball/slider combination and is the Phillies all-time leader in K/9 IP among pitchers with at least 150 innings pitched for the club.

2. Juan Samuel – signed April 29, 1980

Samuel was signed out of the Dominican Republic at age 20 and had his first taste of Major League action in 1983. Samuel was the NL Rookie of the Year runner up in 1984 and was an All-Star second baseman for the Phillies in 1984 and 1987.

1. Carlos Ruiz – signed December 4, 1998

The road to the Major Leagues was long and hard for Chooch. Signed as a 19-year-old second baseman in 1998, Ruiz did not crack a Major League roster until 2006. Chooch's persistence paid off in spades, however, earning a World Series ring in 2008, an All-Star appearance in 2012, and calling a Roy Halladay Perfect Game and No Hitter, a four-pitcher combined No Hitter in 2014, and a Cole Hamels no-no in Hamels' last start as a Phillie in 2015.

#31 *Von Hayes*

Outfielder, First Baseman

Years as a Phillie: 1983-1991
Line as a Phillie: .272/.363/.427, 124 HR, 202 SB in 4988 PA
fWAR Phillies Rank: 19th among position players, 28th among Phillies
Signature Season: Led NL in runs scored and doubles in 1986
Signature Game: Hit two homers in the same inning (June 11, 1985)

Nicknamed "Purple Hayes" and "Five-For-One" Von Hayes was an extremely athletic, versatile 6'5" outfielder/first baseman/fill-in third baseman who showed above-average ability in all five tools no matter what you called him. The lanky native of Stockton, CA would arrive in Philadelphia on December 9, 1982 in a trade that sent five players (Jay Baller, Julio Franco, Manny Trillo, George Vukovich, and Jerry Willard) to Cleveland.

Hayes would start 86 games in the outfield as a 24-year-old for the pennant-winning 1983 squad, hitting 6 HR with 20 SB in 392 PA. Hayes would see his playing time diminish by the time the postseason rolled around, seeing just five plate appearances in the playoffs, ceding playing time in right to the then-recently-acquired Sixto Lezcano.

The fact that Hayes was traded for five players was relatively unusual but perhaps the most unusual and unfortunate development was that all five either had gone on to the Majors or continued their careers in the Majors. Because of the expectations that come with being traded for five players, fans were often critical of Hayes. Lost in the criticism of Hayes was the fact that he was a very, very good ball player. Hayes would start 135 games for the Phillies in 1984, hitting 16 HR and stealing 48 bases with a .292/.359/.447 line.

Hayes would lead the NL in runs scored and doubles in 1986, forming a formidable one-two punch with that year's NL MVP Mike Schmidt for the surprising 1986 second-place Phillies. Hayes would have career highs in batting average and slugging in 1986, en route to an eighth place MVP finish. Hayes would make his only All-Star team in 1989, finishing with 26 HR and 28 SB.

Because Hayes did not have a consistent position (outfielder from 1983 through 1985, first base from 1986 through 1988, outfielder again from 1989 through 1991, with a number of cameos at third base thrown in), it is tougher to pin down comparables. Since his time was spent primarily as an outfielder, that's the criteria we used to compare him to his contemporaries.

Among National League outfielders from 1983 through 1991, Hayes ranked eighth in fWAR, wedged between Andre Dawson and Eric Davis. Hayes ranked 12th in homers, seventh in runs, seventh in RBIs, tenth in steals, fifteenth in OBP, and 28th in slugging among 77 eligible players.

To some, Hayes may have never lived up to the lofty expectations fostered when he was traded for five players. It certainly didn't endear him to fans when one of the players he was traded for, Franco, won a batting title, four Silver Sluggers, and was a three-time All-Star in the same time period that Hayes was in Philadelphia. But Hayes was in the top tier of NL outfielders during his stay in Philadelphia and is one of the Phillies all-time best players.

Phillies' Top 10: **OBP by Phillies' Center Fielders**

Hayes had a knack for drawing walks, placing him near the top of the OBP leaderboard among Phils' center fielders.

1. Billy Hamilton	.468
2. Roy Thomas	.421
3. Richie Ashburn	.394
4. Lenny Dykstra	.388
5. Cy Williams	.380
6. Von Hayes	.363
7. Duff Cooley	.361
8. Tony Gonzalez	.359
9. Dode Paskert	.357
10. Ethan Allen	.356

Bonus

Transactions That Shaped the Phillies: Exploring Five-for-One 32 Years Later

When Pat Gallen and I put together the *Phillies Nation Top 100*, one of the players we had the toughest time placing was outfielder/first baseman Von Hayes. Hayes had nine pretty good seasons in Philly, making one All-Star squad, and received MVP votes once. Hayes generally played on bad teams; aside from being a starter for most of the first half of the 1983 season for the pennant-winning Wheeze Kids, Hayes' Phillies finished above .500 only one other season (1986) and went a combined 609-685 (47.1%) outside of 1983.

Hayes became a lightning rod in Philadelphia for what fans perceived as a laid back, "California" attitude. Hayes' responses, including his famous "They can do whatever they want. I'll still be eating steak every night," comment, gave many fans the impression that Hayes did not care about the game. What didn't help Hayes were the expectations that arrived with him in Philadelphia: Hayes arrived in Philadelphia as a 24-year old outfielder, acquired from Cleveland for five players and quickly became known as "5-for-1".

On December 9, 1982, Hayes was traded by Cleveland to Philadelphia for Jay Baller, Julio Franco, Manny Trillo, George Vukovich, and Jerry Willard. Of that group, everyone but Willard had already acquired some Major League experience already and everyone but Trillo was 26 or younger, with Trillo coming off an All-Star and Gold Glove-winning campaign. Willard would make it to the Majors with Cleveland in 1984, making the tally officially five Major League players for one.

If the trade was just Hayes for Baller, Vukovich, and Willard, it would have likely been considered a major steal for the Phillies. Baller, a righty reliever, would throw only 148.1 MLB innings and would never post positive value per FanGraphs' version of WAR. Baller would never play for Cleveland as he was traded on April 1, 1985 to the Chicago Cubs before making the Majors. Vukovich had earned his stripes in Philly as a bench player on the 1980 World Series-winning club and would spend three seasons with Cleveland as a regular outfielder before retiring. Finally, Willard had one starter-caliber year in 1985 as a catcher for Cleveland (1.3 fWAR) before floating around the game.

But the trade didn't just stop at Baller, Vukovich, and Willard. It also included Franco and Trillo. Let's start with Trillo: Trillo was a fan-favorite in Philadelphia and was the second baseman on the 1980 championship team. Trillo was a two-time All-Star with the Phils in 1980 and 1981. He saw a major drop in production (1.6 fWAR in 1981 in 94 games v. 0.6 fWAR in 1982 in 149 games, slugging dropped from .395 to .319) and at age 33, Trillo was a player on the decline and would never post a season higher than 0.8 fWAR again post 1982.

The point of contention with this trade usually boils down to the inclusion of Franco. Franco had a 16 game cup of coffee with the Phillies in 1982 after hitting .300/.357/.499 with 21 HR for the Triple-A Oklahoma City 89ers that same year. According to Baseball Reference, Franco, at age 22, was two years advanced for his level, making the numbers that much more impressive. Franco made an immediate impact with Cleveland in 1983, finishing second in the Rookie of the Year voting while Hayes was benched down the stretch in favor of Joe Lefebvre and Sixto Lezcano in right field.

Even though Franco had the better year in 1983, Hayes actually outplayed Franco from 1983 through 1988. The time period is used as a period of measurement because those are the seasons that both players spent at their destinations.

In their overlapping time, Hayes outplayed Franco by 3.5 wins according to FanGraphs, hitting .281/.364/.436 with 81 HR and 149 SB v. Franco's .299/.344/.394 with 45 HR and 131 SB.

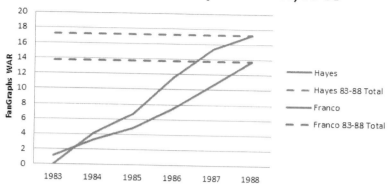

Hayes v. Franco

Hayes would make his first NL All-Star team in 1989, posting a 4.9 fWAR season and would follow it up with a 3.4 WAR 1990. Franco would be traded to the Texas Rangers after the 1988 season for Jerry Browne, Oddibe McDowell, and Pete O'Brien and post three consecutive monstrous seasons of 5.5, 5.8, and 5.8 WAR respectively. The players Texas received in return for Franco posted a combined 5.6 wins over the course of their lifespans in Cleveland while Franco posted 18.7 WAR in five seasons with the Rangers, including three trips to the All-Star game.

If all other players are included in the "5-for-1" analysis, Hayes was nearly as valuable as all combined. Vukovich's pesky 1984, where he was worth 3.9 fWAR was the difference:

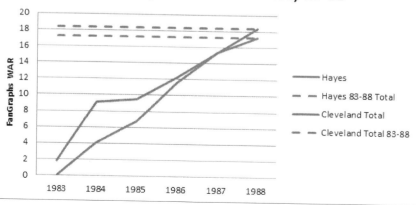

Hayes v. Cleveland

There are a few things with the 5-for-1 deal that are in play that made it a decent deal for the Phillies. First, the composite value the Phillies received by getting all of the production that Hayes brought at one spot allowed them to have a greater opportunity to fill the positions lost in the trade with better players.

A little confusing but bear with me.

Trillo, Baller, Vukovich, and Willard were not particularly good players at those stages of their careers. Vukovich had a freak 1984, where he was worth 3.9 WAR, but other than that, it was three non-prospects and a former All-Star second baseman. There is a bit of opportunity gained when trading them away and being able to play someone better in their stead, particularly in the case of Vukovich, who had struggled to find consistency off the bench.

Secondly, the majority of Franco's success, and I am talking about his run from 1989 through 1991 where he was clearly an All-Star infielder, came after Cleveland had already traded him and was somewhat odd. Franco put together his best three seasons at ages 30, 31, and 32, something that was uncommon in baseball until the late 1980s. Philadelphia made what turned out to be a fair market deal in acquiring Hayes – they shouldn't be punished for Cleveland's secondary trade. There's a wormhole to jump through, here, stating that Franco could have had more market value for the Phillies than Hayes if they kept him, but judging by the return Cleveland got, I'm not sure that was the case at that moment in time.

(For what it's worth, Hayes earned the Phillies 9.3 WAR from 1989 through 1991 and then netted the Phillies an additional 1 WAR from Kyle Abbott and Ruben Amaro, the players netted in return for Hayes after the 1991 season. The 10.3 WAR puts them beyond what Cleveland received (5.6 WAR) for Franco but below Franco himself (18.7))

In short, Hayes nearly out-produced all five players that Cleveland received while Cleveland had them. Hayes out-produced Franco by fWAR by 3.5 wins from 1983 through 1988 and remained an above-average regular for an additional two seasons. As the 5-for-1 trade becomes a footnote in the history of the Phillies, it should be viewed more in a neutral than negative light, as Hayes outplayed the principle player in the deal.

#30 Greg Luzinski
Left Fielder

Years as a Phillie: 1970-1980
Line as a Phillie: .281/.363/.489, 223 HR, 29 SB in 5321 PA
fWAR Phillies Rank: 23rd among position players, 31st among Phillies
Signature Stretch: Four-Straight All-Star Appearances, Four Top-10 MVP Voting Finishes (1975-1978)

"The Bull" was a 6'1" right-handed, Chicagoan bruiser that mashed and crushed his way into the hearts of Phillies' fans everywhere over eleven seasons. After being drafted as the eleventh overall pick in the 1968 draft, Luzinski quickly reached the Majors at age 19 in 1970 and was the Phillies regular left fielder by 1972. The powerful outfielder would be one of the largest contributors to the dramatic turnaround seen under manager Danny Ozark in the early and mid-1970s.

Luzinski would have one of his finest seasons in 1975, the first year the Phillies had been over .500 since 1967. The Bull hit .300/.394/.540 with 34 HR and a league-leading 120 RBIs, finishing second to Joe Morgan in the NL MVP voting in that season who had a pretty out-of-this-world season himself. Luzinski would finish second in NL MVP voting again in 1978, this time to George Foster, wrapping up one of the finest four-year, offensive stretches in Phillies history from 1975 through 1978, hitting .295/.386/.535 with 129 HR.

Luzinski was an unquestioned offensive juggernaut, also coming up big in all four NL Championship Series in which he played for the Phillies, hitting .310/.375/.690 in 64 NLCS PA with five homers. Luzinski would hit the go-ahead, and eventual game-winning, homer in the first inning of Game 1 of the 1977 NLCS, and the go-ahead, and eventual game-winning, homer in Game 1 of the 1980 NLCS against Ken Forsch of the Houston Astros. Luzinski would not register a hit in the 1980 World Series but was one of the few players who had any sort of offensive success in the Phillies four attempts to get to the Fall Classic.

As great as Luzinski was offensively, he did have his warts. According to FanGraphs, Luzinski cost the Phillies 145.9 runs in his eleven seasons in Philadelphia, or the equivalent of about 10 wins, and struck out 20.6% of the time. That never kept Luzinski's bat out of the line-up, though: Luzinski ranks seventh in Phillies history in homers, 25th in runs, 12th in RBIs, and 19th in slugging. Luzinski ranks seventh among NL left fielders from 1970 through 1980 in fWAR, fourth in homers, eighth in runs, second in RBIs, 24th in average, 13th in OBP, and sixth in SLG.

These days, the affable Bull can be found on summer nights at Citizens Bank Park supporting his restaurant, Bull's BBQ. As good a hitter as Bull was, his pulled pork sandwich is equally awesome.

Phillies' Top 10: Doubles by Phillies' Left Fielders, Season

The Bull had a knack for mashing doubles, setting the Phils' single-season record among left fielders with 39 in 1977, breaking the previous record set in 1968 by Dick Allen who spent most of that season in left.

1. Greg Luzinski	39, 1977
2. Pat Burrell	37, 2002
3. Greg Luzinski	35, 1978
4T. Greg Luzinski	34, 1975
4T. Raul Ibanez	34, 2009
6T. Dick Allen	33, 1968
6T. Pat Burrell	33, 2008
8T. Lefty O'Doul	32, 1929
8T. Pat Burrell	32, 2005
10. Chuck Klein	31, 1931

Lenny Dykstra

Center Fielder

Years as a Phillie: 1989-1996
Line as a Phillie: .289/.388/.422, 51 HR, 169 SB in 3374 PA
fWAR Phillies Rank: 20th among position players, 27th among Phillies
Signature Stretch: Three All-Star Appearances (1990, 1994-1995), Silver Slugger (1993), Finished Second in NL MVP Voting in 1993

Affectionately known as "Nails" and "Dude", Lenny Dykstra was a fast-living center fielder from Garden Grove, CA. Listed at 5'10", but definitely a tick or two shorter, Dykstra was the fire cracker in the group that propelled the Phillies from worst-to-first in 1993. Acquired from the Mets with Roger McDowell on June 18, 1989 for fan-favorite Juan Samuel, Dykstra got off to a bit of a slow start as a Phillie, hitting just .222/.297/.330 in 392 plate appearances in 1989 with the Phillies. But Nails would rebound with a 1990 to remember.

According to both FanGraphs' and Baseball Reference's version of WAR, Dykstra was the second-most valuable player in the National League behind only Barry Bonds. Dykstra would hit a career-high .325, lead the league in hits (192) and OBP at .418, hit nine HR and steal 33 bases in 38 attempts (86.84%), a tantalizing preview of what was to come. A few bad decisions and some bad luck cost him significant time in 1991 and 1992, including a drunk-driving accident in 1991, a broken collar bone suffered in Cincinnati in 1991 once he returned, and a broken hand on Opening Day 1992 when Dykstra was hit by a pitch.

Dykstra had the very-rare combination of power, speed, defense, running, and throwing abilities and it made him one of the very best, and perhaps most underrated players in the National League through the early 90's. Dykstra's marquee season was 1993, as he led the National League in PA, AB, runs, hits, and walks with a career-high 19 homers and 37 steals leading to a second-place NL MVP finish and his first, and only, Silver Slugger award. Dykstra's opus, combined with the rest of the serendipitous events that occurred in 1993, drove the Phillies to 97 wins, a victory over the Atlanta Braves in the NCLS, and the NL Pennant.

The success of the Phillies in 1993 was in no small part due to Dykstra's contributions. Dude, who had been a postseason hero with the New York Mets, would get on base at a .400 clip against the Atlanta Braves in the NLCS and nearly single-handedly powered the Phillies offense to a World Series title in 1993, hitting four homers, stealing four bases, and hitting .348/.500/.913 against a stacked Blue Jays pitching staff. The Phillies, of course, ultimately lost in six games.

After 1993, Dykstra's career moved in a downward direction. In 1994 and 1995, the baseball seasons was shortened by a strike and Dykstra battled through injuries in both 1995 and 1996. Dykstra would miss the entire 1997 season before attempting one final comeback prior to the 1998 season. His comeback attempt was unsuccessful and Dykstra quietly retired.

Some folks may question the inclusion of Dykstra on the list because of his alleged steroid use or because of his off-the-field behavior, including guilty pleas in 2011 for bankruptcy fraud, concealment of assets, and money laundering but Dykstra makes the list because he made the Phillies better while in a Phillies uniform.

The 1990 MVP Race

After struggling mightily with the Phillies after being traded to Philadelphia in 1989, Dykstra exploded out of the gates in 1990, leading the National League in hits and on-base percentage.

Nails was featured on the June 4 cover of *Sports Illustrated* and was hitting over .400 until an 0-8 performance in a June 11 double header against the Expos.

Dykstra would finish only ninth in MVP voting despite having a higher average and OBP than winner Barry Bonds.

Bonus

In Their Own Words: Lenny Dykstra

It is hard to tell the story of the greatest Phillies of All-Time without going to the source: the players themselves! Throughout the book, there are excerpts of interviews I conducted for use on Phillies Nation and *Phillies Nation TV*, inserted and edited when appropriate. Some questions and answers may have been omitted but answers from players are presented in full.

This brief interview was conducted for a PN TV offseason special reflecting on the 20th anniversary of the 1993 NL Pennant win.

Ian Riccaboni: What's your favorite memory of the 1993 Phillies team?

Lenny Dykstra: Just the fans coming out. As the summer built, they just kept coming and coming and it was just so exciting to play in front of the fans.

IR: Your teammate on the 1993 team Darren Daulton is recovering from cancer. Any thoughts on playing with Dutch?

LD: Well, he was our horse. He was our leader. My thoughts and prayers are with him – if anyone can beat it, he can. He's a great leader, a great person, and a great teammate.

IR: Anything you'd like to say now that it has been over 20 years since your Phillies team won the NL Pennant?

LD: They're the best, man! I still think about it every day. Every time I see a baseball game, I think about the Phillie fans and it was an honor and a privilege to play in front of them.

Bonus

Transactions That Shaped the Phillies: Nails and McDowell Take the Turnpike

It's easy to forget just how good the 1986 Mets were. And it is amazing to think they traded one of their best players to a division rival that helped said division rival net a pennant four years later.

New York sent four players as starters to the 57th All-Star Game, including 21-year old Dwight Gooden, 24-year old Darryl Strawberry, and a pair of 32-year olds in Gary Carter and Keith Hernandez. While the club was known for being youthful, the club had a tremendous mix of both veterans and young talent that carried them through the playoffs and on to the World Series.

Beyond their four All-Star starters, the Mets had a fifth All-Star, Sid Fernandez, former All-Star third baseman Ray Knight, who hit .298 with 11 homers in 1986, a once-in-a-lifetime season from second baseman Wally Backman, .320/.376/.385 with 13 steals, six pitchers that won 10 games or more, including five that won 14 or more, and two relievers that accumulated at least 21 saves.

The Phillies also had a pretty remarkable season in 1986, tallying an unexpected 86 wins, but would be dwarfed by 21.5 games by the 108-win Mets who were stocked with stars of past, present, and future.

Lenny Dykstra was somewhat of an unsung hero on the late 80's Mets squad. A fan favorite, Dykstra was frequently overlooked when media discussed the team's best attributes. The spunky, 5'10" centerfielder won a starting spot in the Mets outfield midway through 1985 through a Mookie Wilson injury and would hit .295/.377/.445 mostly out of the leadoff spot with eight homers and 31 steals in 1986 to cement his starting role. Dykstra finished 19th in MVP voting that year and hit .300/.352/.540 with three homers and one steal in the playoffs.

Throughout most of 1987, 1988, and 1989 seasons, Dykstra was seen as the stronger half of a platoon with Wilson. However, as the seasons progressed, Dykstra's numbers began to drop. Dykstra finished 1988 with a career-low on-base percentage of .321 and on June 18, 1989, the centerfielder was shipped to Philadelphia with eccentric reliever Roger McDowell and minor leaguer Tom Edens for Juan Samuel.

The June 19, 1989 edition of the *New York Times* referred to Dykstra and McDowell as blithe spirits, possibly referring to their carefree attitudes but also to the perception that both could be better players with a more pronounced focus on baseball. It is unlikely Joseph Durso, the man who labeled the duo had any insight into what Dykstra could become but Dykstra's successes sure make you wonder if he was on to something.

Mets manager Davey Johnson told media that losing Dykstra and McDowell would be difficult but he felt the Mets had received an impact player in Samuel. Samuel had converted from second base to center field in 1989 to accommodate All-Star second baseman Tom Herr. Herr, for his part, held up his end of the bargain, hitting .287/.352/.364 with a pair of homers and 10 steals. Samuel did not, hitting .246/.311/.392 for the Phillies before the trade.

While Samuel had a disappointing start to 1989, there was reason to believe the speedy Samuel could put it all back together. Samuel was an All-Star in 1984 as a rookie with the Phillies and again in 1987, leading the league in triples in both seasons while averaging 50 steals a season between and including his All-Star campaigns. Where Samuel would falter, however, was his ability to draw walks (.309 OBP from 1983 through 1988) and his penchant for striking out, a category he led the National League in each year from 1984 through 1987.

The change of scenery trade looked like a clear victory for the Phillies early on, but it had nothing to do with the play of Nails or Samuel. McDowell, at age 28, certainly had a lot more left in his tank and posted a rather remarkable 1.11 ERA in 44 appearances with 19 saves after the trade in 1989. Combined with the failures of both Dykstra (a very ugly .222/.297/.330 line with just four homers and 17 steals in 28 attempts) and Samuel (.228/.299/.300 with just three homers and 31 steals in 40 attempts), the trade initially appeared as a loss for the in-the-hunt Mets and a small victory in obtaining a high-performance reliever for the Phillies.

But then 1990 happened.

McDowell was nowhere near as incredible as he was in 1989 but he was certainly solid; posting a 3.86 ERA with a league-leading 60 games finished and 22 saves in 86.1 innings pitched. With one year remaining on his contract, Samuel was traded by the Mets for veteran first baseman and right fielder Mike Marshall, who was coming off a .260/.325/.408 line in a year of part-time play. But, to be fair, it wouldn't have mattered what McDowell and Samuel did or where they went because in 1990, The Dude had one of the single-greatest single seasons in Phillies history.

In club history, there have only been four seasons worth nine wins or more in FanGraphs' version of WAR. Three of them were from Mike Schmidt (1974, 1977, 1980), the other belongs to Nails. Taking a .401 average as far as June 11, Dykstra had a season for the ages, leading the National League in hits and on-base percentage while hitting .325 with nine homers, and 33 steals, leading to his first All-Star appearance.

Despite finishing second in the NL in fWAR and rWAR to Barry Bonds, a man who had an even more insane season, Dykstra would finish not second to Bonds in MVP voting but a surprising ninth. The low finish likely had to do with the lack of team success the Phillies saw in 1990, posting a less-than-impressive 77-85 record, finishing fourth in the NL East.

Dykstra would, however, find team success in 1993. In an amazing season where Dykstra led baseball in plate appearances and runs, and led the NL in walks and hits, Nails would lead the Phils to the NL pennant, hitting .313/.450/.729 with six homers and four steals in the playoffs, almost single-handedly willing the '93 Phils to a very unlikely World Series. Samuel would bounce around the Majors, spending time in LA, Kansas City, Cincinnati, Detroit, and Toronto, outlasting Dykstra by one year in Major League play, but certainly not outperforming him. Samuel would hit just .259/.326/.407 against Dykstra's .298/.400/.434.

McDowell was more than just a throw-in, too, posting a 2.90 ERA with 44 saves for the Phillies from 1989 through 1991. McDowell would be flipped in a seemingly inconsequential 1991 trade-deadline deal that netted the Phillies Braulio Castillo and Mike Hartley. Hartley would be flipped to Minnesota for David West, a key contributor on the 1993 NL Pennant winner making the Juan Samuel change of scenery trade a gift that kept on giving and helped the Phillies win a pennant.

Assembling the 1993 Phillies

Dykstra was one of 11 position players on the 1993 Phillies to appear in 90 games or more. Of those players, only three (Darren Daulton, Ricky Jordan, and Mickey Morandini) were drafted and developed by the Phillies organization. Here is how the other eight were acquired:

Wes Chamberlain	Traded from Pittsburgh, 1990
Mariano Duncan	Free Agent Signing, 1992
Lenny Dykstra	Traded from NY Mets, 1989
Jim Eisenreich	Free Agent Signing, 1993
Dave Hollins	Rule 5 Draft, December 1989
Pete Incaviglia	Free Agent Signing, 1993
John Kruk	Traded from San Diego, 1989
Milt Thompson	Free Agent Signing, 1993

Roy Halladay

Right-Handed Starter

Years as a Phillie: 2010-2013
Line as a Phillie: 55-29, 3.25 ERA, 1.119 WHIP in 702.2 IP
fWAR Phillies Rank: 19th among pitchers, 60th among Phillies
Signature Moments: Threw a regular season Perfect Game against the Marlins and a postseason No Hitter against the Reds in 2010

The days and nights surrounding December 15, 2009 were some of the most exciting and confusing times of my existence as a sports fan. The rumors were piling up that the Phillies were getting ready to pull the trigger on a trade for Roy Halladay of the Toronto Blue Jays for some combination of Kyle Drabek, Travis d'Arnaud, Michael Taylor, Domonic Brown, Andrew Carpenter, and J.A. Happ to name a few.

There was also a very quiet side rumor that the Phillies were working on a deal to trade Cliff Lee, who had won them two games in the 2009 World Series, to Seattle. Halladay would arrive in Philadelphia for Drabek, d'Arnaud, and Taylor and, suddenly, the team that had reached the World Series in 2009, but started an aging Pedro Martinez twice, had acquired undoubtedly the best pitcher in baseball. What happened next confused and surprised Phillies fans: Lee was dealt to Seattle.

Suddenly, the joy of acquiring the best pitcher in baseball to pair with a sturdy but not spectacular rotation was sucked out of the air. Despite two straight World Series appearances, including their 2008 win, the Phillies would seemingly needlessly walk the line between big market spenders and penny pinchers. The first order of business after trading for Halladay was signing Halladay to an extension. He was signed for a three-year, $20 million per year extension, just a hair under market value.

Soon, Philadelphia would know the wonder of Roy Halladay: the intense training regiment, the emotionless soul taker that took the hill every five games. Halladay's first game was in Washington, the first opposing pitcher to toe the rubber at Nationals Park. He struck out nine in seven innings, earning his first of 55 wins as a Phillie. Halladay's starts were suddenly events for the two-time defending NL Champs with that excitement coming to a head on May 29, 2010. With the Flyers down the dial playing in Game One of the Stanley Cup Finals, Doc stole all of the headlines in Philadelphia: throwing 115 pitches, Halladay struck out 11 Marlins, allowing no hits or base runners, throwing the 20th Perfect Game in MLB history.

After leading the National League in innings pitched in 2010, Halladay would take the hill for the first time in his career in the postseason and no-hit a potent Reds offense in Game 1 of the NLDS. In two starts in the NLCS against the Giants, Halladay would drop Game 1 against Tim Lincecum but rebound to take the must-win Game 5 in San Francisco.

Unfortunately, the Phillies would get bumped in the very next game. Having posted a 21-10 record with a 2.44 ERA and a league-leading nine complete games and four shutouts, the awards would roll in after the season, as Halladay would earn the NL Cy Young, as well as Pro Athlete of the Year by the Sporting News and the Clutch Performer of the Year by MLB. Halladay was the first Phillie since Steve Bedrosian to win the Cy Young Award and was the first Phillie since Steve Carlton in 1982 to win 20 games.

Lee and Halladay would be united in the same rotation in 2011 in what many thought had the makings of the greatest rotation of all-time. Halladay would post a 19-6 record, improve his ERA to 2.35 and finished second in the Cy Young voting. Halladay would have a second shot at the postseason, defeating former Phillie Kyle Lohse in Game 1 of the NLDS. With the series against the St. Louis Cardinals knotted at 2-2, Halladay allowed only one earned run and just six hits, but the Phillies could only muster three hits and couldn't advance into their fourth-straight NLCS.

Halladay would slow down due to injuries in 2012 and would make only 13 starts in his final season in Philly. From 2010 through 2013, despite injuries, Halladay would rank fourth in the NL in fWAR, behind only Clayton Kershaw, Cole Hamels, and Cliff Lee. And despite these injuries, he would rank fourth in wins despite only ranking 18th in appearances and 12th in innings pitched. Halladay would rank 29th in K/9 IP, third in

BB/9 IP, and tenth in FIP. If narrowed to 2010 and 2011, Halladay was the best on the planet: first in ERA, FIP, xFIP, wins, innings pitched, and K/BB.

Some will undoubtedly question Halladay's position on this list but for two seasons, Halladay was considered the premier pitcher in baseball and was also pretty impressive in the postseason, too (2.37 ERA and 0.737 WHIP in 38.0 IP). Had the Phillies offense shown up in the 2010 NLCS or in Game 5 of the 2011 NLDS, Halladay would have had a World Series opportunity.

Unfortunately, injuries slowed down Halladay, probably in no small part to him retiring fifth on the active list for innings pitched and first complete games. Halladay earns his spot on this list for his two years of absolute dominance and his outstanding postseason record.

Phillies' Top 10: K/9 IP among Starting Pitchers, Career

Halladay was a dominant strikeout artist and his success is evident in his placement among Phillies' starting pitchers in strikeouts per nine innings pitched.

1. Cliff Lee   8.84 K/9 IP, 2009, 2011-2015
2. Cole Hamels   8.61 K/9 IP, 2006-2015
3. Curt Schilling   8.42 K/9 IP, 1992-2000
4. Roy Halladay   7.97 K/9 IP, 2010-2013
5. Robert Person   7.94 K/9 IP, 1999-2002
6. Brandon Duckworth   7.54 K/9 IP, 2001-2003
7. Randy Wolf   7.40 K/9 IP, 1999-2006
8. Steve Carlton   7.38 K/9 IP, 1972-1986
9. Brett Myers   7.35 K/9 IP, 2002-2009
10. Kevin Millwood   7.29 K/9 IP, 2003-2004

Bonus

Transactions That Shaped the Phillies: Amaro Makes a House Call

The 2009 Phillies came just two wins short of repeating as World Series champions. Throughout the series, the Phillies deficiency was clear: despite getting two memorable performances, and more importantly wins, out of midseason acquisition Cliff Lee, the Phillies lacked starting pitching. Relying on two starts from 37-year old Pedro Martinez, the Phillies dropped a very winnable World Series in six games.

Lee was the reigning AL Cy Young winner heading into the 2009 season. The Phillies snagged Lee in a midseason deal that sent Carlos Carrasco, Jason Donald, Jason Knapp, and Lou Marson to Cleveland in exchange for Lee and outfielder Ben Francisco.

At the conclusion of the season, Toronto made the league aware that 2003 AL Cy Young winner Roy Halladay was available. During the 2009 All-Star break, rumors went wild that Halladay would be willing to become a Phillie. The Phillies, facing fears that they would not be able to resign Lee beyond his $9 million option for 2010, saw Lee as a player they may not be able to afford

The dots all started to connect in December, 2009.

As the well-documented, but still-murky story goes: General Manager Ruben Amaro and ownership believed that Lee would not be amenable to a long-term, team-friendly extension whereas Halladay had, in some form or another, indicated he was amenable to sign a three-year extension beyond 2010 for $60 million. Amaro pulled the trigger on a deal that sent Lee to Seattle and negotiated an adjacent deal to acquire Halladay from Toronto for catcher Travis d'Arnaud, pitcher Kyle Drabek, and outfielder Michael Taylor.

In a vacuum, acquiring Halladay was one of the finest moves in Phillies history. Halladay took the mound for the first time for the Phillies on April 5, 2010 in the opening game at Nationals Park. Halladay pitched seven innings and struck out nine, earning a win in his first decision. Doc would win his first four decisions with the Phillies including a complete game shutout on April 21 in Atlanta. On May 29, Halladay had thousands of households in Philadelphia switching their televisions from the Stanley Cup Finals of the Flyers and Blackhawks to the perfect game Halladay was throwing. Halladay struck out 11 en route to completing the perfect game.

In 2010, Halladay would win 21 games, throw 9 complete games, including 4 shutouts across 250.2 innings, leading the Majors in all categories en route to winning the National League Cy Young award, an NL All-Star birth, and a sixth-place MVP finish. Halladay's magic ride would continue on October 6: in his first postseason game, Halladay threw a no-hitter against the Cincinnati Reds, striking out 8, allowing just one walk in an economical 104 pitches. Halladay would lose his next start 4-3 in Game One of the NLCS against the San Francisco Giants but would win a must-win Game Five to keep the Phillies alive. The Phillies would be eliminated in six.

With the mission of winning a World Series not accomplished, Halladay went in to 2011 looking to carry his team even further. Halladay would win 19 games, losing just 6, lowering his ERA to 2.35 ERA, leading the NL in complete games and ERA+ while leading the Majors in Fielding Independent Pitching (FIP). Halladay would win Game One of the NLDS against the Cardinals, pitching eight innings, allowing three earned against eight strikeouts. He would take the mound in the decisive Game Five, allowing only a first-inning run. Despite going eight innings, allowing just one run while striking out seven, the Phillies would be held scoreless and would be eliminated from the playoffs.

Still one of the undisputed best pitchers in baseball heading into the 2012 season, Halladay would win his first three decisions but his velocity would drop and his strikeout totals would dip. Following a May 27 game where Halladay left after two innings, he would be placed on the disabled list, making under 30 starts for the first time in his career since 2005. Halladay would win 11 games in 2012 with a 4.49 ERA before slowing down to 4-5 record with a 6.82 ERA in just 13 starts in 2013.

And what about the talent the Blue Jays received in exchange for Halladay? Catcher Travis d'Arnaud, a five-time *Baseball America* Top 100 prospect and 2007 first-round pick of the Phillies, would be traded prior to the 2013 season for Cy Young winner R.A. Dickey and would make his Major League debut at age 24 for the Mets on August 17, 2013. D'Arnaud has struggled to put it all together in the Majors so far, hitting just .189/.277/.269 with four homers in 257 MLB PA, battling through various injuries.

Drabek, a two-time *Baseball America* Top #100 prospect and the Phillies' 2006 first-round pick, would reach the Majors on September 15, 2010, pitching six innings, striking out five in a losing effort against the Baltimore Orioles. While young, Drabek has struggled to remain healthy, posting a career 8-15 mark thus far with a career 5.37 ERA.

Finally, Taylor, ranked by *Baseball America* as the 29th best prospect in baseball prior to the 2010 season, has seen just 81 plate appearances in the Majors. Taylor was traded twice on December 16, 2009, first from the Phillies to the Blue Jays and then from the Blue Jays to the Oakland Athletics for infielder Brett Wallace. Taylor was traded to the Chicago White Sox on June 14, 2014 at which time he was hitting .135/.210/.189 with just one homer in his Major League career.

The Phillies acquisition of Halladay could have been one of the greatest trades in club history. It had all of the elements of a great trade: the Phils gave up prospects that didn't live up to their superstar potential or, in some cases, their potential of becoming Major League regulars, and acquired a pitcher who won the Cy Young in his first season and finished second in his second season, and rode Halladay into the playoffs two years in a row.

In the scheme of great Phillies trades, this one is a win for the Phillies, but it has its limitations. The Phillies only got two awesome seasons from Halladay. Another was only average while another was downright awful. Second, while the Phillies earned surplus value on Halladay's $20 million per year contract in 2010 and 2011, according to FanGraphs, Halladay was worth a net negative $32.9 million against the last two years of his contract and a net negative $12.2 million over his entire deal. Third, the Phillies didn't win a championship during Halladay's run, but that certainly wasn't entirely Halladay's fault.

#27 Ryan Howard

First Baseman

Years as a Phillie: 2004-active
Line as a Phillie: .263/.349/.519, 355 HR, 12 SB in 6144 PA
fWAR Phillies Rank: 30th among position players, 41st among Phillies
Signature Season: Led the NL in HR, RBI, and Total Bases en route to winning 2006 NL MVP
Signature Stretch: Six-Straight Top-10 NL MVP finishes (2006-2011), NL MVP (2006)

The "Big Piece" was a fifth-round draft pick out of Missouri State in 2001 and quickly accelerated through the Phillies minor league ranks. Howard's name would appear in trade rumors almost immediately after his 2002 campaign in Lakewood when he hit .280/.367/.460 with 19 HR.

Howard would have an even better 2003 with Clearwater, hitting .304/.374/.514 with 23 HR, coinciding directly with the Phillies' signing of Jim Thome, making Howard seemingly that much more expendable. Howard would get his first taste of the Major Leagues after he set the Phillies minor league home run record with 46 in 2004. Howard would hit two pinch-hit homers in his brief September stay that would pique Phillies' fans interest.

Despite all of Howard's rapid minor league success, Howard was blocked by Thome at first base and would start 2005 in Triple-A Scranton-Wilkes Barre. But an injury to Thome would open the doors for Howard to have a shot at the starting first base gig. Howard would hit .288/.356/.567 with 22 HR en route to winning the 2005 National League Rookie of the Year.

In 2006, Howard would take over the first base job when Thome was traded to the Chicago White Sox and deliver for the Phillies: Howard led the NL in homers, RBIs, and total bases, winning the MVP in large part due to his huge August and September, hitting .365/.513/.750 with 22 HR, nearly willing the Phillies into the playoffs.

Through the next five seasons, Howard was a threat for 30+ homers and would finish in the Top 10 in NL MVP voting. He would also be a driving force in the Phillies' postseason success, hitting .259/.357/.488 with 8 HR. Howard would have particular success in the 2008 World Series, hitting three homers, including one as the second half of back-to-back homers with Chase Utley in Game 4 off of Matt Garza. Howard had huge success in three NLCS appearances, hitting .316/.435/.561 in 69 NLCS PA, and he would win the 2009 NLCS MVP.

Howard would suffer an unfortunate torn Achilles' tendon to close out the 2011 NLDS. Howard's 2012 and 2013 seasons were riddled with injury and Howard saw only 71 and 80 games respectively in each season. Had Howard stayed healthy, he may have approached 500 HRs. But instead, Howard sits at 355, good enough for second in Phillies history, third in RBIs, and eighth in SLG. Howard also holds the single-season record among Phillies in homers with 58.

Regardless, Howard's game, predicated on power, walks, and strikeouts, has many holes. Having only played parts of eleven seasons, Howard already ranks 33rd in MLB history in strikeouts and with 100 in 2014, would jump firmly into the 50s. Howard has also cost the Phillies 135 runs according to FanGraphs on defense or the equivalent of about eight and a half wins.

Howard, along with Roy Halladay, Von Hayes, and Cliff Lee, was one of the hardest players to place on the list. Some of Howard's calling cards are homers (a result of his talent) and RBIs (a result of the hitters getting on base in front of him), so while many want to give him credit for the RBIs, the RBIs were not necessarily a result of Howard's success. We ultimately ranked Howard a bit higher than his FanGraphs' rating because of the 2006 MVP, his postseason success and contributions, and quite frankly, the fact that he is the greatest first baseman in Phillies' history.

Cliff Lee
Left-Handed Starter

Years as a Phillie: 2009, 2011-present
Line as a Phillie: 48-34, 2.94 ERA, 1.098 WHIP in 827.1 IP
fWAR Phillies Rank: 11th among pitchers, 38th among Phillies
Signature Season: 17-8 with a 2.40 ERA and a 1.027 WHIP in 2011, finishing third in NL Cy Young Voting
Signature Moment: Catch in Game 1 of the 2009 World Series

On July 29, 2009, the Phillies found themselves up six games in the NL East but facing a number of injuries. General Manager Ruben Amaro, in an effort to bolster the starting rotation that now featured various combinations of Cole Hamels, Joe Blanton, Jamie Moyer, Antonio Bastardo, J.A. Happ, Rodrigo Lopez, and Chan Ho Park, had just signed former Cy Young award winner Pedro Martinez who wouldn't be ready until mid-August.

Anticipating the need for a top-flight pitcher in order to be successful in the playoffs, the Phillies' GM had been linked in rumors to Roy Halladay. With Phillies fans clamoring for an ace, and reporters asking Halladay his thoughts of Philadelphia during the All-Star festivities, Amaro delivered Philadelphia an ace.

It just wasn't the one Phillies fans had expected.

Yet, Cliff Lee, the 2008 reigning AL Cy Young winner, seemed to be the ace the Phillies needed. The Phillies acquired Lee for Carlos Carrasco, Jason Donald, Jason Knapp, and Lou Marson, and went 35-18 down the stretch, with Lee going 7-4 with a 3.39 ERA.

Lee would be a postseason hero for the 2009 NL Pennant-winning squad, posting a 4-0 record with two complete games, striking out 33 batters in 40.1 IP with a 1.56 ERA in what was likely the finest single postseason run of any Phillies pitcher ever. Despite Lee winning Games 1 and 5 for the

Phillies, the Fightins would ultimately fall short in 2009 in six games to the Yankees.

What happened in the offseason still has some confused to this day: on December 15, 2009, the Phillies would acquire Roy Halladay, forming unquestionably the top rotation in baseball only to trade Lee to Seattle in what was referred to at the time as a move that needed to be made for salary reasons. After an All-Star season with the Mariners and a World Series appearance after being traded in the same season with the Rangers, Lee would return to Philadelphia as a free agent for the 2011 season. He would finish third in the Cy Young voting in 2011, posting a career-low 2.40 ERA en route to his first All-Star appearance with the Phillies. Lee would meet a rocky end to the 2011 season, blowing an early 4-0 lead in Game 2 of the 2011 NLDS to the St. Louis Cardinals at home.

Despite going just 6-9, Lee led the National League in BB% and K/BB ratio with a stellar 1.114 WHIP in 2012. Lee would once again lead the NL in BB% and K/BB ratio, while lowering his ERA and WHIP to reach his second All-Star game as a Phillie in 2013 and a sixth-place Cy Young finish.

Among all Phillies starters, Lee ranks first in K/9 IP, second in BB/9 IP, first in K/BB, 18th in ERA, and 13th in FIP. From 2011 through 2013, Lee ranks 27th in starts, sixth in innings pitched, ninth in K/9 IP, first in BB/9 IP, and first in K/BB.

Among the players in the upper-echelon of the Phillies Nation 100, Lee has among the shortest tenures but, like Lenny Dykstra, was a Phillie that almost single-handedly willed the Fightins to a World Series title on his own.

Bonus

Transactions That Shaped the Phillies: Midseason Swap Nets Cy

If you looked only at their record, you wouldn't have guessed the 2009 Phillies necessarily needed any starting pitching. Heading into the July 31st trade deadline, 2008 World Series MVP Cole Hamels was seemingly turning his season around, winning his last three decisions, and the Phillies had just wrapped up a 10-game winning streak winning four in a row as they headed into their July 29 match-up against the Arizona Diamondbacks.

But a look at the names that figured into the decisions certainly told a different story. The Phillies were relying on Hamels and a whole lot of offense to dispatch their opponents. The 2009 Phils would use 12 different starting pitchers that season and had been ravaged by injury to the point that their rotation became Hamels, Joe Blanton, rookie J.A. Happ, and Rodrigo Lopez, while, for a spell, Chan Ho Park, Antonio Bastardo, and Kyle Kendrick held down the back end of the starting rotation.

The Phillies were looking to defend their World Series crown and take advantage of their NL-best offense; leading the NL in homers, runs, homers, and slugging while ranking second in stolen bases in 2009. In an effort to bolster a return trip to the playoffs for a third straight year, the Phillies knew they had to upgrade their starting rotation. The Phillies had just taken a flyer on former Cy Young winner and future Hall of Famer Pedro Martinez in July but Martinez would not be ready until August. Additionally the Phillies had more than one opening in their starting rotation.

The rumors, at the time, suggested that Roy Halladay may have been on his way to Philadelphia. A perennial Cy Young contender, and former Cy Young winner himself, Halladay had made overtures toward the Phillies by way of acknowledging rumors during an All-Star week press conference when he stated: "I think Philadelphia is a great city." That was all it took for the rumor mill to start churning.

The Phillies, reportedly unwilling to part with Domonic Brown, could not pry away Halladay away from the Jays but they would not let the trade deadline pass empty handed. No, the Phillies would acquire outfielder Ben Francisco and 2008 Cy Young award winner Cliff Lee for pitching prospects Carlos Carrasco and Jason Knapp, catcher Lou Marson, and infielder Jason Donald.

The move wasn't necessarily seen as a slam dunk at the time of its completion. The Phillies, up seven games in the NL East and in the middle of a four-game winning streak, were seemingly fine with the hulking offense that took the field each night. And Lee was no sure thing, either: while he had won 22 games with a 2.54 ERA in 2008 for Cleveland, he was omitted from Cleveland's 2007 playoff roster after a demotion during the season. Sure the Phillies were acquiring a relatively young former Cy Young winner seemingly in his prime, there were several outstanding questions as to whether or not his prime performance was a fluke.

Thankfully for the Phillies, it wasn't.

Lee provided more than just a standard reliable arm for a team seeking reinforcements. Lee would go 7-4 for the Phillies in 12 starts with a 3.39 ERA with a 1.130 WHIP with a then-career-high 8.4 K/9 IP, helping the Phillies cruise to a 93 win season, out-performing the second-place Marlins by six games.

Lee's value increased multiple times over as he piled up playoff victory after playoff victory. Looking to avenge their NLDS loss of 2007, the Phils sent Lee to the mound for Game One of the 2009 NLDS against the Colorado Rockies, where he scattered six hits, struck out five, and allowed just one run. Lee took the mound next in the fourth and deciding game of the NLDS, picking up a no decision, allowing just one earned with five strikeouts, scattering five hits.

The lefty seemed to get better as the playoffs continued, throwing eight innings of shutout ball with ten strikeouts in Game Three of the NLCS in front of a sold-out Citizens Bank Park while picking up a single and run of his own in the eighth inning of an 11-0 thrashing of the Dodgers. The Arkansas native stymied the Yankees in Game One of the World Series at Yankees Stadium, striking out ten again, allowing only one unearned run while scattering six hits. In a do or die Game Five, Lee bent but did not break, earning his fourth win of the postseason, matching Cole Hamels' club record for wins in a single postseason set the year before.

But, just like that, in a flash, Lee was gone. With an opportunity to acquire Halladay right in front of him, General Manager Ruben Amaro, who brilliantly engineered the trade to acquire Lee, sent him packing for a package of pitchers Phillippe Aumont and J.C. Ramirez and outfielder Tyson Gillies.

In Lee, Amaro acquired a slightly risky arm with a brilliant previous season but not much of a track record beyond that. The gamble paid off in spades and the Phillies acquired a much needed starting pitcher who not only helped them maintain their division lead but also helped them win the 2009 pennant. And I'd be remiss to omit any mention of Francisco: Francisco was solid in the fourth and fifth outfielder role for the Phillies from 2009 through 2011, posting a .259/.332/.420 line and a go-ahead, pinch-hit homer in Game 3 of the 2011 NLDS against the Cardinals off of Jaime Garcia.

What helps this trade is that none of the players who were acquired for Lee became anything more than regular Major Leaguers at best while one never made a Major League roster.

The most successful of the group, Carrasco, reached the Majors in 2009 but posted an 8.87 ERA while averaging an uncharacteristically-low 4.43 K/9 IP. Carrasco improved but has only pitched more than 100 innings in the Majors once (2011) while posting a 5.08 ERA. Knapp succumbed to elbow issues and was out of professional baseball from 2010 until 2014 when the Rangers signed him and stashed him in High-A Myrtle Beach.

Marson, believed at one point to be the Phillies' power-hitting catcher of the future, became a career .219/.309/.299 Major League hitter and has not played professional baseball in 2014 after becoming a Spring Training casualty of the Phillies. Donald, projected to be a second-division regular, has spent most of the five-plus seasons since the trade in Cleveland, Cincinnati, Kansas City, and Texas' Triple-A clubhouses. Donald is a career .257/.309/.362 Major League hitter.

In acquiring Lee, Amaro used pieces that had no immediate use to a competing team and turned them into a top-flight starting pitcher. The pieces went on to middling Major League careers despite being Major League-ready at young ages at the time of the trade. The Arkansan southpaw put the Phillies on his back and took them all the way to the pennant in 2009 and may have been called upon on short-rest to start Game 7 had the Phillies been able to stretch the series any longer.

This trade could have ranked as the second best, possibly even best trade in Phillies history, had the Phillies actually kept Lee for the 2010 season at the $9 million price tag his contract commanded. A 2010 pairing of the NL Cy Young Halladay and AL Cy Young contender Lee could have been lethal and would have likely negated the necessity to deal midseason for Roy Oswalt. Lee would win three games for the Texas Rangers in the 2010 playoffs before dropping two in the World Series.

Sam Thompson
Right Fielder

Years as a Phillie: 1889-1898
Line as a Phillie: .334/.388/.509, 95 HR, 192 SB in 4835 PA
fWAR Phillies Rank: 15th among position players, 23rd among Phillies
Signature Season: Hit .415/.465/.696 with 147 RBIs in 1894

On October 16, 1888, the Philadelphia Quakers purchased the 28-year old "Big" Sam Thompson from the Detroit Wolverines. Thompson would waste no time becoming a big-time star in Philadelphia: in his first season with the Phillies, Thompson would win the NL homer crown with 20 HR, a feat he would repeat in 1895. Thompson had a perfect combination of power and speed, averaging 12 homers and 24 steals a season from 1889 through 1896, leading the league in both SLG and RBI in 1894 and 1895.

It wasn't until 1974 when the Veterans' Committee finally honored Thompson in the Hall of Fame and it is difficult to imagine what took so long. Thompson retired as second all-time in Major League history in homers, 29th in runs scored, eighth in RBIs, and fourth in slugging.

From 1889 through 1898, the outfielder led all of baseball homers, ranked in 17th in runs, fourth in RBIs, 53rd in steals, and tenth in OPS. During Thompson's best season, he was one-fourth of the best-hitting outfield quartet of all-time of Ed Delahanty, Billy Hamilton, Thompson, and Tuck Turner. In 1894, they became the only outfield in Major League history to hit above .400 for the season. And Thompson did that after having part of a fingertip amputated.

Thompson's career would seemingly conclude following the 1898 season, when injuries limited him to just 17 games between the 1897 and 1898 seasons. But Thompson just could not shake baseball out of his system, returning to the Major Leagues in 1906 to play eight games in the outfield for the Detroit Tigers.

Thompson, in large part, is overlooked because he played with such talented players, including Delahanty, Hamilton, and Nap Lajoie. However, Thompson had some of the best individual seasons in Phillies history, including the second and fifth-best SLG in a season in 1894 and 1895. Thompson was one fourth of the best outfield in Phillies history and usually is passed over in favor of Delahanty and Hamilton but is absolutely a Top 25 Phillie in his own right.

Phillies' Top 10: Single-Season Slugging

Sam Thompson's 1894 was one of the best seasons in Phillies history. The outfielder hit .404 with a .458 OBP and a .686 SLG with 13 homers and 24 steals. The .686 SLG was the club's single-season mark until Chuck Klein broke it in 1930.

1. Chuck Klein - .687, 1930
2. Sam Thompson - .686, 1894
3. Ryan Howard - .659, 2006
4. Chuck Klein - . 657, 1929
5. Sam Thompson - .654, 1895
6. Chuck Klein - .646, 1932
7. Mike Schmidt - . 644, 1981
8. Dick Allen - .632, 1966
9. Ed Delahanty - . 631, 1896
10. Mike Schmidt - .624, 1980

Cy Williams

Center Fielder

Years as a Phillie: 1918-1930
Line as a Phillie: .306/.380/.500, 217 HR, 77 SB in 5786 PA
fWAR Phillies Rank: 17th among position players, 25th among Phillies
Signature Season: Hit 41 HR with 11 SB with a .293/.371/.576 SLG

Part power hitter, part product of his environment, Fred "Cy" Williams was a 6'2" power-hitting, lefty center fielder who pounded the short, 280 foot right field fence in the Baker Bowl. Williams was acquired on December 26, 1917 from the Chicago Cubs for Dode Paskert.

The trade ultimately ended up being one of the few bright spots of the 1920s: Williams led all Phillies in the 1920s in plate appearances, homers, runs, RBIs, steals, and OPS. During Williams' tenure in Philadelphia, the Phillies were a miserable 720-1222, good enough for 37.08% winning percentage, nevertheless Williams was among the best center fielders of the time.

From 1918 through 1930, Williams was a model of durability and was in the upper echelon of center fielders, leading all NL center fielders in games, RBIs and homers, second in runs, and third in OBP, SLG, and OPS.

Williams retired as the second-leading home run hitter in National League history, with 251 HR, due in no small part to the short porch at the Baker Bowl but still impressive. Williams' 251 HR ranks tenth all-time among center fielders and is tied for seventh in Phillies history in homers. Williams ranks 13th in team history in runs and RBIs, 15th in SLG, and 16th in OPS.

Williams' stunning numbers and historic power among center fielders earns him high praise on this list but his inclusion suffers from the lack of team success during his tenure and the ballpark that Williams played in. Williams' career reputation suffers because he was never on a winning team.

And that's a literal statement: no Phillies team that Williams played on was ever above .500. Interestingly, most of Williams' top seasons came after the age of 30. He held the record for most homers by a 39-year old, an NL-leading 30 in 1927, until Hank Aaron broke the mark in 1973.

<hr>

Did You Know: Regulars at age 39

Cy Williams set the MLB record for most home runs by a 39-year old with 30 in 1927. The Phillies have had just four regulars at 39 garner enough at bats to qualify for the batting title. According to FanGraphs' version of WAR, only two contributed positive value to the Phillies.

1906 – Kid Gleason hit .227/.281/.269 with 0 HR, 17 SB in 562 PA, worth -0.1 WAR

1927 – Cy Williams hit .274/.365/.502 with 30 HR, 0 SB in 570 PA, worth 1.6 WAR

1980 – Pete Rose .282/.352/.354 in 739 PA, worth 0.3 WAR

2011 – Raul Ibanez .245/.289/.419 in 575 PA, worth -1.7 WAR

Del Ennis

Left Fielder

Years as a Phillie: 1946-1956
Line as a Phillie: .286/.344/.479, 259 HR, 44 SB in 6939 PA
fWAR Phillies Rank: 14th among position players, 22nd among Phillies
rWAR Phillies Rank: 13th among position players, 18th among Phillies
Signature Season: Led NL in RBI while hitting .311/.372/.551, finishing fourth in 1950 NL MVP voting

A star in baseball and football at Olney High School, Del Ennis was the local boy that made good. And good may be one of the largest understatements possible. A Petty Officer Third Class who saw action in the Pacific during World War II, Ennis was able to hone his baseball skills while in the Navy, playing with Major Leaguers Billy Herman, Johnny Vander Meer, and Schoolboy Rowe in the Honolulu League.

Ennis impressed so much during his stay in Hawai'i that New York Yankees owner, and fellow serviceman, Dan Topping offered Ennis $25,000 to sign with the Yankees, a sum 500 times larger than his original Phillies signing bonus. Ennis declined and became a Major Leaguer with the Phillies just a few weeks after returning from duty in 1946.

Had there been a Rookie of the Year Award in 1946, Ennis would likely have won it as he led all rookies in RBI, runs scored, batting average, and slugging while hitting 17 HR and accumulating the most WAR out of any rookie batter or pitcher.

His rookie performance was good enough for an eighth-place NL MVP finish. The six-foot, right-handed slugging outfielder was among the first of the Whiz Kids to join the Phillies to help turn the tide of the franchise and he guided them with his power throughout the 1950s.

Ennis would receive MVP votes seven times in eleven years with the Phillies with his highest finish, fourth place, coming in 1950 after hitting

.311/.372/.551 with a then-Phillies record for HR (31) by a right-handed batter. The Phillies would win the pennant in 1950 and like many Phillies, and quite a few Yankees for that matter, Ennis would struggle at the plate during the Fall Classic, hitting just .143/.200/.214. Ennis was traded by the Phillies to the St. Louis Cardinals for Bobby Morgan and Rip Repulski. The trade ended up being a relatively even swap: the Cardinals got a very solid year from Ennis and the Phillies got a solid year from Repulski.

As Ennis' time in Philadelphia drew to a close, he left as the All-Time franchise leader in home runs, a record that would last for 25 years until Mike Schmidt broke it. Ennis currently ranks third in team history in HR, tenth in runs scored, third in RBIs, and 26th in SLG.

From 1946 through 1956, Ennis was in an elite class of left fielders, leading all Major League left fielders in games played, plate appearances, and RBI, ranked third in HR and runs, and ninth in slugging.

Ennis was an excellent outfielder for eleven seasons, among the best in baseball. He was inducted onto the Phillies Wall of Fame in 1982 and in 1983 was chosen to the Phillies Centennial Team.

Phillies' Top 10: Doubles by Left Fielder, Career

Ennis had a fine power stroke that resulted in many doubles, triples, and homers. He ranks third among Phillies left fielders.

1. Ed Delahanty	442, 1888-1901
2. Sherry Magee	337, 1904-1914
3. Del Ennis	310, 1946-1956
4T. Greg Luzinski	253, 1970-1980
4T. Pat Burrell	253, 2000-2008
6. Raul Ibanez	100, 2009-2011
7. Irish Meusel	99, 1918-1921
8. Gregg Jefferies	95, 1995-1998
9. Johnny Mokan	92, 1922-1927
10. Morrie Arnovich	86, 1936-1940

Garry Maddox

Center Fielder

Years as a Phillie: 1975-1986
Line as a Phillie: .284/.320/.409, 85 HR, 189 SB in 5039 PA
fWAR Phillies Rank: 21st among position players, 29th among Phillies
Signature Achievement: Won Eight-Straight Gold Gloves from 1975 through 1982

"Two-thirds of the world is covered by water. The other one-third is covered by Gary Maddox."

- Harry Kalas, 1975

At 6'3" 175 lbs., the "Secretary of Defense" was one of the smoothest, and best, defensive center fielders in Major League history. The winner of eight-straight Gold Gloves from 1975 through 1982, Maddox's defensive play often looked effortless as he secured the Phillies approximately five and a half wins over 12 seasons in Philadelphia. Maddox led the NL in Total Zone Runs in 1976 and 1979, put outs in center in 1976 and 1979, assists in center 1975 and 1976, Total Zone Runs as a center fielder in 1976, 1978, 1979, and 1980, and led the NL in range factor as a center fielder in 1975, 1976, 1978, and 1979. And as great as Maddox was defensively, he was also a key contributor offensively for a championship Phillies squad.

Maddox was acquired from the San Francisco for Willie Montanez on May 4, 1975 and made an instant impact, stealing 24 bases in 27 chances, hitting .291/.359/.433 with the Phillies en route to his first Gold Glove season. Maddox would follow '75 with an even better 1976, having the absolute best season of his career hitting .330/.377/.456 with six homers, 29 steals, and his second straight Gold Glove. Maddox finished fifth in NL MVP voting, one of five Phillies in the top 16, and contributed to the Phillies' first playoff appearance since 1950.

From 1975 through 1986, Maddox led center fielders in FanGraphs' version of defensive runs saved. Maddox ranked fourth among his NL contemporary center fielders in WAR while with the Phillies, eighth in batting average, 14th in SLG, and fifth in steals.

Despite Maddox's stellar defensive reputation, Maddox would have two errors in the tenth inning of Game 4 of the 1978 NLCS against the Los Angeles Dodgers. Maddox would misplay a Dusty Baker fly ball and then a Bill Russell single. The end result was Ron Cey scoring the pennant-winning run on Russell's single, ending the Phillies 1978 season.

Just two years later however, Maddox would redeem himself by driving home a go-ahead, and eventual pennant-winning, run of his own in the tenth inning of Game 5 of the 1980 NLCS. Maddox would appear six times in the playoffs with the Phillies, hitting .271/.307/.374, including the eventual game-winning homer of Game 1 of the 1983 World Series.

Maddox is one of the rare defensive talents who passed the eye test during his time whose successes are supported by modern, advanced statistics. Maddox remains one of the most underrated contributors to the 1980 World Series-winning club.

Phillies' Top 10: Doubles by Center Fielder, Season

Maddox hit 37 doubles in 1976, good for ninth among Phillies' center fielders.

1. Ethan Allen	46, 1935
2. Aaron Rowand	45, 2007
3. Lenny Dykstra	44, 1993
4. Ethan Allen	42, 1934
5T. Kiddo Davis	39, 1932
5T. Shane Victorino	39, 2009
5T. Willie Montanez	39, 1972
8. Doug Glanville	38, 1999
9T. Garry Maddox	37, 1976
9T. Dode Paskert	37, 1912

Bonus

Transactions That Shaped the Phillies: Phils Enlist Secretary of Defense

Rusty Staub was a fine outfielder and first baseman in the National League. From 1963 through 1974, Staub hit .279/.366/.430 with 178 homers, earning MVP votes five times and making five-straight All-Star squads from 1967 through 1971. Staub was often the best player on bad teams, spending 1963 through 1968 with the expansion Houston Colt .45s and Astros, 1969-1971 with the expansion Montreal Expos, and then with the recently-created Mets from 1972 through 1975.

The Phillies, sensing an opportunity to improve in 1975, had signed veteran first baseman Dick Allen for a return to the team. Third baseman Mike Schmidt was coming off one of the single-greatest seasons in Phillies history (MLB-leading 36 homers, NL-leading .546 slugging) and Bob Boone, Larry Bowa, and Greg Luzinski all were developing into cornerstone pieces for the franchise. After signing Allen, incumbent first baseman Willie Montanez became redundant and the club attempted to trade Montanez to the Mets for Staub.

It resulted in one of the best non-trades in club history.

The non-trade was a positive but not for reasons you may assume. Montanez didn't become a superstar and Staub didn't flame out. No, the Mets reluctance to trade Staub for Montanez became a huge win for the Phillies because of the direction they were forced to move in instead. On May 4, 1975, the Phillies acquired center fielder Garry Maddox from San Francisco for Montanez.

Maddox was a second round pick in the January 1968 amateur draft by the San Francisco Giants. At age 18, Maddox would perform well enough in Rookie ball to earn a brief cameo in Single-A Fresno. The defensively-gifted outfielder would be drafted into the Vietnam War midway through the 1968 season and would serve his country in the conflict until he returned to baseball for the 1971 season.

After hitting 30 homers with a .299/.356/.562 line for Single-A Fresno despite not having played competitive baseball for two-plus seasons, Maddox spent 11 games in Triple-A Phoenix in 1972 before earning a permanent spot on Major League rosters in 1972.

In his best seasons, Maddox was as close to being a five-tool player as there was in baseball. There were hints of the player Maddox could become scattered in his early stats, as well: in his age 22 through 24 seasons, 1972 through 1974, Maddox would hit .292/.324/.431 with San Francisco, averaging 10 homers and 19 steals a season. After a slow start in 1975 where Maddox hit just .135/.237/.212 with one steal and one homer through his first 17 games, Maddox was shipped to Philly for Montanez.

After one season, the trade looked like a small win for San Francisco. Montanez earned MVP votes by hitting .302/.353/.415 across the whole season with 10 homers and 101 RBI. Meanwhile, Maddox rebounded from his slow start but finished with a line of just .272/.344/.406 with five homers and 25 steals. Nevertheless, an annual tradition began: Maddox snagged his first Gold Glove.

It was during the 1976 season, however, that Maddox definitely became the better player in the trade and left the pretty solid Montanez in the dust. Maddox would hit .330/.377/.456 with six homers and a career-high 29 steals while winning his second of eight-consecutive Gold Gloves in a row and earning a fifth-place NL MVP finish. Maddox frequently hit seventh between right fielder Jay Johnstone and catchers Boone and Tim McCarver, helped lead the Phillies to a 15-win improvement and was a big piece of their first-ever 101-win season in 1976.

Maddox's strong performance contributed to a squad that would make its first playoff appearance since 1950. Maddox was not only terrific in the regular season but his numbers translated about as well as you would expect to the postseason, hitting .271/.307/.374, driving in the eventual pennant-winning run in the 1980 NLCS, winning a World Series ring in 1980, and hitting a memorable homer in the 1983 World Series. But beyond his above-average offensive, Maddox was an other-worldly defender.

Sure, many remember the slogan "Two-third of the world is covered by water. The other one-third is covered by Garry Maddox" or the catchy, Harry Kalas-appointed nickname, the "Secretary of Defense". Yet, somehow, Maddox lived up to that billing. From 1975 through 1986, Maddox led center fielders in FanGraphs' version of defensive runs saved, led the NL in Total Zone Runs in 1976 and 1979, put outs in center in 1976 and 1979, assists in center 1975 and 1976, Total Zone Runs as a center fielder in 1976, 1978, 1979, and 1980, and led the NL in range factor as a center fielder in 1975, 1976, 1978, and 1979. Maddox ranked fourth among his NL contemporary center fielders in WAR while with the Phillies, eighth in batting average, 14th in SLG, and fifth in steals.

Maddox has longevity and an eye-popping accomplishment, eight-straight Gold Gloves in the defensively-difficult center field, in his corner. The man he was traded for, Montanez, would be an All-Star more times than Maddox, once, but would play through only 1982 while Maddox lasted in the Majors through 1986. Montanez would put up a .275/.322/.392 line while averaging 10 homers and two steals a season as a first baseman from 1976 through 1982 against Maddux's line of .287/.318/.416 with an average of 10 homers and 22 steals a season across the same time period while playing parts of an additional four seasons.

While the numbers are surprisingly similar, Maddox's fantastic speed, best-of-class defense at a premium defensive position, and his ability to carry his regular season numbers into the playoffs make this trade a huge win for the Phillies.

Chris Short

Left-Handed Starter

Years as a Phillie: 1959-1972
Line as a Phillie: 132-127, 3.38 ERA, 1.283 WHIP in 2253 IP
fWAR Phillies Rank: 8th among pitchers, 21st among Phillies
Signature Season: Went 17-9 with a 2.20 ERA in 1964
Signature Game: Threw 15 shutout innings against the Mets on October 2, 1965

The 6'4" lefty from Milford, DE, Chris Short finds himself scattered across many Phillies all-time pitching leader boards. Short ranks fourth in innings pitched, wins, and complete game shutouts, and fourth in strikeouts in Phillies club history.

Somewhat lost in history is the fact that Short was among the best pitchers in the National League during his stay with the Phillies. From 1959 through 1972, the versatile Short was 15th in the NL in wins, seventh in appearances, seventh in games started, sixth in innings pitched, and 64th out of 185 in ERA.

Short's solid accomplishments often went unnoticed while pitching in the same staff as the legendary Jim Bunning. Short would make two All-Star teams including one in 1964, his finest season, where he would go 17-9 with a 2.20 ERA. Like many of the Phillies, the carriage turned back into a pumpkin for Short in September 1964 where he went just 3-2 with a 3.00 ERA in the month. Not horrible at all but definitely a downgrade from the other-worldly pitching he had going through August 26 (14-6, 1.69 ERA).

Short would be converted from primarily a starter into a full-time reliever for 1972. Following the 1972 season, Short was released from the Phillies and signed with the Milwaukee Brewers. He would pitch in 42 games, including seven starts, for the Brew Crew, posting a 3-5 record with a 5.13 ERA. The Milford, DE native would retire at the conclusion of the 1972 season.

Short passed away on August 1, 1991 after slipping into a coma from a ruptured aneurysm. He was inducted on to the Phillies Wall of Fame in 1992.

Phils from the First State

Chris Short was one of 53 Major Leaguers that was born in Delaware. Here is a list of every Phillie from the First State.

P Huck Betts (1920-1925)
P Bill Crouch Jr. (1941)
P Bert Cunningham (1890)
P Dallas Green (1960-1964, 1967)
P Harry Hoch (1908)
P Broadway Jones (1923)
3B Hans Lobert (1911-1914)
1B John Mabry (2002)
P Renie Martin (1984)
P John Morris (1966)
P Al Neiger (1960)
1B Costen Shockley (1964)
P Chris Short (1959-1972)
P Barney Slaughter (1910)
P Happy Townsend (1901)
P Augie Walsh (1927-1928)

Gavvy Cravath

Right Fielder

Years as a Phillie: 1912-1920
Line as a Phillie: .291/.381/.489 with 117 HR, 80 SB in 4237 PA
fWAR Phillies Rank: 13th among position players, 18th among Phillies
rWAR Phillies Rank: 14th among position players, 20th among Phillies
Signature Season: Hit .285/.393/.510 with 24 HR, 115 RBI and 11 SB in 1915
Signature Accomplishments: Six-time NL HR King (1913-1915, 1917-1919), Led NL in OPS (1913-1915)

If it wasn't for an administrative error, Gavvy Cravath wouldn't have made this list. The Minneapolis Millers of the American Association forgot the word "not" in a telegram and that allowed a then-30 year old to make a return to the Major Leagues after close to three seasons elsewhere.

The offensive standout of the 1915 pennant-winning club, Cravath was the finest power hitter of his generation. From 1912 through 1920, Cravath edged out Babe Ruth for most homers in that time period and ranked 15th in OBP, fifth in slugging, and sixth in OPS behind Babe Ruth, Ty Cobb, Tris Speaker, Joe Jackson, and George Sisler. Not bad company. Cravath was the prototypical power hitter before there was a prototypical power hitter: with great power came great strikeout totals, ranking 247 out of 264 qualified batters in K%. Cravath would hold the team's all-time home run record from 1917 through 1924 until it was broken by Cy Williams, as well as the single-season home run record which Williams broke in 1922.

Cravath had an interesting career path: not making it to the Majors until age 27, Cravath spent 1908 and 1909 bouncing between the Boston Red Sox, Chicago White Sox, and the Washington Senators. Cravath would reemerge in the Majors in 1912 after the Phillies purchased his contract from Minneapolis of the American Association after the clerical error. Cravath made the full leap from obscurity into superstardom in 1913 as a 32-year old right fielder for the Phillies when he led the NL in hits, HR, RBI,

SLG, and OPS en route to a second-place MVP finish and a second-place finish in the NL for the Phillies.

The 1910s were the prime of the late-blooming Cravath's career as he would lead the NL in homers six times during the decade, including during the 1915 season when he hit a career-high 24 to drive the Phillies to their first National League pennant.

Like most of the Phillies hitters, Cravath's bat disappeared during the 1915 World Series (.125/.222/.313) but Cravath would continue to hit, hit, and hit some more through the rest of the decade. Cravath gets credit on this list for being the primary offensive force of the 1915 pennant-winning squad, the nucleus of which also have three second-place finishes in the decade.

Cravath was an interesting man off the field, reportedly getting the nickname "Gavvy" due to hitting a ball that killed a seagull while playing with the Los Angeles Angels of the Pacific Coast League. *Gaviota* is seagull in Spanish. Cravath was also nicknamed "Cactus" and was criticized by fans and reporters for his easy-going style during his time in Philadelphia. I guess some things just don't change.

Cravath was inducted on to the Phillies Wall of Fame in 2000.

Kings of the Long Ball: Phillies NL Home Run Kings

Cravath won six NL home run titles as a Phillie. A Phillie has led the NL in homers 27 times.

Ed Delahanty	1893, 1896
Sam Thompson	1895
Gavvy Cravath	1913-1915, 1917-1919
Cy Williams	1920, 1923, 1927
Chuck Klein	1929, 1931-1933
Mike Schmidt	1974-1976, 1980-1981, 1983-1984, 1986
Jim Thome	2003
Ryan Howard	2006, 2008

#19 Johnny Callison
Right Fielder

Years as a Phillie: 1960-1969
Line as a Phillie: .271/.338/.457 with 185 HR, 60 SB in 4237 PA
fWAR Phillies Rank: 11th among position players, 16th among Phillies
rWAR Phillies Rank: 8th among position players, 12th among Phillies
Signature Season: Hit .274/.316/.492 with 30 2B, 10 3B, and 31 HR in 1964 to finish second in NL MVP voting
Signature Moment: Hit a three-run, walk-off homer in the 1964 All-Star Game off of Dick Radatz to earn MVP honors

Standing just 5'10", Johnny Callison packed power into everything he did. Whether it was his rocket arm (led the NL in assists by a right fielder from 1962 through 1965) or his powerful bat (his 185 homers from 1960 through 1969 ranked fourth in the NL among right fielders, only behind Hank Aaron, Billy Williams, and Frank Robinson), Callison packed a big punch in whatever he did. Callison had among the game's greatest arms of all-time and currently ranks 23rd in putouts by a right fielder, 11th in assists, and 22nd in double plays. He also produced particular speed and cunning, leading the NL in triples twice.

Callison was acquired from the Chicago White Sox in a December 9, 1959 deal for third baseman Gene Freese. It would be a fortuitous trade for the Phillies: Callison would win the starting right field job in 1960 and not relinquish it for ten seasons while Freese would only last in the Majors until 1966, hitting .253/.299/.416 after the trade. Callison's addition in 1960 was one of the big steps in turning the cellar-dwelling Phillies into a contender during the mid-60's.

Callison would earn All-Star appearances in 1962, 1964, and 1965, as well as MVP votes in every season from 1962-1965. The star of the 1964 squad that squeaked away a 6.5 game lead with 12 to play, Callison was one of the few Phillies who did not collapse down the stretch of that infamous season. Callison would hit .277/.317/.508 in September with 8 HR, including a three-homer game on September 27, 1964 against the Braves that the Phillies would lose 14-8. Despite having a statistically-better season in 1963, Callison would finish in second place to St. Louis' Ken Boyer in the MVP voting in 1964, a 13-place increase from his position in MVP voting in 1963. Callison managed to play every single game in 1964 despite battling the flu during the latter stages of the season. The durable Callison ranks 23rd in games played in right field in MLB history.

Callison's most famous moment, perhaps, is his walk-off homer to end the 1964 All-Star game. While Callison would fall short of having a Hall of Fame career after being traded from the Phillies to the Cubs for Oscar Gamble and Dick Selma in November 1969 and later to the Yankees in 1972, he was one heck of a ball player. Others thought so, too, as he was inducted on to the Phillies Wall of Fame in 1997.

All-Stars in the Outfield

Callison is one of 19 Phillies' outfielders to be named to an all-star team since the game's creation in 1993.

Chuck Klein	1933
Herschel Martin	1938
Morrie Arnovich	1939
Danny Litwhiler	1942
Del Ennis	1946, 1951, 1955
Harry Walker	1947
Dick Sisler	1950
Richie Ashburn	1951, 1953, 1958
Johnny Callison	1962, 1964-1965
Greg Luzinski	1975-1978
Glenn Wilson	1985
Von Hayes	1989
Lenny Dykstra	1990, 1994-1995
Bobby Abreu	2004-2005
Aaron Rowand	2007
Raul Ibanez	2009
Shane Victorino	2009, 2011
Jayson Werth	2009
Domonic Brown	2013

Roy Thomas

Center Fielder

Years as a Phillie: 1899-1908, 1910-1911
Line as a Phillie: .290/.413/.333 with 7 HR, 244 SB in 6575 PA
fWAR Phillies Rank: 8th among position players, 11th among Phillies
rWAR Phillies Rank: 9th among position players, 13th among Phillies
Signature Season: Hit .327/.453/.365 with 107 BB in 1903
Signature Accomplishment: Led National League in Walks in Seven of Eight Seasons (1900-1904, 1906-1907)

So often we forget two of the most basic tenants of baseball: get on base and score runs. There was one Phillie that did that better than just about every other player and that was turn of the century center fielder Roy Thomas. Thomas ranks third in Phillies history with a .413 OBP, second in BB%, and seventh in runs scored. His single-season marks are almost as impressive: Thomas led the National League in walks in seven out of eight seasons from 1900 through 1907 and led all of baseball in OBP in 1903.

Thomas was one of the first modern lead-off men in baseball. At 5'10", 150 lbs., Thomas was small but fast and dynamic on the base paths. A native of Norristown and a graduate from the University of Pennsylvania, Thomas is believed by Bill James to be the only regular player in Major League history to score three-times as many runs as he drove in.

Thomas was among the top lead-off hitters during his career; he also had the fourth-best OBP, sixth in runs, and 26th in steals between 1899 through 1911.

Among National League center fielders, Thomas ranked first in fWAR, second in runs, fourth in steals, and first in OBP. Thomas' all-time stats hold up well, too: Thomas ranks 20th in BB%, 29th in OBP, and 84th all-time in total walks.

Thomas was purchased in 1908 by the Pittsburgh Pirates and returned to the Phillies as a free agent in 1910. He would spend the remainder of his career with the Phillies and begin coaching at Penn in 1909. If the dates seem a little funky, it is because Thomas was the head coach of the Quakers while he was still an active Major Leaguer for the Boston Doves. Thomas is one of Philadelphia's great baseball men – as a native son of Norristown, he was a fantastic Phillie and he would go on to post a winning percentage of .632 (106-46-3) as Penn's manager.

The Greatest Phillie Walkmen, NL Leaders in Walks

Roy Thomas led the National League in walks seven times in eight years. Seven Phillie have led the NL in this category 20 times.

Jim Fogarty	1887
Billy Hamilton	1891, 1894-1895
Roy Thomas	1900-1904, 1906-1907
Gavvy Cravath	1915
Richie Ashburn	1954, 1957-1958
Mike Schmidt	1979, 1981-1983
Lenny Dykstra	1993

Phillies' Top 10: Walks, Career

Thomas was one of the most prolific walkers in Phillies' history and sits tied for third in franchise history with 946.

1. Mike Schmidt	1507, 1972-1989
2. Bobby Abreu	947, 1998-2006
3T. Richie Ashburn	946, 1948-1959
3T. Roy Thomas	946, 1899-1908, 1910-1911
5. Pat Burrell	785, 2000-2008
6. Jimmy Rollins	753, 2000-2014
7. Puddin' Head Jones	693, 1947-1959
8. Ryan Howard	677, 2004-Present
9. Ed Delahanty	643, 1888-1889, 1891-1901
10. Chase Utley	625, 2003-Present

Curt Simmons
Left-Handed Starter

Years as a Phillie: 1947-1960
Line as a Phillie: 115-110, 3.66 ERA, 1.332 WHIP in 1936.2 IP
fWAR Phillies Rank: 6th among pitchers, 19th among Phillies
Signature Season: Returned to the Major Leagues for 1952 season after being called to active military service in September 1950 and had best statistical year of career (2.82 ERA, 1.192 WHIP, named an All-Star)

Oh, what might have been in 1950.

The pride of Egypt, PA, Curt Simmons, pitching for Whitehall High School at the time, struck out eleven Phillies in a 1947 exhibition game. On the Phillies radar after leading the Whitehall Zephyrs to three-straight league titles and the Coplay American Legion team to two state titles, Simmons was signed shortly after the game to a $65,000 signing bonus. By the end of 1947, the 18-year old Simmons was in a Phillies uniform, pitching the Phillies to a 3-1 complete-game victory in his only start of the season.

Simmons was used as a swingman in 1948 and 1949 before finding his groove as a top-flight pitcher in 1950. Simmons went 17-8 with a 3.40 ERA, finishing 16th in the 1950 NL MVP voting, despite missing most of September after being called into duty for the Korean War. The Whiz Kids would hang on and win the NL Pennant and Simmons would be granted a 10-day leave to join his teammates for the World Series. But rosters had been finalized and Simmons had to watch from the stands. One only wonders what may have been had the Fightins had Simmons in their rotation during a Fall Classic that featured three one-run games and, despite being a sweep, was decided by six total runs.

Simmons' most memorable season, however, may have been 1952. Having missed the entirety of the 1951 season, Simmons posted career-lows in ERA and WHIP, going 14-8 in over 200 IP. Simmons ranks fifth all-time in Phillies history in victories and innings pitched, 16th in complete games, and seventh in shutouts. During his time with the Phillies, Simmons ranked ninth in the NL in wins, 30th in ERA, seventh in complete games, and tenth in shutouts.

Like all good stories, Simmons' has a happy ending. Released midseason by the Phillies in 1960, Simmons would sign with the St. Louis Cardinals. In 1964 with the Cardinals, Simmons would get his shot at the World Series. Starting Games 2 and 6, Simmons would leave Game 2 with a 1-1 tie in the ninth and would be on the losing end of Game 6. Ultimately, the Cardinals would win the 1964 World Series and Simmons would be rewarded with a World Series ring.

Somewhat surprisingly, there are few people who say Simmons release in 1960 contributed anything to the Phillies falling apart down the stretch in 1964 to the Cardinals. Hindsight being 20/20, it probably would have helped the 1964 Phillies had they had a pitcher down the stretch who went 18-9 with a 3.43 ERA, including four wins in September. Simmons would finish his career in 1967 after spending time with the Cubs and Angels and was inducted on to the Phillies Wall of Fame in 1993.

Phillies' Top 10: Wins in the 1950's

Simmons paired with Robin Roberts to form an effective 1-2 punch at the top of the Phillies rotation through the 1950's.

1. Robin Roberts   199
2. Curt Simmons   103
3. Bob Miller   42
4. Jim Konstanty   41
5T. Russ Meyer   30
5T. Jack Sanford   30
7. Karl Davis   25
8. Bubba Church   23
9T. Harvey Haddix   22
9T. Murry Dickson   22

Bonus
In Their Own Words:
Curt Simmons

It is hard to tell the story of the greatest Phillies of All-Time without going to the source: the players themselves! Throughout the book, there are excerpts of interviews I conducted for use on Phillies Nation and *Phillies Nation TV*, inserted and edited when appropriate. Some questions and answers may have been omitted but answers from players are presented in full.

This interview was conducted as part of a four-part feature for *Phillies Nation TV* and *Lehigh Valley TV*.

Ian Riccaboni: When you were growing up, how did you become a baseball fan and were you a Phillies fan or an A's fan, since the A's were the more successful team in that time?

Curt Simmons: Well, you know I was born in '29 and the Phillies were around but nobody knew it because they were real bad. I just liked sports; I played baseball as a kid. There wasn't much to do in those days: the father went to the cement mill, the mother stayed in the house, and for the kids they would say "go play".

I was from a small town, Egypt, and we'd go down to the playground at the old grade school, there. That's where I used to go with the gang and we'd choose sides and play ball. You just got out of the house and went and played.

IR: Whitehall was much different than it was now, there weren't the big shopping malls and Allentown actually had a few professional baseball teams. Did you ever go see the Allentown Cardinals play?

CS: I went down there, the old park, Fairgrounds Park. I got a couple passes and got to see a couple games in high school.

IR: How did you keep track of the Cardinals or even the Phillies back then? There was very little TV and not all games were broadcast on the radio.

CS: Back in those days, I was playing. I played Copley Legion and I played for Whitehall High School. For Whitehall High School, by the middle of June, it was over. For Copley Legion, we'd play our league schedule and then we would play some other teams.

And I would play with the Egypt AA team in the Twilight league. When I wasn't playing for Copley Legion, I was playing for Egypt. I was playing baseball quite a few days of the week.

IR: You played for Babe Ruth and Ty Cobb in a series of All-Star games. What was it like meeting them?

CS: I was 16 and they chose a kid from each state. They split it up East versus West. Babe Ruth was the East manager and Ty Cobb was the West manager. Ruth chewed tobacco and smelled of booze a little bit but he was a happy, jolly guy and Cobb was a grump, always saying "our team is gonna beat ya!"

I started the game and got a couple runs. The first guy bunted for the other team and my third baseman threw it into the stands at the Polo Grounds. The Polo Grounds aren't there anymore but you had to throw it *very* high to get it into the stands on a fly! I pitched four innings until Babe Ruth said "Go play right field!" because I got a base hit and I ended up hitting a triple. We ended up beating them 5-4 – we were losing 4-2 in the ninth. Nobody did that much, so they gave me a trophy! At 16 years old I was *The All-American Boy*.

IR: Not to long after that, there was the famous exhibition between the Phillies and the Egypt AA team.

CS: It was the Egypt AA team and we picked up a catcher from Northampton. But it was mostly our guys, the Egypt AA team.

Cy Morgan was a scout from Allentown for the Phillies and he had been hanging around all the time when I was 16 already. He'd be giving my mother and my sisters, during the war, they couldn't get nylon stockings, so he'd get some nylon stockings and give them to them. Occasionally, he'd get a couple Eagle tickets and give them to me. So, he was bribing me a bit the best he could do – he wasn't supposed to be doing any of it!

They were building Egypt Memorial Park and Cy Morgan says "How 'bout we bring the Phillies up and have your kid pitch against us," to my father. My father said "Yeah, bring 'em on!" I was a bashful kid and there was a good chance I was gonna get smacked around! I pitched well and we shoulda won – a couple of our guys ran into each other on a fly ball. It ended up a 4-4 tie, there were no lights so it was dark.

After the game, the Detroit Tigers bid $50,000 and the Yankees bid $60,000 and my father told the Phillies he'd give them the last shot. So, my father tells the Phillies "He'll sign for $65,000," and they say "Ok, you got it!" So, that's how I ended up with the Phillies! My father was my agent and all the guys at the cement mill were telling him how to handle this!

It worked out well; I struck out 11 Phillies.

IR: At the end of that year, you made your Major League debut.

CS: Yeah, the end of the year. I had been with Wilmington, the Class B league team, and at the end of the year, the Phillies had to bring me up and keep me because I was classified as a bonus player or else they would lose me to some kind of draft. So I pitched the last game of the season against the New York Giants. Johnny Mize was tied with Ralph Kiner going into the day for the home run lead and hit lead off, to maybe get an extra at bat or something. I broke a couple of his bats! We beat 'em 3-1 – I walked a few guys, but it was a nice start anyways.

IR: Of course, 1950 was the year the Phillies won their first pennant in 35 years. Could you take us through a little bit of that season? Was there any indication that that team was going to be special?

CS: We were OK but we had a lot of young guys. They called us the "Whiz Kids", ya know. The Dodgers were the cream of the crop. In those days, they didn't have drafts or anything. You couldn't leave a team unless they sold you or got rid of you. But anyway, we start playing well. (Robin) Roberts starts winning and I start winning and a lot of guys have good years. Jim Konstanty was outstanding as our so-called "closer", he won 15 games and a Most Valuable Player award.

And of course, in the beginning of September, I had to go into the service. I was in the National Guard that was activated and a guy named Bob Miller was a pitcher and he hurt his back. A guy named Bubba Church was a pitcher and Ted Kluszewski was a big first baseman for the Reds and he hit a line drive that hit (Church) right in the eye. How he didn't kill him or really hurt him or die, I don't know, it was that bad. So three pitchers are out and Roberts is pitching every three days. Finally, he pitched ten innings the last game of the year against the Dodgers to win the pennant.

IR: Were you able to follow along while you were in training?

CS: Well, I was in boot camp in Atterbury, IN so I would listen to the games on the radio. That was before TV, of course. So the last game of the season, I out playing touch football with the boys. We're out playing football and a guy hollered out the back "(Dick) Sisler hit a home run! The Phillies are up 4-1!"

I got a call from the boys at their party. Most of them weren't too coherent! Robin Roberts told me "I'm tired, I'm going home." His wife was pregnant, so they didn't hang around the party too long.

IR: You missed the entire 1951 season and came back in 1952 and had statistically one of your best seasons.

CS: Yeah, in '52, I came back Opening Day, no Spring Training. I was in Germany and some guy, some PR guy from Washington calls me and says "Can you be at the show?" The Gimbel Brothers were having some sort of show on Opening Day and they wanted me to be there. A lot of my buddies were jealous that I got to fly home and didn't have to take the bumpy ship!

IR: Through the '50's, you faced a lot of great, Hall of Fame players. Willie Mays, Jackie Robinson, Hank Aaron. Could you walk us through preparing for someone of Mays or Aaron's caliber?

CS: Well, I had good stuff, good fastball. My problem was throwing strikes and moving the ball around pretty good. I didn't really go over the hitters that finely. I remember '52, I was starting the All-Star Game in Philadelphia and I got to the ballpark pretty early but I was actually late! They were having a meeting going over the hitters and Leo Durocher, the manager, says "Simmons, where the hell you been?!"

He said "Get the ball over the plate!" I pitched three innings and shut em out. I had good stuff but my problem was control and of course, walked too many guys.

I had some good years. In 1953, I cut my toe with a lawn mower and I was out for a month but I still won 16 games that year.

IR: You had a lot of success throughout the '50's but weren't able to win another pennant.

CS: Yeah, we never were able to come back. A couple guys started having bad years so they started trading them and so forth. We never got back to where we were until they started rebuilding.

In '64, of course, they start winning. I'm with the Cardinals. They had a 6.5 game lead with 12 to play. We played three games against them in Philadlephia, beat 'em three in a row. We played three games in St. Louis, beat 'em three in a row. We snuck up on them and won the pennant on the last day of the season.

IR: Did you feel any measure of revenge because the Phillies had released you in 1960?

CS: Well, they'd ask me that! We had a team who could hit and we'd win a couple games against them 9-7, but I pitched some good ones, too. I said I hope I'm trying real hard against everyone! I wanted to beat them, of course, but I wanted to beat everyone!

IR: How was the reception pitching in Philadelphia as a Phillie versus pitching in Philly as a Cardinal?

CS: I'm sure they didn't like it when I was beating 'em! Philly fans have a reputation for booing but when you're pitching, you are concentrating on the hitter and the catcher and you go from there.

Curt Schilling

Left-Handed Starter

Years as a Phillie: 1992-2000
Line as a Phillie: 101-78, 3.35 ERA, 1.120 WHIP in 1659.1 IP
fWAR Phillies Rank: 5th among pitchers, 14th among Phillies
rWAR Phillies Rank: 5th among pitchers, 15th among Phillies
Signature Season: Went 17-11 with a 2.97 ERA and MLB-best 319 K in 1997 for the 68-94 Phillies
Signature Moment: Threw a complete-game shutout in Game 5 of the 1993 World Series at Veterans Stadium to force a Game 6

After losing Game 1 of the 1993 World Series, Curt Schilling found himself taking the mound at the Vet, his team down three-games-to-one, and less than 24 hours removed from one of the toughest-to-swallow losses in franchise history. Just one night earlier, Larry Andersen and Mitch Williams had combined to cough up a 14-9 lead in the 8th inning of Game 4, a sequence that concluded in a go-ahead two-run triple off the bat of Devon White. If the Phillies wanted to have any chance of winning the 1993 World Series, they needed to turn to an ace; someone to stop the bleeding.

Luckily, they had just the guy.

Schill would go the distance in front of 62,000+ screaming fans at the Vet, striking out six and shutting out the very team that had put up a 15-spot the night before. Schilling got the 1993 Phillies one more game. And arguably, Schilling was the pitcher most responsible for getting them to the World Series in the first place: the eventual 1993 NLCS MVP had pitched 16 innings in the Championship Series with a 1.69 ERA to help dispatch the two-time defending NL Champion Braves in six games.

Schilling's dominant performance was, at that point, very unexpected. Acquired for Jason Grimsley on April 2, 1992 after spending time in Boston, Baltimore, and Houston's systems, Schilling would very quietly have a very impressive season: in his first year with the Phillies, Schilling would start 26 games, appear in 16 more, post a 2.35 ERA, and throw ten complete games. In a time when advanced statistics weren't very popular among analysts, Schilling led the NL in WHIP (0.990) and was the toughest pitcher off whom to get (6.6 H/9 IP). Despite declining stats across the board in 1993, casual fans began to notice Schilling's performance when he posted a 16-7 record for the Macho Row Phils.

If casual Phillies fans didn't know who Schilling was, they certainly did by the end of the 1993 season. By 1999, Schilling had made three-straight NL All-Star teams, and finished fourth in NL Cy Young voting in 1997. Schilling led the NL in strikeouts in 1997 and 1998 and pitched an astonishing 15 complete games in 1998.

Among Phillies, Schilling ranks third among Phillies starters in K/9 IP, only behind Cliff Lee and Cole Hamels. Schilling ranks sixth in Phillies history in wins, seventh in starts, eighth in IP, 37th in ERA among starters, and fourth in strikeouts. Schilling went 101-78 (56.4%) games for the Phillies playing for teams that went a combined 717-751 (48.8%). From 1992 through 2000, Schilling ranked second only to Greg Maddux in FanGraphs' version of WAR among NL pitchers, ranking sixth in starts, third in IP, 22 in K/9 IP, first in total strikeouts, and second in complete games and shutouts.

By 2000, Schilling was frustrated with the Phillies' lack of success and gave then-General Manager Ed Wade a list of six teams to which he would accept a trade to. The teams included St. Louis, who offered Matt Morris and J.D. Drew (!), Seattle, and Arizona, Schilling's eventual destination. Schilling was traded on July 26, 2000 for Omar Daal, Nelson Figueroa, Travis Lee, and Vicente Padilla and would win a share of the 2001 World Series MVP with Randy Johnson. Schilling's career would conclude following the 2007 season, ending with 3116 strikeouts (15th all-time) and 216 wins (82nd all-time).

Schilling missed induction into the Hall of Fame in 2012 and 2013, getting 38.8% and 29.2% in each respective year but is undoubtedly a Hall of Fame pitcher.

Bonus

Transactions That Shaped the Phillies: Switch Snags Schill

It's difficult to explain to folks who didn't watch the early 90's Phillies squads how simultaneously exciting yet disappointing those teams were. Aside from an exciting-but-never-a-threat second place finish in 1986, the late 80's Phillies squads were a mix of decent young players like Von Hayes and Juan Samuel, aging veterans like Greg Gross, Lance Parish, and Mike Schmidt, and a groan-inspiring pitching staff led by Shane Rawley and Don Carman with Steve Bedrosian and Kent Tekulve in the bullpen. General Manager Lee Thomas took over as the club's general manager from Woody Woodward in June 1988 and began to shape the roster rather quickly.

On July 15, 1988, Thomas' first move was a rather subtle one: Thomas dealt Luis Aguayo, a sometimes-starting shortstop, for Amalio Carreno, a pitcher that would appear in three games for the Phillies in 1991. In his first offseason steering the Phillies' ship, Thomas would trade Shane Rawley to Minnesota for Tom Nieto, Eric Bullock, and Tom Herr, a move that allowed the Phillies to experiment with Samuel in center field by playing the former All-Star Herr at second and indirectly allowing the Phillies to trade Samuel for Roger McDowell and Lenny Dykstra.

Up next on Thomas' winter to-do list was to reshape the entire outfield, trading Phil Bradley to Baltimore for reliever Gordon Dillard and starter Ken Howell, who would lead the team with 12 wins and a 3.44 ERA in 1989, and Milt Thompson to St. Louis for back-up catcher Steve Lake and reserve outfielder Curt Ford. Trading Bradley was a win, while the Thompson trade was a bust. It was likely the only major blemish on Thomas' record.

Soon, everything Thomas would touch turned to gold, even if it was a few years later. The Phillies would acquire John Kruk and Randy Ready from San Diego for Chris James on June 2 and Dykstra and McDowell from the Mets for Samuel on June 18, 1989. No player was untouchable, not even 1987 Cy Young winner Steve Bedrosian; Bedrosian would be dealt for Dennis Cook, Charlie Hayes, and Terry Mulholland on June 18. In December, 1989, the Phils stole Sil Capusano and Dave Hollins away from the Toronto Blue Jays and San Diego Padres respectively in the Rule 5 draft. The Phillies, finally, had a plan.

The Phillies would go from 67 wins in 1989 to 77 in 1990 to 78 in 1991. Younger talent like Darren Daulton, Dykstra, and Kruk were hitting their strides while unexpected contributions from veterans Dickie Thon and Dale Murphy in 1991 boosted their record. Not satisfied with third and fourth place finishes, Thomas pulled the trigger on the best trade of his tenure, sending then 24-year-old, full-of-promise Jason Grimsley to Baltimore for the suddenly 25-year-old journeyman Curt Schilling.

Schilling once had been one of the best pitching prospects in baseball; Schilling was drafted as a 19-year old flamethrower out of Yavapai College in the second round of the January 1986 Amateur Draft. Schilling was durable and successful in the minor leagues and earned his first taste of Major League action in 1988 with the Orioles, who he was traded to with Brady Anderson for Mike Boddicker. Oops.

The 6'5" Arizonan righty would be a part of another lopsided deal in 1991, after gaining little traction as a reliever with the Orioles, the orange birds would package him with Steve Finley and Pete Harnisch and send him to Houston for outfielder Glenn Davis. Despite switching from the AL to the NL, Schilling's ERA would jump by 1.27 points and would be dealt in the offseason in the third lopsided trade of his young career, this time landing in Philadelphia for Grimsley.

Schilling became the star of perhaps one of the most frustrating Phillies clubs in recent memory. The 1992 Phillies had all the makings of a team that was ready to turn the corner and compete with the Pirates for the NL East crown. Instead, a second wave of young, home-grown and acquired talent the Phillies were relying on to make the jump to the Majors, including shortstop Juan Bell, outfielder Ruben Amaro, and pitchers Kyle Abbott, Ben Rivera, Andy Ashby, Mike Williams, and Tommy Greene didn't make the jump as expected.

Schilling seemed unaffected by the chaos surrounding him: he went 14-11 with a 2.35 ERA, leading the team in wins and ERA while leading the NL in WHIP as a swing man that started 26 games and appeared in 16 more. The 1992 Phillies would win just 70 games but it was clear they had something special in Schilling.

1993 would be quite a year for Schilling and the Phillies. Schilling would win a career-high 16 games but would see his ERA rise by 1.67 points. His WHIP remained low, his walk rate decreased, and his K/9 IP increased. The wins piled up for Schilling and the rest of the Phillies, as the Fightins won 97 games, ended the Pirates brief run as the class of the NL East, and vanquished the Braves in the NLCS to win the National League pennant.

It was in the 1993 NLCS that Schilling would begin his run as one of the all-time great postseason pitchers. Schilling would strike out 19 Braves in 16 innings allowing just three earned runs earning the NLCS MVP despite not earning a decision. And, when the spotlight was shining the brightest, Schilling threw a complete game shutout in Game 5 of the 1993 World Series with the Phillies down 3-1 in the series against a historically offensively-gifted Toronto Blue Jays less than a day after the Jays plated 15.

We all know how the 1993 World Series ended and any mention of Joe Carter's homer would just be another painful reminder of the result. The Phillies were seemingly never the same. Schilling wasn't either, but in a completely different, much better way. Schilling would become one of the NL's best pitchers: from 1996 through 1999, Schilling won 56 games with a 3.22 with 38 complete games with a WHIP of 1.088 for a team that had a winning percentage of 44.12% in that span. Schilling was the ace the Phillies needed, not the one they deserved.

Schilling's stats are eye-popping, both in Phillies' history but also against his contemporary NL pitchers. Among Phillies, Schilling ranks third among Phillies starters in K/9 IP, only behind Cliff Lee and Cole Hamels. Schilling ranks sixth in Phillies history in wins, seventh in starts, eighth in IP, 37th in ERA among starters, and fourth in strikeouts. From 1992 through 2000, Schilling ranked second only to Greg Maddux in FanGraphs' version of WAR among NL pitchers, ranking sixth in starts, third in IP, 22 in K/9 IP, first in total strikeouts, and second in complete games and shutouts.

Schilling desired to play for a winner and was dealt to Arizona on July 26, 2000 for Omaar Daal, Nelson Figueroa, Travis Lee, and Vincente Padilla in what amounted to be, you guessed it, the fourth lopsided deal in which Schilling was involved. When it was all said and done, Schilling was a three-time All-Star as a Phillie and only their third NLCS MVP, ever. Schilling would win three World Series rings, one with Arizona and a pair with Boston, earning six total All-Star births and a World Series MVP win in 2001.

As for Grimsley, well, he was one of the first Major Leaguers to admit he was using performance-enhancing drugs. Grimsley never filled the promise of becoming a top-flight starter but did spend 15 seasons in the Majors, going to the World Series in 1995 with Cleveland and winning a pair of World Series rings with the Yankees in 1999 and 2000. After the trade, Grimsley posted a 4.84 ERA, going 37-46 primarily in a relief role for six different clubs.

Schilling's acquisition by General Manager Lee Thomas led directly to the Phillies fifth NL pennant and gave them arguably the second-best pitcher in the National League for parts of nine seasons. Even though Grimsley displayed similar longevity to Schilling, Schilling is a Hall of Fame caliber pitcher that was acquired for a career long reliever. Not a bad deal.

Billy Hamilton

Outfielder

Years as a Phillie: 1890-1895
Line as a Phillie: .361/.468/.459 with 23 HR, 510 SB in 3629 PA
fWAR Phillies Rank: 9th among position players, 13th among Phillies
rWAR Phillies Rank: 10th among position players, 14th among Phillies
Signature Season: Hit .403/.521/.523 with a professional baseball-leading 100 steals and 128 walks with an all-time, single season-record 198 runs in 1894. Was one-fourth of group of Phillies' outfielders, including Sam Thompson, Ed Delahanty, and Tuck Turner, to all hit over .400.
Signature Accomplishments: Owns single-season, MLB runs scored record (198, 1894), is Phillies' all-time steals leader (508), is Phillies' all-time leader in batting average for players over 1500 PA (.361), all-time Phillies leader in OBP, owns single-season Phillies records for steals and OBP

"Sliding Billy" arrived in Philadelphia via Kansas City, having being purchased from the American Association's Kansas City Cowboys for $6,000 prior to the 1890 season. It may have been the best $6,000 the then-Quakers, future Phillies had or would ever spend.

Hamilton wasted no time adjusting to the National League, hitting .325/.430/.399 with 102 SB in his first season with the Quakers. The following season, Hamilton would win the batting title, lead the league in OBP, runs, hits, walks, and steals. In all, Hamilton would win two batting titles with the Quakers, lead the league in runs and walks three times, and steals four times. Hamilton is the franchise's all-time leader in steals and OBP.

Hamilton would set single-season franchise records for steals, OBP, and runs scored. Hamilton's runs scored record still stands as an MLB record, a likely untouchable 192 achieved in 1894. His skills of getting on base and his speed have given Hamilton a claim at being the best baseball player to ever play in a Phillies uniform. Hamilton led all of baseball in steals and OBP during his time with the Phillies.

The fact that Hamilton is peppered all over Phillies' leader boards in counting stats, including steals (first) and runs (eleventh), despite playing just six seasons in Philadelphia is a testament to how great of a player Hamilton was. Hamilton ranks just 15th and not higher on the countdown because of his short stay and because, in spite of the incredible offensive talent on the clubs for which he played, Hamilton's clubs never finished higher than third.

Hamilton would be dealt to the Boston Beaneaters on November 14, 1895 for third baseman Billy Nash in one of the worst trades in Quakers or Phillies history. Hamilton would go on to steal 274 more bases with the Beaneaters and retire with the most steals in Major League history, a record that stood until Lou Brock broke it in 1978.

Hamilton would be a Veterans' Committee inductee to the Baseball Hall of Fame in 1961, a somewhat curious omission until that point. Hamilton currently ranks third all-time in steals and fourth all-time in OBP, behind only Ted Williams, Babe Ruth, and John McGraw.

Phillies' Top 10: OBP, Single-Season

Hamilton reached base at a rate greater than every-other at-bat in 1894, setting the Phillies' single-season OBP mark at .523.

1. Billy Hamilton	.523, 1894
2. Ed Delahanty	.500, 1895
3T. Billy Hamilton	.490, 1895
3T. Billy Hamilton	.490, 1893
5. Ed Delahanty	.478, 1894
6. Ed Delahanty	.472, 1896
7. Lefty O'Doul	.465, 1929
8. Ed Delahanty	.464, 1899
9. Sam Thompson	.458, 1894
10. Roy Thomas	.457, 1899

Sherry Magee
Outfielder

Years as a Phillie: 1904-1914
Line as a Phillie: .299/.371/.447, 75 HR, 387 SB in 6314 PA
fWAR Phillies Rank: 5th among position players, 7th among Phillies
rWAR Phillies Rank: 5th among position players, 8th among Phillies
Signature Accomplishment: Led the Major Leagues in homers from 1904 to 1914

Signed as a 19-year old amateur free agent, Sherry Magee of Clarendon, PA made his Phillies debut two days after signing with the club in 1904. Magee would replace Shad Berry in the outfield and become one of best outfielders in club history.

During his run with the Phillies, Magee led the Major Leagues in HR, was fourth in runs scored, third in RBI, third in steals, 22nd in batting average, 29th in OBP, and tenth in SLG. Magee occupies similar places in Phillies history, ranking eighth in runs, seventh in RBI, fourth in steals, and 44th in SLG.

Magee's clubs were unable to accomplish much during his time in Philadelphia, posting an 838-835 record with no finishes higher than second place in 1913. This detail becomes more important when put in the context of what the Phillies did the season after Magee was traded: the Phillies would trade Magee for Oscar Dugey and Possum Whitted and the 1915 squad would win the NL Pennant but fall short in the World Series in five games.

Dugey hit .154 in the 1915 regular season and was used only as a defensive replacement in the World Series while Whitted hit .281 in the regular season and .067 in 17 World Series PA. In a World Series where all Phillies' losses were decided by one run, Magee, who hit .280/.350/.392 for the Boston Braves, may have made the World Series closer. Magee, however, would win a World Series title of his own with the Cincinnati Reds in 1919 before retiring.

These days, Magee is notable for being on the short-list of top players of all-time to not be in the Hall of Fame. Magee ranks 96th in baseball history among position players in fWAR, in front of a number of Hall of Famers.

National League Leaders in Slugging

Sherry Magee led the National League in SLG two times. Nine Phillies have led the NL in this category 21 times.

Sam Thompson	1894-1895
Nap Lajoie	1897
Ed Delahanty	1892-1893, 1896, 1899
Sherry Magee	1910, 1914
Gavvy Cravath	1913, 1915
Cy Williams	1926
Chuck Klein	1931-1933
Dick Allen	1966
Mike Schmidt	1974, 1980-1982, 1986

Chuck Klein

Right Fielder

Years as a Phillie: 1928-1933, 1936-1939, 1940-1944
Line as a Phillie: .326/.382/.553, 243 HR, 71 SB in 5772 PA
fWAR Phillies Rank: 12th among position players, 17th among Phillies
rWAR Phillies Rank: 12th among position players, 17th among Phillies
Signature Achievements: Won Triple Crown and led the NL in all triple-slash categories in 1933 but finished second in MVP voting (.368/.422/.602, 28 HR, 15 SB, 120 RBI) one year after winning the NL MVP (.348/.404/.646, 38 HR, 20 SB, 137 RBI)

In 1928, the Phillies outbid the Yankees to obtain the services of a left-handed outfielder in the Class B Central League. The 23-year old outfielder was hitting .331/.378/.652. No sooner after they acquired him, the Phillies inserted Chuck Klein into their line-up. After all – what did a team that would end up 43-109 have to lose? Klein rewarded them with a .360/.396/.577 line with 11 HR in 275 PA.

In Klein's first full season, the 6'0" lefty from Indianapolis, IN would hit an NL-leading 43 HR, benefiting from the short right field porch of the Baker Bowl. Klein would win the HR title three more times, including in 1932, when his 38 HR propelled him to the NL MVP, and 1933, when Klein won the NL Triple Crown and led the NL in every triple-slash category. In addition to being a fine offensive right fielder, Baker Bowl or not, Klein had one of the finest arms in baseball, setting the single-season assist record in 1930 and leading the NL in assists at his respective position (right field in 1930, 1932-1933, left field in 1931) from 1930-1933.

Klein would be traded to the Chicago Cubs on November 21, 1933 for Harvey Hendrick (a below-average utility player), Ted Kleinhans (a below average reliever), and Mark Koenig (a fine defensive infielder who was dealt a few weeks later). Klein's numbers, his SLG in particular, would see a precipitous drop, leading some to speculate his phenomenal numbers were due, in large part, to the friendly confines of the Baker Bowl. On

May 21, 1936, Klein returned to Philadelphia in a trade for Ethan Allen (a fine outfielder for 1934 and 1935) and Curt Davis (led the NL in appearances in 1934).

At age 31, Klein concluded the 1936 season with 25 HR, the last season he would hit more than 20. Some speculated that the Baker Bowl was to blame but his stats somewhat dispute this. In parts of the following eight seasons, everything but three-quarters of 1939, Klein called the Baker Bowl his home park and would not slug over .500 again while achieving career-highs in BB% and career-lows in K%. Klein became a more selective-but-less-successful hitter.

Klein's greatness, however brief, leaves him in rare air also Phillies' history. Klein retired the all-time leader in homers in Phillies history and now ranks fifth. Klein ranks fifth in runs scored, fourth in RBI, eight in batting average, 14th in OBP, and second in SLG. In Klein's prime years with the Phillies, 1928-1933, he ranked third in the NL in fWAR, only behind Mel Ott and Bill Terry while leading the NL in homers, runs scored, RBI, and SLG, ranking second in batting average behind Rogers Hornsby, and fourth in OBP.

Klein's totals were good enough for a 1980 Veteran's Committee selection to the Hall of Fame and an induction onto the Phillies Wall of Fame in the same year.

Wasted Greatness on the 1928-1933 Phillies

Despite having one of baseball's best offensive threats in Klein, the Phillies surrounded him with downright poor offensive counterparts.

Of the nine players that qualified for the batting title during this period, only six were above replacement-level per fWAR while only Klein had an fWAR above 13.5 (32.7).

Klein accounted for 54.41% of the team's offensive production per fWAR while the team went 370-549 (40.26%).

#12 Jim Bunning

Right-Handed Pitcher

Years as a Phillie: 1964-1967, 1970-1971
Line as a Phillie: 89-73, 2.93 ERA, 1.111 WHIP in 1520.2 IP
fWAR Phillies Rank: 7th among pitchers, 20th among Phillies
Signature Accomplishment: Won 17 or more games in four straight seasons (1964-1967)
Signature Moment: Threw seventh Perfect Game in Major League History on June 21, 1964, Father's Day

If you asked Jim Bunning what his signature achievement in life has been, he would likely tell you that it has nothing to do with baseball. Senator Bunning spent two full terms, or twelve years, serving the people of Kentucky in the United States Senate from 1999 through 2011, elected just three years after his Baseball Hall of Fame induction in 1996. Bunning was a Veteran's Committee selection in 1996 after fifteen years on the ballot and was elected as a Phillie. Make no mistake: Bunning was one of the finest pitchers in Phillies history.

Bunning, a five-time All-Star by that point, was acquired on December 5, 1963 for super-utility player Don Demeter and reliever Jack Hamilton. The trade was as much of a steal as it looks like on paper: Demeter would be solid but under-perform his Phillies' stats and Hamilton would float around for six seasons before retiring. Meanwhile, Bunning would win 74 games in four seasons and make two All-Star teams.

Bunning's tenure in Philadelphia got off of to a great start, posting a 2.17 ERA with a .215 BAA through August 28, 1964 including the seventh perfect game in baseball history on June 21, 1964 against the Mets.

And then, September happened: manager Gene Mauch had Bunning take the mound for ten starts, posting a 5-5 record with a 4.06 ERA with a .286 BAA as the Phillies blew a 6.5 game lead with 12 to play to the Cardinals.

Bunning would finish no worse than fifth in the NL in ERA from 1964 through 1967, no worse than fourth in WHIP, and would lead the NL in BB% in 1964 and shutouts in 1966 and 1967. From 1964 through 1967, Bunning led MLB pitchers in fWAR and innings pitched, ranked second in the NL in wins, ranked second in the NL in games started, and ranked third in the NL in ERA.

Bunning would be traded for Woodie Fryman, third baseman Don Money, Bill Laxton, and Harold Clem after finishing second in the Cy Young voting in 1967. While the Phillies did not get a huge return for Bunning, Bunning's era would jump by a point and a half and the trade would seemingly be a wash.

After a season and a half with the Pirates and half of 1969 with the Dodgers, Bunning would return to the Phillies for the 1970 season. Bunning would go a combined 15-27 in 1970 and 1971 for the Phillies with a 4.57 ERA and would retire after the 1971 season.

Bunning ranks 14th in Phillies history in wins, 11th in IP, 24th in ERA, and fourth in WHIP. Bunning's stints with the Phillies were short but he was one of the most dominant pitchers in the Major Leagues while with the Phillies. Bunning was elected on to the Phillies Wall of Fame in 1984 and had his number 14 retired by the Phillies in 2001.

Bonus

Transactions That Shaped the Phillies: Phils Dupe Detroit

The 1963 Phillies were a successful squad without an identity. Led by left fielder Wes Covington, then 31, and right fielder Johnny Callison, then 24, the Phillies had successfully blended veteran leadership with a small youth movement. Throughout the line-up, there was a solid blend of youth and experience: for every 26-year-old Clay Dalrymple there was a 36-year old Roy Sievers, for the 26-year-old Tony Gonzalez, there was 35-year-old Don Hoak.

The mix of veterans and youngsters was less pronounced on the pitching staff where youth dominated the ranks. In addition to and including 19-year-old spot starter Marcelino Lopez, the 1963 Phillies featured nine pitchers at age 26 or younger out of the 14 that appeared for them in 1964. Four out of five starting pitchers that started 16 games or more for the Phillies were 25 or under. The exception? 37-year old Cal McLish, who went 13-11 with a 3.26 ERA with 10 complete games.

The '63 Phils had the unenviable task of competing with some of the finest dynasties and mini-dynasties of the time in the National League. The eventual World Series' winning Dodgers won 99 games to run away with the National League pennant. The Phils finished a solid fourth, twelve games behind the Dodgers, six back of the second-place Cardinals, and just one behind the third place Giants, a line-up that featured Willie Mays, Willie McCovey, and Orlando Cepeda. Not bad, right?

In a rare aggressive move for a Phillies team of this time period, the Phillies sensed an opportunity to add a top-of-the-line pitcher to their young staff. With Detroit becoming skeptical of a then-31-year old Jim Bunning's increasing ERA (2.79 to 3.19 to 3.59 to 3.88) from 1960 through 1963 and the fact that Bunning failed to complete 10 games or more for the first time since 1957, the Tigers decided it was the right time to move the 6'3" Kentuckian before the wheels fell off too fast for the then five-time All-Star.

The Tigers' move proved to be about four years too early.

Bunning was traded on December 5, 1963 with former three-time All-Star Gus Triandos to Philadelphia for outfielder Don Demeter and pitcher Jack Hamilton. Demeter was a .267/.313/.464 hitter at the time of the trade and earned a twelfth-place MVP finish in 1962 and a twenty-first-place MVP finish in 1963. Hamilton appeared primarily as a 24-year old reliever with the Phillies in 1963 after going 9-12 primarily as a 23-year old starter in 1962.

At the time, and even in retrospect, all signs pointed to this trade being at best a wash for the Phillies or, at worst, a possible small win for the Tigers. After all, the Tigers were receiving an outfielder who had garnered MVP consideration in each of the last two seasons and Hamilton was a young arm that was worth a gamble. Meanwhile, the Phillies received a catcher who hadn't had 500 PA since 1958 who was entering his age-33 season and was coming off the two worst seasons of his career and a starting pitcher entering his age-32 season whose ERA kept climbing as he got older.

But, a funny thing happened when Bunning got to Philadelphia. At age 32, Bunning was better than he ever was. The apex of his fantastic 1964 campaign came on Father's Day, June 21, when Bunning dazzled Mets hitters, tossing a No Hitter in the recently-opened Shea Stadium. Bunning would be named to his sixth All-Star team in 1964, his first in the National League, while pitching 284.1 innings, posting a 2.63 ERA and winning 19 games for the Phillies.

Bunning's final numbers for 1964 might have been even better had he received proper rest. With a clear shot at their first pennant since 1950, up 6.5 games with 12 to play on the second-place Cardinals, Phillies' manager Gene Mauch decided to increase his chances of winning the pennant by pitching Bunning on four days' or less rest nine times in the month of September, including four complete games. While four days' rest was not uncommon until most teams expanded to five-man rotations, the three starts on just three days' rest may have did him in, including two down the stretch where Bunning made it through just the third inning on both his September 27 and September 30 starts.

As you may know, the Phillies would cede the 1964 pennant to the St. Louis Cardinals, led by a late season hot-streak on the mound by former Phil Curt Simmons. But Bunning would remain an impact pitcher, one of the best in the game, for the next three seasons. Bunning went 74-46 with a 2.48 ERA over the first four years he was with the Phillies, pitching 60 complete games and 23 shoutouts. Bunning also recorded three saves in four relief appearances.

Bunning, whose 224 wins, 3.27 ERA, and no Cy Young Awards put him on the fringe of Hall of Fame candidacy, earned him a 1996 Veteran's Committee selection, inducted as a Phillie. I am one of the many who believe his four-year, dominant run with the Phillies sealed his Hall of Fame induction.

Triandos, the catcher the Phillies received with Bunning, went on to have a solid season as the club's back-up behind Dalrymple, hitting .250/.339/.426 with eight homers in 220 PA. Bunning would be traded to Pittsburgh in a solid deal for Woodie Fryman, Bill Laxton, and Don Money on December 15, 1967 while Triandos was purchased from the Phillies on June 14, 1965 by the Houston Astros.

Bunning would return for the 1970-1971 seasons, posting a 15-27 mark with a 4.57 for some pretty bad squads before retiring. Afterwards, Bunning would hold numerous political positions before becoming a United States Senator in 1998. Bunning would serve two terms before choosing not to seek re-election in 2010.

As for the players the Phillies traded away, well, they didn't amount to a whole lot, at least in comparison to the Hall of Fame-dominance Bunning gave the Phillies. Demeter would hit .262/.297/.452 over four seasons with Detroit, Boston, and Cleveland before retiring following the 1967 season. Hamilton would post a 21-27 record with 17 saves after the trade across six seasons with a 4.21 ERA, pitching for the Tigers, Mets, Angels, Indians, and White Sox.

Bunning was not able to get the Phillies a pennant, but it certainly was not his fault. From 1964 through 1967, Bunning led MLB pitchers in fWAR and innings pitched, ranked second in the NL in wins, ranked second in the NL in games started, and ranked third in the NL in ERA. Considering how little the Phillies gave up to acquire both Bunning and Triandos, this trade ranks as one of the best in club history.

Bobby Abreu
Right Fielder

Years as a Phillie: 1998-2006
Line as a Phillie: .303/.416/.513, 195 HR, 254 SB in 5885 PA
fWAR Phillies Rank: 7th among position players, 10th among Phillies
rWAR Phillies Rank: 6th among position players, 9th among Phillies
Signature Moment: Hit 41 total home runs, including 24 first-round homers, to win the 2005 Home Run Derby
Signature Stretch: Back-to-Back All-Star Selections (2004-2005), Won Silver Slugger (2004), Won Gold Glove (2005)

For someone who ranks fourth in team history in doubles, 11th in home runs, ninth in runs scored, tenth in RBI, seventh in steals, third in BB%, 24th in batting average, ranks 9th in SLG, leads all Phillies with 1500 or more PA in OBP after 1910, and ranks second in OPS under the same criteria, Bobby Abreu gets very little respect from Phillie fans.

Acquired from the Devil Rays for Kevin Stocker in one of the greatest trades in Phillies history, Abreu won the starting right field job out of camp in 1998 and never looked back, hitting .312/.409/.497 in his first full season in the Majors. Arguably, Abreu's best season with the Phillies came in 2004 when he hit 30 HR and stole 40 bags while hitting .301/.428/.544. Abreu led the league in doubles in 2002 and triples in 1999 and was top 10 in OBP in every year he was with the Phillies aside with the exception of 2001.

Abreu was traded with pitcher Cory Lidle on July 30, 2006 for reliever Matt Smith and some prospects that did not pan out. Abreu's time in Philly ended with no World Series rings, or even playoff runs, to show for it but he certainly made an impact on the Phillies all-time leader boards.

Abreu's stats hold up comparatively well for his time: from 1998 through 2006, Abreu led all Major League right fielders in fWAR , plate appearances, runs, steals, BB%, and he ranked 11th in homers, sixth in

RBI, 11th in BA, third in OBP, 11th in SLG, and eighth in OPS. Abreu's consistent well-above-average play also puts him fifth among all Major Leaguers in WAR from 1998 through 2006.

Abreu returned to the Phillies organization on a minor league contract with an invitation to Spring Training in 2014 one year removed from last playing in the Majors. The Venezuelan outfielder was released in Spring Training and signed with the Mets.

Abreu is a player whose value is found in more advanced rather than traditional statistics. Does he have a shot at the Hall of Fame? Well, Abreu's Hall of Fame case is an interesting one; a man who did so many things right but never was a true standout in any one category.

He resides 114th all-time in rWAR, 77th all-time in OBP, 80th in runs scored, 22nd in walks, 74th in steals, 51st in total times on base, and is 13th overall in Major League history in Baseball Reference's Power/Speed numbers. He is certainly surrounded by Hall of Fame company, however: Abreu is just one of four players, joining Barry Bonds, Rickey Henderson, and Joe Morgan as players with 200+ HR, 1,200+ BB, and 400 SB.

The Phillies' 100/100 Club

In 2001, Abreu became the first Phillie to hit 30 home runs while stealing 30 bases in the same season. He repeated the feat in 2004 while teammate Jimmy Rollins became just the second Phillie to accumulate those numbers.

In Phillies' history, just six players have hit 100 or more home runs while stealing 100 or more bases:

Mike Schmidt	548 HR, 174 SB, 1972-1989
Juan Samuel	100 HR, 249 SB, 1983-1989
Von Hayes	124 HR, 202 SB, 1983-1991
Bobby Abreu	185 HR, 254 SB, 1998-2006
Jimmy Rollins	216 HR, 453 SB, 2000-2014
Chase Utley	232 HR, 142 SB, 2003-2015

Bonus

Transactions That Shaped the Phillies: Thomas Steals Abreu from Devil Rays

Lee Thomas had put together a pretty solid playing career. An All-Star first baseman/outfielder in 1962 for the Los Angeles Angels, Thomas spent eight years in the Major Leagues with the Yankees, Angels, Red Sox, Braves, Cubs, and Astros, accumulating 106 career homers before spending a year in Japan with the Nankai Hawks.

After retiring following the 1969 season, Thomas became a coach and, eventually, the director of player development with the St. Louis Cardinals. In the 1980s, Thomas helped assemble and develop the Cardinals clubs that won three pennants and the 1982 World Series. In June 1988, the Phillies tapped Thomas to steer the ship as their general manager.

Thomas won *The Sporting News* Executive of the Year in 1993 after guiding the Phillies from worst to first and a World Series appearance. Thomas made several shrewd trades in addition to the ones that will appear in this countdown but struggled with keeping talent for reasonable prices.

Thomas would sign players like Darren Daulton and Lenny Dykstra to long-term deals which made sense in the context of their 1992 through 1994 seasons. The deals look less favorable when injuries and bad decisions cost both players significant time in future seasons. And while Gregg Jefferies, Benito Santiago, and Todd Zeile were solid ballplayers for the Phillies, a team mired in the basement close to their payroll threshold probably wasn't equipped to take on three multi-million dollar contracts as their attendance dwindled and the excitement from 1993 faded away.

Before being replaced in 1998 by Ed Wade, Thomas gave the Phillies one final gift. On November 18, 1997, the Philadelphia Phillies received then-24-year-old outfielder Bobby Abreu from the Tampa Bay Devil Rays for shortstop Kevin Stocker. In Thomas' last move of substance with the Phillies, he added one of the greatest players in franchise history for an overpaid and under-producing shortstop.

Thomas found a willing trade partner in Tampa Bay general manager Chuck LaMar. LaMar may be a name Phillies fans remember from his tenure with the squad as their assistant general manager of player development & scouting, a position he held from November 2008 through September 2011. Previously, LaMar had been the Devil Rays' first general manager, earning the position soon after the franchise was awarded. From 1998 through 2005, LaMar was the Devil Rays general manager, compiling a 518-777 record.

LaMar had earned his stripes working alongside then-Atlanta general manager John Schuerholz from 1991 through 1995 as director of player development and scouting and later assistant general manager and director of player personnel. LaMar and Schuerholz assembled the 1995 World Series-winning Atlanta Braves.

Thomas and LaMar hooked up on the deal when the Houston Astros left Abreu unprotected in the expansion draft prior to the 1998 season. The Devil Rays selected Abreu in the third round, sixth overall, with the sole intention of trading him to the Phillies. LaMar opined a year later to the Inquirer's Jim Salisbury that the Devil Rays simply "could not go into our first season without a shortstop".

While LaMar's views were progressive, shortstops are indeed scarcer than your average outfielder, Stocker's salary was $1.8 million in 1998, $2.4 million in 1999, and $3.3 million in 2000, a steep price to pay for a hitter with a .262/.347/.350 line at that time.

The contrast in the seasons Abreu and Stocker had couldn't have been any starker: while he possessed one of the best gloves at shortstop in 1998, Stocker hit just .208/.282/.313 with six homers and five steals against Abreu's .312/.409/.497 line with 17 homers and 19 steals. Abreu would hit under .300 just twice in his full seasons with the Phillies, ranking fifth in baseball in fWAR during that period while Stocker would be out of the Majors following the 2000 season.

In Phillies history, Abreu ranks sixth among position players and ninth among all Phillies in WAR with a .303/.416/.513 line and 195 HR and 254 SB in 5885 PA. Abreu ranks fourth in team history in doubles, eleventh in homers, ninth in runs scored, tenth in RBI, seventh in steals, third in BB%, 24th in batting average, ninth in slugging, leads all Phillies with 1500 or more PA in OBP after 1910, and ranks second in OPS under the same criteria.

Abreu never reached the playoffs with the Phillies but he was part of the group that radically changed the Phillies fortunes and the perception of the fans who were attending games at Veteran's Stadium and Citizens Bank Park. Abreu was a back-to-back All-Star in 2004 and 2005, winning the Home Run Derby in 2005 with an astonishing 41 home runs, 24 of which came in the first round. Needless to say, Stocker did not do these things.

It is sort of amazing that the Phillies were able to acquire one of the best players in baseball for an overpaid shortstop, proving that sometimes, things do go the Phillies way. When the Phillies appeared to be out of contention midway through the 2006 season, the Phillies sent Abreu and pitcher Cory Lidle to the New York Yankees for reliever Matt Smith and a handful of prospects. The follow-up trade wasn't one of the team's best trades but it did afford them additional payroll flexibility heading into the 2007 season, the year the Fightin' Phils would finally return to the playoffs.

Abreu finished his career just 12 homers away from reaching and stole exactly 400 bases. Meanwhile, Stocker was believed to be a front-runner for one the vacant Phillies' broadcasting positions that opened up prior to the 2014 season. Stocker has spent the last 14 baseball seasons as a color analyst, currently working for the Pac-12 Network.

Constructing the 1993 Phillies

General Manager Lee Thomas took the 1993 Phillies to the pennant with the benefit of just six of 40 players used drafted under his watch. Here is where the pieces of the 1993 team came from:

Drafted by Thomas:

RHP Paul Fletcher	RHP Tim Mauser	SS Kevin Stocker
RHP Tyler Green	2B Mickey Morandini	RHP Mike Williams

Drafted by previous GMs:

3B Kim Batiste	C Darren Daulton	C Doug Lindsey
RHP Brad Brink	1B/OF Ricky Jordan	

Rule 5 Draftees by Thomas:

3B Dave Hollins	C Todd Pratt

Free Agent Signings by Thomas:

RHP Larry Andersen	RF Jim Eisenreich	INF Joe Millette
RHP Jose DeLeon	LF Pete Incaviglia	OF Milt Thompson
2B Mariano Duncan	INF Jeff Manto	

Purchased:
RHP Bob Ayrault

Acquired via Trade by Thomas:

OF Ruben Amaro Jr.	RHP Tommy Greene	RHP Don Pall
SS Juan Bell	RHP Danny Jackson	RHP Ben Rivera
OF Wes Chamberlain	1B/OF John Kruk	RHP Curt Schilling
LHP Mark Davis	OF Tony Longmire	RHP Bobby Thigpen
CF Lenny Dykstra	RHP Roger Mason	LHP David West
RHP Kevin Foster	LHP Terry Mulholland	LHP Mitch Williams

Dick Allen

Third Baseman

Years as a Phillie: 1963-1969, 1975-1976
Line as a Phillie: .290/.371/.530 with 204 HR, 86 SB in 4511 PA
fWAR Phillies Rank: 10th among position players, 15th among Phillies
rWAR Phillies Rank: 11th among position players, 16th among Phillies
Signature Stretch: 1964 Rookie of the Year, Three-Straight All-Star Selections (1965-1967)

Bursting on to the scene in 1964 with one of the greatest rookie seasons of all-time, Dick Allen was one of the most feared hitters of the 1960s. Allen hit an incredible .318/.382/.557 in his rookie year of 1964, leading the Major Leagues in runs scored and triples, while his 8.3 fWAR is fourth-best among rookie years, ever. During the Phillies' historic collapse in 1964 where the Phillies blew a 6.5 game lead with 12 to play, Allen hit .429/.462/.796 with 5 2B, 2 3B, and 3 HR.

During his first stint with the Phillies, Allen would hit .300/.380/.554 with 177 HR and 64 SB. During this stretch, Allen led all Major League third basemen in batting average, SLG, and OPS, ranked third in OBP, HR, and runs among all third basemen, and fourth in RBI. Allen would make three-straight All-Star teams from 1965 through 1967 and start the games in '65 and '67. Despite his successes, Allen would also lead the league in strikeouts in 1964 and 1965 and led the league in errors committed in 1964 and 1967.

Even though Allen was mashing baseballs on a regular basis, he would face frequent racist comments and objects thrown at him from the stands while at third base. Allen also reportedly hated the nickname "Richie" and got into a fist-fight with teammate Frank Thomas in 1965 where it is alleged that Thomas hit Allen with a bat after Thomas reportedly made racist remarks toward Allen. For all Allen went through, Allen maintained his status as an elite offensive third baseman of his time.

Allen would miss a twilight double-header with the Mets after reportedly spending time at a horse race in New Jersey in the morning. Following the 1969 season, Allen would be traded to the St. Louis Cardinals in a mega-deal that would land the Phillies, among others, Tim McCarver and Curt Flood, who would refuse to report to Philadelphia and accelerate the birth of free agency. Allen would wind up as a first baseman with the Chicago White Sox in 1972 and win the AL MVP.

In 1975, Allen would be traded to the Atlanta Braves from the White Sox but would not take the field for the team before being traded to the Phillies on May 7, 1975 with Johnny Oates for Barry Bonnell and Jim Essian. Allen would hit 27 HR and 23 SB with a .248/.335/.424 line between 1975 and 1976, helping the Phillies reach the playoffs for the first time since the 1950 World Series.

Allen, who was also a successful lead singer with the group The Ebonistics, still ranks among the top hitters in Phillies history. Allen ranks ninth in team history in HR, 19th in runs, 19th in RBI, fifth in SLG, and 12th in OPS. One of baseball's best hitters for the first seven seasons he was with the Phillies, Allen earns his place on the Phillies Nation 100 for his ability to crush baseballs.

Phillies' Top 10: Home Runs by a Rookie

Allen set the Phillies' rookie home run record in 1964 with 29 before Willie Montanez broke it with 30 in 1972.

1. Willie Montanez	30, 1972
2. Dick Allen	29, 1964
3. Ryan Howard	22, 2005
4. Larry Hisle	20, 1969
5T. Don Hurst	19, 1928
5T. Puddin' Head Jones	19, 1949
7T. Buzz Alret	18, 1931
7T. Greg Luzinski	18, 1972
7T. Mike Schmidt	18, 1973
7T. Pat Burrell	18, 2000

Bonus
Top Ten Phillies' Rookie Seasons of All-Time

Dick Allen's 1964 year was one of not only the greatest Phillies' rookie seasons of all-time but also one of the all-time great rookie seasons in baseball history.

Allen would be the second Phillie to win the NL Rookie of the Year award, the first being right-handed pitcher Jack Sanford in 1957. Third baseman Scott Rolen would win the award in 1997 and first baseman Ryan Howard would be the fourth and most recent Phillie to win the hardware in 2005.

10. Ryan Howard, first baseman, 2005: .288/.356/.567, 22 HR, 52 R, 63 RBI, 0 SB

9. Jimmy Rollins, shortstop, 2001: .274/.323/.419, 14 HR, 97 R, 54 RBI, 46 SB

8. Juan Samuel, second baseman, 1984: .272/.307/.442, 15 HR, 105 R, 69 RBI, 72 SB

7. Roy Thomas, center fielder, 1899: .325/.457/.362, 0 HR, 137 R, 47 RBI, 42 SB

6. Del Ennis, right fielder, 1946: .313/.364/.485, 17 HR, 70 R, 73 RBI, 5 SB

5. Richie Ashburn, center fielder, 1948: .333/.410/.400, 2 HR, 78 R, 40 RBI, 32 SB

4. Jack Sanford, starting pitcher, 1957: 19-8, 3.08 ERA in 236.2 IP

3. George McQuillan, starting pitcher, 1908: 23-17, 1.53 ERA in 359.2 IP

2. Grover Cleveland Alexander, starting pitcher, 1911: 28-13, 2.57 ERA in 367 IP

1. Dick Allen, third baseman, 1964: .318/.382/.557, 29 HR, 125 R, 91 RBI, 3 SB

#9 Jimmy Rollins

Shortstop

Years as a Phillie: 2000-2014
Line as a Phillie: .267/.327/.421 with 216 HR, 453 SB in 9511 PA
fWAR Phillies Rank: 6th among position players, 9th among Phillies
rWAR Phillies Rank: 7th among position players, 10th among Phillies
Signature Stat: All-time Phillies' hit king
Signature Season: Led the league in PA, AB, runs, and triples in 2007 with .296/.344/.531 line with 30 HR and 41 SB en route to winning the 2007 MVP after proclaiming in Spring Training the Phillies were the "team to beat" in Spring Training.

The word swagger, and in turn, its slang equivalent "swag", has been around for years and is defined by Merriam Webster as "a very confident and typically arrogant or aggressive gait or manner." It is often associated with persons who exhibit a certain savoir-faire, a confidence exhibited when one knows exactly what to do. Sometimes someone with swagger often can have savoir-faire but the two are mistaken for each other. In Spring Training 2007, Jimmy Rollins displayed both.

"I think we are the team to beat in the NL East — finally. But that's only on paper," Rollins told reporters. How right he would be.

The Atlanta Braves stranglehold of the NL East was finally broken in 2006 by the New York Mets. The Mets finished 12 games ahead of the second-place Phillies, which were just three behind the Wild Card-winning Dodgers. As spring brings hope eternal, statements like the one Rollins made usually come and go, particularly when they are targeted at a team that was just a few outs away from the World Series the season prior.

Rollins' comments were not taken particularly seriously until the Phillies swept the Mets in a four-game set in August in Philly and then again in a three-game set in September at Shea. The Phillies would erase a seven game Mets lead with 17 to play and win their first NL East title since 1993, due, in large part, to Rollins' MVP season.

Rollins became only the second Phillie ever to hit 30 HR and steal 30 bags in a season in 2007. He has also been the club's undisputed greatest shortstop. Rollins leads all Phillies' shortstops in HR, runs scored, RBI, SB, SLG, and OPS and ranks third in BA and seventh in OBP. In club history, Rollins ranks second in games played, PA, and steals, ninth in HR, third in runs scored and eighth in RBI.

Including the historic 2007 squad, Rollins was the starting shortstop on each of the five NL East winners from 2007 through 2011. He was a .250/.314/.372 hitter in the playoffs, including three homers. Rollins most memorable postseason hits include a Game 5 lead-off homer against Chad Billingsley in the 2008 NLCS and his two run, game-winning double in Game 4 of the 2009 off of Jonathan Broxton to help put the Phillies up three-games-to-one en route to their second straight pennant.

From 2000 through 2013, Rollins played the most games at shortstop, stole the most bases, and hit the most doubles while trailing only Derek Jeter in fWAR and runs scored, Miguel Tejada in HR, Jeter and Tejada in RBI, and Jose Reyes in triples. Rollins also played stellar defense, leading all MLB shortstops in defensive runs saved according to FanGraphs' version of the stat during that time period as well as having the third-best fielding percentage at shortstop of all-time.

As Rollins continues to add to his career totals, he will also join the rare air of the elite shortstops. Rollins ranks eighth in homers among shortstops, 18th in runs scored, and tenth in steals. Rollins finished his time in red pinstripes as the second-most tenured Phillie of all-time while compiling the most hits, has won an MVP, is a multiple-time All-Star and Gold Glove winner, and was part of the 2008 Championship squad. For this, he is ranked ninth on the Phillies Nation Top 100 Countdown.

Cole Hamels

Left-Handed Pitcher

Years as a Phillie: 2006-2015
Line as a Phillie: 114-90, 3.30 ERA, 1.145 WHIP in 1930.0 IP
fWAR Phillies Rank: 4th among pitchers, 12th among Phillies
rWAR Phillies Rank: 4th among pitchers, 11th among Phillies
Signature Season: Posted a 1.80 ERA in 35 IP in the 2008 postseason en route to winning the 2008 NLCS and World Series MVP Awards after leading the NL in WHIP with a 14-10 record and 3.09 ERA.

When Philadelphia acquired a scrawny 6'3 18-year-old lefty prep pitcher from San Diego with the 17th pick in the 2002 draft, they were taking a considerable risk. The player the Phillies were selecting, Cole Hamels, had broken his humerus bone in his left arm as a sophomore in high school and there seemed to be a few safer picks with considerable talent left on the board, namely the University of Kentucky's Joe Blanton and Stanford's Jeremy Guthrie.

Yet, the Phillies had Hamels, who had been clocked at 94 MPH in high school, fall into their lap after San Diego, who was believed to have interest in Hamels, selected shortstop with Khalil Greene at pick 13 instead. As we know from *Moneyball*, this was one of the many moves that allowed the A's to snag Nick Swisher with the 16th pick and, subsequentially, the Phillies Hamels at 17.

I would say the move worked out pretty well for them.

But things weren't always rosy: Hamels would impress in 2003 for Lakewood and Clearwater but be limited to just four games in the minors in 2004 and eight in 2005, tanking his 2004 *Baseball America* prospect ranking from #17 in 2004 to #71 in 2005 to #68 in 2006. To complicate things, Hamels was involved in a bar fight in 2005 where he would break his pitching hand, raising concerns about both his durability and his make-up. But Hamels was able to put that all behind him, going from Lakewood to Clearwater to Scranton in 2006 before making his big league debut on May 12, 2006, striking out seven in five shutout innings to beat the Reds.

Hamels would spend the rest of 2006 with the Phillies and make his first All-Star team in 2007 while finishing sixth in NL Cy Young voting. In his last 13 starts of 2007, Hamels was a tough man to beat, posting a 6-2 record with a 2.82 ERA, helping the Phillies catch the Mets down the stretch and reach the playoffs for the first time since 1993. Hamels would be the starter for the Phillies' first playoff home game since Curt Schilling shutout the Toronto Blue Jays in Game 5 of the 1993 World Series. Hamels gave up three runs in 6.2 IP while striking out seven, losing Game 1. The Phillies would get swept by the Rockies but the season ended with the feeling that this wasn't the last time fans would see the Phillies, or Hamels, in the playoffs.

Hamels would lead the NL in WHIP in 2008 and entered the playoffs with unfinished business on his mind. Hamels would throw eight shutout innings against a potent Milwaukee Brewers' line-up in Game 1 of the NLDS to give the Phillies a 1-0 series lead. Hamels would get the ball for Game 1 of the NLCS and out-duel Derek Lowe, pitching seven innings, giving up only two earned while striking out eight. Hamels got the ball next with a chance to clinch the NL pennant in Los Angeles. This time facing Chad Billingsley, Hamels threw seven innings, surrendering only one earned, and striking out five on his way to winning his second decision of the NLCS and earning NLCS MVP honors.

In what was becoming a trend, Hamels took the ball in Game 1 of the World Series against the Rays at Tropicana Field. The Phillies struck first on a two-run Chase Utley homer and later on a Carlos Ruiz ground-out. The three runs were all Hamels needed to pick up his fourth winning decision of the playoffs as Hamels threw seven strong innings, surrendering just two earned, striking out five. Hamels made his last start of the 2008 postseason under the bright lights of Citizens Bank Park with a 3-1 series lead in the favor of the Phillies and a chance to close out the World Series in the Phillies' house. Armed with a two-run lead after a first-inning Shane Victorino two-out single, Hamels would strike out three in six innings as the rain started to pour down.

With the Rays down one run in the sixth, Hamels began to lose his stellar command as the rain poured down harder and Hamels would surrender his second run of the night before the game was paused once the third out in the first half of the sixth inning was made. After some clutch hitting by Geoff Jenkins, a lucky flare by Jayson Werth, even clutch-er hitting by Pat Burrell and Pedro Feliz, and a Brad Lidge strikeout, the Phillies could breathe easy as champions and Hamels was awarded the Series MVP trophy.

What Hamels did in 2008 alone would be enough for most organizations' Top 50 or even Top 25 lists. Since then, however, Hamels has proved he is one of the best Phillies in club history. In the same number of starts, Hamels has more postseason wins than Steve Carlton, ranks seventh in club history in wins, just one shy of number six, Curt Simmons, ranks fourth in starts in club history. Hamels trails only Cliff Lee in K/9 IP in team history while ranking tenth in WHIP. Hamels ranks third in strikeouts in Phillies' history, falling just 27 behind Robin Roberts in second place.

And make no mistake: Hamels' excellence extends beyond his place in franchise history. From 2006 through 2013, Hamels ranked second in the NL in wins, third in games started and innings pitched, 19th in ERA, and first in strikeouts.

With trade rumors swirling, Hamels no-hit the Cubs on July 25, 2015 in his final start as a Phillie. And with the club in full on rebuild mode, Hamels was dealt on July 31, 2015 with teammate Jake Diekman to the Texas Rangers for five prospects and pitcher Matt Harrison.

Bonus

Top Five Moments in Citizens Bank Park History

Citizens Bank Park held its first MLB game on April 12, 2004, a 4-1 Phils' loss to the Reds. Since then, there have been many memorable moments. Here are the top five.

5. Chooch Scores Bruntlett on a Dribbler

It looked like the Phillies had squandered a 4-1 lead. The Rays had scored two in the seventh and one in the eighth to knot Game 3 of the 2008 World Series up at 4-4. With Rays' reliever J.P. Howell on the mound as the clock approached 2 AM in a rain-delayed game, Eric Bruntlett was hit by a pitch and advanced to third on a wild pitch and poor throw to second base by Dioner Navarro. Howell issued two intentional walks to load the bases for Carlos Ruiz, who would end the game on a dribbler up the third base line, scoring Bruntlett from third to give the Phillies a 2-1 World Series lead.

4. Thome Hits 400th Homer

In the first of many memorable events in the recently-opened ballpark, slugger Jim Thome blasted his 400th career homer off of Jose Acevedo in the bottom of the first inning. A plaque still remains in Citizens Bank Park to celebrate "Gentleman Jim's" accomplishment.

3. J-Rol Breaks the Club Hit Record

In the fifth inning of the June 14, 2014 match-up between the Phils and the Cubs, Jimmy Rollins came to the plate and ripped a single to right field to pass Mike Schmidt on the Phillies' all-time hits leaderboard. Rollins was surprised at first base when Schmidt came to great him and presented him with a ceremonial bat to celebrate the achievement while fireworks erupted at Citizens Bank Park.

2. J-Rol Walks Off 2009 NLCS Game 4

Down 4-3, facing Dodgers' shutdown closer Jonathan Broxton, the Phillies faced a grim fate. Lead-off hitter Raul Ibanez grounded out before pinch hitter Matt Stairs walked. Broxton would hit catcher Carlos Ruiz to put runners on first and second with one out. Broxton would get pinch hitter Greg Dobbs to line out to third to get the second out. Just one out away from knotting the NLCS up at two games apiece, shortstop Jimmy Rollins hit a line drive that split the gap between right and center on a 1-1 fastball, scoring pinch runner Eric Bruntlett and Dobbs, getting the Phillies a 4-3 victory and a 3-1 series lead.

1. Phillies Close Out the 2008 World Series

Cole Hamels took the mound in a rainy, blustery Monday night, on October 27, 2008 for Game 5 of the World Series with a chance to pitch the Phillies to their first World Series victory since 1980. Hamels was pitching with a 2-1 lead in the sixth inning when the skies opened up. The Rays scored a run to knot the game at two before the game was suspended due to the rapidly escalating storm.

The game was suspended for nearly fifty hours, a World Series first, before resuming on Wednesday October 29. Pinch hitter Geoff Jenkins started the chilly night in the bottom of the sixth inning with a double, was sacrificed to third by Jimmy Rollins, and was singled home by Jayson Werth. Rocco Baldelli would hit a homer in the seventh off of Ryan Madson to tie the game at two before Eric Bruntlett, pinch running for Pat Burrell, scored from third on a Pedro Feliz single. Brad Lidge would save his 48th game of the season, striking out Eric Hinske to wrap up the World Series for the Phillies, and creating one of the most memorable visuals of in Phillies' history: Lidge dropping to his knees, embracing catcher Carlos Ruiz.

Grover Cleveland Alexander

Right-Handed Pitcher

Years as a Phillie: 1911-1917, 1930
Line as a Phillie: 190-91, 2.18 ERA, 1.075 WHIP in 2513.2 IP
fWAR Phillies Rank: 3rd among pitchers, 8th among Phillies
rWAR Phillies Rank: 3rd among pitchers, 4th among Phillies
First Phillie to be elected to Baseball Hall of Fame (1938)
Signature Accomplishments: Led the NL in Wins Five Seasons, ERA three times, Ks five times, IP six times, CG five times, SO four times, and WHIP twice. Last Phillies Pitcher to win 30+ games (30, 1917) in a season. Won Pitching Triple-Crown as a Phillie from 1915 through 1917
Oddball Fact: Was the first and only Phillies pitcher to have a win in the World Series for 65 years (1915 to 1980, Bob Walk)

The 6'1" right-handed pitcher from Elba, NE nicknamed "Old Pete" was born Grover Cleveland Alexander on February 26, 1887, directly in the middle of President Grover Cleveland's first of two non-consecutive terms. Just like President Cleveland having two non-consecutive terms as president, Alexander would have two non-consecutive runs for as a Phillie. And like President Cleveland, Alexander's first term was much better received than his second.

Alexander had one of the all-time historic rookie campaigns, bursting on the scene like a flash of lightning. Alexander would set the modern, rookie record with an NL-leading 28 wins and throwing 31 complete games. He would also be dominant in every sense of the word in his seven-year tenure with the Phillies: Alexander led the NL in Wins in five seasons, ERA three times, Ks five times, IP six times, CG five times, SO four times, and WHIP twice. Among his contemporaries, Alexander was neck and neck with Walter Johnson for the title of best pitcher in the Major Leagues and was clearly the National League's finest.

From 1911 through 1917, Alexander led the National League in wins, appearances, games started, IP, complete games, shutouts, and strikeouts by over 400 more than the next closest pitcher. Despite Alexander's undisputed individual success, the Phillies would merely flirt with .500 (.516%) from 1911 through 1914. Alexander, however, would get even better for 1915, starting his string of three-straight NL Pitching Triple-Crowns with the Phillies en route to a 90-win season and the NL Pennant.

Alexander would win Game 1 for the Phillies, the only World Series game the Phillies would win for nearly 65 years. Alexander, however, would lose a 2-1 pitcher's duel to Dutch Leonard of the Red Sox in Game 3 and the Phillies would not see World Series baseball for another 35 years.

Alexander was traded from Philadelphia to the Chicago Cubs in what is the worst trade in Phillies, and perhaps Philadelphia sports, history. The Phillies received Pickles Dillhoefer and Mike Prendergrast for Alexander prior to the 1918 campaign. Dillhoefer was a light-hitting catcher who saw 13 PA with the Phillies in 1918 before being traded to St. Louis. Prendergrast was a Federal League standout who started just 31 games total for the Phillies in 1918 and 1919.

While Alexander would slow down a bit in Chicago, he never the less reeled off 128 wins in nine years with a 2.84 ERA before picking up 55 more with the Cardinals in four more seasons. "Old Pete" was 43 years old when he returned to the Phillies through a December 11, 1929 deal and would go 0-3 with a 9.14 ERA before hanging it up.

"Old Pete" was elected to the Baseball Hall of Fame in 1938 and is enshrined as a Phillie. Alexander wound up winning 373 games total, good for third all-time, ranks 15th in baseball history by Baseball Reference's version of Wins Above Replacement-Level and fourth among pitchers. Alexander's stretch wasn't super long and didn't result in a title but it was one of the most dominant in baseball history. Because Alexander did not wear a number during his playing days, the Phillies have instead retired an English-script P in his honor. Alexander was elected on to the Phillies Wall of Fame in 1981 as part of the third class of inductees.

#6 Richie Ashburn

Center Fielder

Years as a Phillie: 1948-1959
Line as a Phillie: .311/.394/.388, 22 HR, 199 SB in 8223 PA
fWAR Phillies Rank: 4th among position players, 6th among Phillies
rWAR Phillies Rank: 4th among position players, 7th among Phillies
Veteran's Committee Selection to Hall of Fame (1995)
Signature Accomplishments: Made Four NL All-Star Teams as a Phillie (1948, 1951, 1953, 1958). Won two batting titles and led the NL in OBP four times, led MLB in hits during the 1950s.

For many folks who grew up in the Delaware Valley and its surrounding suburbs, it is not uncommon for them to say they knew the voices of Whitey Ashburn and Harry Kalas before they could recognize their own father's or mother's voice. While that is certainly hyperbolic, it isn't entirely too far off from the truth. And before Whitey excelled at broadcasting, generations before ours remember that Whitey was one of the finest center fielders in Major League Baseball and left the game as one of the finest Phillies of all-time.

Ashburn signed with the Phillies shortly before the start of the 1945 season out of Tilden HS in Tilden, NE. Ashburn would spend a year with the Class-A Utica Blue Sox before serving a year in the military. In 1948, after hitting .362 the previous season as a 20-year old in Utica, Ashburn cracked the Phillies roster. Ashburn would hit .333/.410/.400 with an NL-leading 32 SB in his rookie season to snag an All-Star selection while finishing third in Rookie of the Year voting and 11th in MVP voting.

Ashburn was just 23 years old when the famed Whiz Kids won the pennant in 1950; Whitey would have a pivotal play in the pennant-clinching game, throwing out the Dodgers' Cal Abrams at home plate to maintain the 1-1 tie. Like many of the other Whiz Kids hitters, Ashburn struggled in the World Series, going just 3 for 17 off the potent Yankees' pitching.

Ashburn would prove to be anything but a flash in the pan during the 1950s, leading the Majors in hits with 1875. Ashburn's lofty hit total was in large part due to his ability to hit the ball to all parts of the field but also due to his ability to stay on the field. From June 7, 1950 through September 26, 1954, Ashburn did not miss a game, appearing in 730 straight games which ranked fifth-best in baseball history at the time. Ashburn's mark still stands as the Phillies' franchise record and currently ranks 14th in Major League history.

Whitey retired as the all-time Phillies leader in games played, PA, hits, and walks. Ashburn now resides at third, third, second, and third respectively in those categories. Additionally, he ranks 11th in team history in SB, fourth in runs scored, and ninth in team history in OBP. During his active years with the Phillies, Ashburn led the Majors in games, PA, hits, triples, and SB while ranking second in runs, and 11th in batting average. While Whitey was able to hit the gaps and use his speed to earn triples, Ashburn had just 22 HR in 12 seasons with the Phillies.

On January 11, 1960, the Phillies traded White to the Chicago Cubs for John Buzhardt, Al Dark, and Jim Woods. Ashburn would lead baseball with a .415 OBP in his first season with the Cubs but then see a limited role with them in 1961. The Cubs certainly won the trade as Buzhardt would post a 11-34 record as a starter from 1960-1961, the 38-year old Dark would hit .242 before being traded for the other Joe Morgan, and Woods hit .207 in 92 PA from 1960-1961. In 1962, Ashburn was the Mets first-ever All-Star after joining the team as a free agent. In 1963, Whitey retired and joined the Phillies broadcast team. From 1971 until his death on September 9, 1997, Whitey broadcast games with the incomparable Kalas as his colleague.

Ashburn's #1 was retired in 1979 and he was the second Phillie inducted on to the Phillies Wall of Fame the same year. Whitey was a Veteran's Committee selection to the Baseball Hall of Fame for 1995 after exhausting his 15 years of ballot eligibility in 1982. Whitey passed away on September 9, 1997 after calling a game with Kalas at Shea Stadium, ending 47 years of service in one capacity or another with the Phillies organization. In 2004, the Phillies named the center field corridor (Ashburn Alley) and the radio broadcast booth (The Richie "Whitey" Ashburn Broadcast Booth) of Citizens Bank Park after Whitey.

#5 *Ed Delahanty*

Outfielder

Years as a Phillie: 1888-1889, 1891-1901
Line as a Phillie: .348/.414/.508, 87 HR, 411 SB in 7141 PA
fWAR Phillies Rank: 2nd among position players, 3rd among Phillies
rWAR Phillies Rank: 2nd among position players, 5th among Phillies
Second Phillie ever inducted into Baseball Hall of Fame in 1945 via Old Timers' Committee
Signature Achievments: Has highest single-season batting average in team history (.410 in 1899), hit over .400 three times, last Phillie to have OBP of .500 or greater (.500, 1895)
Signature Game: Hit four HR in a losing effort on July 13, 1896
Is also known for: Mysterious death near Niagara Falls

"Big Ed" was one of Major League Baseball's earliest and most well-known sluggers. At age 20, the future right-handed slugging outfielder Delahanty joined the then-Quakers in 1888 when the team purchased his contract from Wheeling of the Tri-State league. Delahanty jumped to the Cleveland Infants of the Players' League prior to the start of the 1890 season. Following the 1890 season, the Players' League's only season, Delahanty jumped back to the Quakers.

By 1892, Delahanty would begin to show flashes of what made him a top power-hitter in baseball, leading the NL in triples and slugging percentage. By 1893, Delahanty had arrived: from 1893 through 1899, Delahanty put together a seven-year stretch matched by very few in baseball history: .384/.457/.568 with 65 HR and 255 SB.

During his time second run with the Phillies, Delahanty was among the leaders in all major offensive categories in baseball. Delahanty ranked third in games played, PA, and runs, first in HR and RBI, 16th in steals, fourth in BA, seventh in OBP, and second in hits, SLG and OPS. As a Phillie, Delahanty led the NL in BA in 1899 with a .410 average, the last time any Phillie hit above .400, in OBP with a .500 mark in 1895, the last time any

Phillie got on base at a .500 clip, and led the NL in SLG and OPS four times. Delahanty has the fifth-best batting average in Major League history and ranks 31st in OBP, 88th in SLG, and 51st in OPS. Delahanty would sign with the Washington Senators for the 1902 season and play with them until his death on July 2, 1903, when Delahanty died near Niagara Falls in a mysterious incident that has been described as an accident, suicide, as well as a murder.

Delahanty's numbers hold up well with others in Phillies' history, even over 100 years later. Delahanty ranks fifth in PA, second in runs and RBI, third in steals, third in BA, sixth in OBP, eleventh in slugging, sixth in OPS, ahead of, among others, Mike Schmidt, and first in triples. Delahanty retired as the club leader in hits, a mark that stood until Richie Ashburn broke it in 1959; doubles, a mark that stood until Jimmy Rollins broke it in 2013; runs, a mark that stood until Schmidt broke it; and RBI, a mark also broken by Schmidt. Delahanty was arguably the greatest player in Phillies history until the Whiz Kids came around, having both the standout seasons and cumulative numbers to prove it.

Delahanty might have been ranked even higher on the Top 100 had his teams had any success during his playing days in Philly. The highest any of his teams ever finished was second during his final season with the Phils in 1901, finishing 7.5 games behind the pennant-winning Pirates. Delahanty's teams played exactly .500 baseball (955-955) during his tenure in Philadelphia, meaning one of the league's most mediocre teams during the two stretches Delahanty was in Philly had one of the game's best players.

Delahanty was an Old Timers' Committee selection to the Baseball Hall of Fame in 1945 and was inducted to the Phillies Wall of Fame in 1985. Despite being one of the best players in Phillies' history, and having a top-five all-time batting average, Delahanty is not among the ranks of those who have had their jersey, or in the case of more-appropriate-for-comparison Grover Cleveland Alexander and Chuck Klein, their scripted P, retired.

Chase Utley

Second Baseman

Years as a Phillie: 2003-2015
Line as a Phillie: .287/.373/.498, 217 HR, 129 SB in 5617 PA
fWAR Phillies Rank: 3rd among position players, 5th among Phillies
rWAR Phillies Rank: 3rd among position players, 6th among Phillies
Signature Stat: All-time leader in SB% (88.75%, 142 out of 160)
Signature Stretch: Selected to five-straight NL All-Star teams (2006-2010), won four-straight Silver Sluggers (2006-2009)
Signature Series: Tied a World Series record with five homers in the 2009 World Series
Signature Moment: Hit 2-run HR in first inning of Game 1 of the 2008 World Series

Taken as the 15th overall pick in the 2000 MLB Draft out of UCLA by the Phillies, Chase Utley stormed through the Phillies minor league system, playing for short-season Batavia in 2000, skipping A-ball and going straight to Clearwater for 2001. Utley handled Triple-A pitching well for a 22-year old in 2002, hitting 17 homers in a season where they switched the lefty-hitting Utley's position from second to third base. Utley switched back for 2003, earned a cup of coffee with the Phils and by 2005, Utley was a regular for the Fightins.

In 2005, his first full season in the Majors, Utley hit .291/.376/.540 with 28 HR and 16 steals, earning 13th place in MVP voting. In 2006, Utley would earn his first All-Star nod, his first of five straight, and would win his first of four straight Silver Slugger awards. Utley was in the middle of an MVP caliber season before John Lannan broke his hand with a fastball on July 26, 2007. Utley, who was hitting .336/.414/.581, would finish the year with a .332/.410/.566 line with 22 HR and 9 SB, helping the Phillies break their 14-year playoff drought.

While Utley wouldn't deliver in 2007's playoffs (2-11 in a 3-0 Rockies sweep), Utley would shine the brightest during the postseason. Utley hit

10 postseason homers for the Phillies, second only to Jayson Werth's 11, including a 2-run homer off of Scott Kazmir in the first inning of Game 1 of the 2008 World Series and the first half of a pair of back-to-back dingers off of Matt Garza in the sixth inning of Game 3 en route to a 4-1 series win over the Rays. When the Phillies returned to the World Series in 2009 to face the Yankees, Utley was a monster, hitting five homers in six games, tying Reggie Jackson's single-World Series record in a 4-2 series loss.

Utley has a rare combination of power, speed, and defensive ability at second base. From 2003 through 2013, Utley has accumulated the fourth most fWAR in baseball, ranking first among second baseman. Among second baseman from 2006 through 2013, Utley ranks first in runs scored, is second in homers, second in RBI, sixth in steals, second in OBP, second in SLG, second in triples, ranks first in defensive runs created, and ranks fifth in all of baseball across all positions in that metric during that time frame. Among Phillies, Utley leads all second baseman in HR, runs, and RBI.

Had injuries in 2007, 2012, and 2013 not slowed Utley down, he likely would be approaching Hall of Fame status. Utley currently is ranked as the 16th most productive second baseman of all-time according to FanGraphs' version of WAR. He ranks eighth among second baseman of all time in homers. No slouch in the field, Utley ranks 17th all-time in defensive runs preserved.

Utley earned the nickname "The Man" from Hall of Fame broadcaster Harry Kalas when he scored from second base on a ground ball hit to Atlanta pitcher Macay Macbride by attempting to steal third during the pitch and then taking off as Macbride was throwing to first to put out Ryan Howard. Utley's smarts and hustle also makes him Major League Baseball's all-time SB% leader.

On August 19, 2015, Utley was dealt to the Los Angeles Dodgers for pitcher John Richey and utility player Darnell Sweeney. Though no longer a Phillie, when Utley decides to retire, his #26 will no doubt be retired and his face will appear on the Phillies Wall of Fame.

Bonus
The Top Ten Drafted, Home-Grown Players

From 1993 through 2007, every one of the Phillies first round and supplemental first round draft picks reached the Majors. With a knack for drafting and a keen eye for talent, the Phillies relied on drafting their top talent during the days their budget was lean.

10. Pat Burrell – Drafted first overall in the 1999 amateur draft from the University of Miami (FL). Won World Series ring in 2008.

9. C Mike Lieberthal - Drafted third overall in the 1990 amateur draft from Westlake High School in Westlake Village, CA. Made two All-Star teams and won one Gold Glove as a Phillie.

8. RHP Larry Christenson – Drafted third overall in the 1972 amateur draft from Marysville High School in Marysville, WA. Won World Series ring in 1980.

7. C Darren Daulton – Drafted in the 25th round of the 1980 amateur draft from Arkansas City High School in Arkansas City, KS. Made three All-Star teams and won one Silver Slugger as a Phillie.

6. 3B Scott Rolen – Drafted in the second round of the 1993 amateur draft from Jasper High School in Jasper, IN. Made one All-Star team and won two Gold Gloves as a Phillie.

5. LF Greg Luzinski – Drafted 11th overall in the 1968 amateur draft from Notre Dame High School in Niles, IL. Made four All-Star teams and earned four top eight NL MVP voting finishes as a Phillie. Won World Series ring in 1980.

4. SS Jimmy Rollins – Drafted in the second round of the 1996 amateur draft from Encinal High School in Alameda, CA. Made four All-Star teams, won four Gold Gloves, one Silver Slugger, and the 2007 NL MVP award as a Phillie. Won World Series ring in 2008.

3. LHP Cole Hamels – Drafted 17th overall in the 2002 amateur draft from Rancho Bernardo High School in San Diego, CA. Made three All-Star teams and earned three top eight NL Cy Young voting finishes as a Phillie. Won NLCS and World Series MVP honors in 2008.

2. 2B Chase Utley – Drafted 15th overall in the 2000 amateur draft from UCLA. Made five All-Star teams and won four Silver Slugger awards as a Phillie. Won World Series ring in 2008.

1. 3B Mike Schmidt – Drafted in the second round of the 1971 amateur draft from Ohio University. Won three NL MVPs, nine Gold Glove awards, six Silver Slugger awards, and was an All-Star 12 times. Won 1980 World Series MVP and was inducted into the Baseball Hall of Fame on his first ballot in 1995.

Phillies' Top 10: **Home Runs, Career as Phillie**

Six players drafted and developed by the Phillies occupy six of the top ten spots on the Phillies' all-time, home run leaderboard.

1. Mike Schmidt	548, 1972-1989
2. Ryan Howard	355, 2006-Present
3. Del Ennis	259, 1946-1956
4. Pat Burrell	251, 2000-2008
5. Chuck Klein	243, 1928-1933, 1936-1938, 1939-1944
6. Chase Utley	235, 2003-2015
7. Greg Luzinski	223, 1971-1980
8. Cy Williams	217, 1918-1930
9. Jimmy Rollins	216, 2000-2014
10. Dick Allen	204, 1963-1969, 1975-1976

Robin Roberts

Right-Handed Starter

Years as a Phillie: 1948-1961
Line as a Phillie: 234-199, 3.46 ERA, 1.171 WHIP in 3739.1 IP
fWAR Phillies Rank: 2nd among pitchers, 4th among Phillies
rWAR Phillies Rank: 1st among pitchers, 2nd among Phillies
Inducted into the Baseball Hall of Fame in 1976
Signature Stat: Ranks first in Phillies history in IP, CG
Signature Stretch: Won 20 games or more in six-straight seasons (1950-1955), led MLB in games started in six-straight seasons (1950-1955), threw 20 or more complete games in seven-straight seasons. Made seven-consecutive NL All-Star teams (1950-1956), Five Top 7 NL MVP finishes.

There isn't a whole lot to say about Robin Roberts, the greatest right-handed pitcher in Phillies history, that hasn't already been said. Roberts is the all-time leader in Phillies' history in appearances, innings pitched, and complete games, and ranks second in wins, strikeouts, and games started, and third in shutouts. Roberts also was selected to seven-straight NL All-Star teams and started on the hill for five of them. But it is perhaps his link to one of the biggest underdog stories of all-time, the 1950 NL Pennant-winning Whiz Kids, which has pushed Roberts' rank so highly on this list.

In 1950, Roberts would lead baseball with 39 games started and five shutouts, going 20-11 with a 3.02 ERA, starting the All-Star game, and finishing seventh in MVP voting for the NL Pennant-winning Phillies. The group, collectively known as the Whiz Kids with an average age of 26.4 years old, shocked baseball, winning the pennant by two games over Brooklyn. Roberts, just 23 at the time, would lead them into the 1950 World Series, where he would lose a 2-1 ball game in the tenth inning. Yes, Roberts pitched all ten innings. Roberts would throw a scoreless eighth inning in relief in Game 4, but the damage was done, and the Phillies would lose 5-2 in Game 4 and the series 4-0.

Roberts was just about everything you could ask of a starting pitcher. Roberts was reliable: Roberts led the National League in games started in six-straight years while throwing 20 or more complete games in seven-straight years. Roberts was durable: from 1951 through 1955, Roberts led the MLB in innings pitched. And he was a winner: from 1948 through 1961, his years as a Phillie, Roberts led all right handers in wins across MLB.

From the day he was signed prior to the 1948 season through October 16, 1961, when the Yankees purchased his contract, Roberts was among the best pitchers in baseball: he ranked second in wins, third in appearances, second in starts, second in complete games, third in shutouts, second in innings pitched, and third in strikeouts. Aside from a 1-10 hiccup in 1961, Roberts was remarkably consistent. He won 10 or more games in 12-straight seasons (1949-1960) and won 20 games or more in six-straight seasons (1950-1955).

Roberts would be traded from the Yankees to the Orioles prior to the start of the 1962 season, spending parts of four seasons in Baltimore, parts of two seasons in Houston, and his final season, 1966, with the Cubs.

Roberts was elected to the Hall of Fame on his fourth appearance on the ballot in 1976 and was the first Phillie elected to the Phillies Wall of Fame in 1978. Roberts died of natural causes at the age of 83 on May 6, 2010 at his home in Florida. There has never been, and may never be, a better right-handed pitcher for such a consistent period of time than the Phillies had with Robin Roberts.

The Top Ten Amateur Free Agent Signings in Phillies' History

Prior to the introduction of the Amateur Draft in June 1966, the primary route of bringing amateur talent into your system was to scout and sign. These days, the Phillies sign amateur players outside of the draft through international scouting.

In the 1940s, the Phillies hit a significant hot streak, landing the team a plethora of talent that would end up on the 1950 NL Pennant-winning Wiz Kids. The Wiz Kids had 11 players that either made the All-Star team with the Phillies prior to 1950, during the 1950 season, or after the 1950 season. One of those players, Hall of Famer Robin Roberts, leads the list of the Top 10 Phillies Amateur Free Agent Signings of All-Time. Here are the others:

10. Larry Bowa (1970-1981) – 12 seasons, .264/.301/.324, 13 HR, 288 SB. Five-time All-Star, two-time Gold Glove winner as a Phillie. Signed out of Sacramento City College in 1965.

9. Stan Lopata (1948-1958) – 11 seasons, .257/.355/.459, 116 HR, 18 SB. Two-time All-Star as a Phillie. Signed out of Southwestern High School in Detroit, MI in 1946.

8. Carlos Ruiz (2006-Present) – 9 seasons, .275/.361/.411, 59 HR, 18 SB. One All-Star appearance as a Phillie. Signed out of Chiriqui High School in Chiriqui, Panama in 1998.

7. Rick Wise (1964-1971) – 7 seasons, 75-76 record, 3.60 ERA, 1.302 WHIP. One All-Star appearance as a Phillie. Signed out of Madison High School in Portland, OR in 1963.

6. Jack Clements (1884-1897) – 14 seasons, .289/.352/.426 with 70 HR, 54 SB. Signed out of Philadelphia, PA in 1884.

5. Del Ennis (1946-1957) – 11 seasons, .284/.340/.472 with 288 HR, 45 SB. Three-time All-Star as a Phillie. Signed out of Olney High School in Philadelphia, PA in 1943.

4. Chris Short (1959-1972) – 14 seasons, 132-127 record, 3.38 ERA, 1.283 WHIP as a Phillie. Made two All-Star teams as a Phillie. Signed out of Bordentown Military Institute in Bordentown, NJ in 1957.

3. Curt Simmons (1947-1960) – 13 seasons, 115-110 record, 3.66 ERA, 1.332 WHIP as a Phillie. Made three All-Star teams as a Phillie. Signed out of Whitehall High School in Whitehall, PA in 1947.

2. Richie Ashburn (1946-1959) – 12 seasons, .311/.394/.388 with 29 HR, 234 SB. Four-time All-Star as a Phillie who was inducted as a Phillie into the Hall of Fame in 1995. Signed out of Tilden High School in Tilden, NE in 1945.

1. Robin Roberts (1948-1961) – 14 seasons, 234-199 record, 3.46 ERA, 1.171 WHIP as a Phillie. Made seven consecutive All-Star teams as a Phillie and was inducted as a Phillie into the Hall of Fame in 1976. Signed out of Michigan State University in 1948.

Phillies' Top 10: **Wins, Career as a Phillie**

Robin Roberts was the Phillies' all-time wins leader until Steve Carlton topped his mark in 1985.

1. Steve Carlton	241, 1972-1986
2. Robin Roberts	234, 1948-1960
3. Grover Cleveland Alexander	190, 1911-1917
4. Chris Short	132, 1959-1972
5. Curt Simmons	115, 1947-1960
6. Cole Hamels	114, 2006-2015
7. Curt Schilling	101, 1992-2000
8. Al Orth	100, 1895-1901
9. Charlie Ferguson	99, 1884-1887
10. Jack Taylor	96, 1892-1897

Steve Carlton

Left-Handed Starter

Years as a Phillie: 1972-1986
Line as a Phillie: 241-161, 3.09 ERA, 1.211 WHIP in 3697.1 IP
fWAR Phillies Rank: 1st among pitchers, 2nd among Phillies
rWAR Phillies Rank: 2nd among pitchers, 3rd among Phillies
First-Ballot Hall of Fame Selection in 1994 as a Phillie
Signature Stat: Franchise leader in games started, wins, and strikeouts
Signature Stretch: Won Four Cy Young Awards as a Phillie (1972, 1977, 1980, 1982), seven NL All-Star Selections as a Phillie, one Gold Glove (1981), 20-games winner five times and won 13 games or more in 13-straight seasons as a Phillie.
Signature Season: Went 27-10 for the 59-97 Phillies in 1972 with a career-low 1.97 ERA en route to his first Cy Young
Signature Series: Went 2-0 with a 0.66 ERA in 13.2 IP in the 1983 NLCS
Signature Game: Went seven innings, giving up only one earned in the 1980 Series-clinching Game Six en route to a win and the Phillies' first World Series victory

Lefty, as Steve Carlton was known, was the greatest pitcher in Phillies history. Acquired from the Cardinals in a trade for Rick Wise, Carlton joined the Phillies a year after they had won just 67 games. Carlton came to the Phillies with an impressive pedigree: a World Series champion in 1967 with St. Louis, Carlton, at age 27, had already been a three-time selection to the NL All-Star team. Because of a contractual situation that decreased the Cardinals leverage, the Phillies were able to execute perhaps the greatest trade in franchise history: trading a very good pitcher for a pitcher that ranks among the greatest in not only franchise but baseball history.

Carlton would arrive in 1972 in time for Spring Training and immediately set a higher standard for pitching. Despite the team winning eight less games in 1972 than the season before (67 to 59), Carlton would win 27 decisions on his own, the highest in club history since Robin Roberts won

28 in 1952 on a team that went 87-67. Carlton earned the winning decision in 45.76% of his team's games and was worth an astounding 12.1 fWAR to his team. Wise was worth 5.5 WAR that season, meaning, had the trade not happened, the Phillies likely would have hovered around 51-53 wins, making them one of the worst teams in history.

The Phillies trade for Steve Carlton single-handedly altered the directions that both the Phillies and Cardinals would take. From 1973 through 1980, the Cardinals would come close but fall short of a series of NL East crowns before breaking through in 1981. The Phillies, on the other hand, would put the pieces together in 1976 and win four division titles and a World Series crown in that time. During his parts of 15 seasons with the Phils, Carlton led baseball in wins while ranking second in WAR, games started, innings pitched, and strikeouts. His iconic 1972 Cy Young win would be his first of four with the Phillies, earning the award for the league's best pitcher in 1977, 1980, and 1982 as well.

One of the very few knocks on Carlton is the fact during his time with the Phillies, Lefty briefly struggled in the postseason. In his first three Phillies' postseasons, Lefty posted a 1-2 record with a 5.53 ERA and a .269/.355/.472 BAA, dropping Game One of the 1976 NLCS against the Reds and the series ending Game Four of the 1977 NLCS against the Dodgers. In the Phillies return to the postseason in 1980 after missing the playoffs in 1979 for the first time in three seasons, Lefty was a different pitcher. Carlton went 3-0 in the 1980 playoffs, including wins in Game Two and Game Six of the 1980 World Series. Carlton would channel similar postseason dominance in 1983, putting up a League Championship series for the ages, going 13.2 innings against the Dodgers, striking out 13, and earning the win in Game One and the pennant-winning Game Four at the Vet.

Carlton's time with the Phillies would conclude at age 41 when the Phillies released him on June 24, 1986. Carlton would play through 1988, spending time with the Giants, White Sox, Indians, and Twins. Carlton's 329 career wins rank 11th all-time, fourth in strikeouts, sixth in games started, 75th in complete games, and 14th in shutouts. Carlton was inducted to the Baseball Hall of Fame in 1994 as a first-ballot selection and on to the Phillies Wall of Fame in 1989, when his number 32 was also retired.

Bonus
Transactions That Shaped the Phillies: Wise Move For GM Quinn

Let's look at two players, once traded for one another, in a blind comparison:

Player A: Age 25, 75-76, 3.60 ERA, 1.302 WHIP, 5.2 K/9 IP, One-time All-Star

Player B: Age 26, 77-62, 3.10 ERA, 1.279 WHIP, 6.8 K/9 IP, Three-time All-Star

Player B was better but with better defense, Player A's stats might look better. And whichever person was on the better team would benefit the most, right? Player A is right-hander Rick Wise, a player the Phillies signed as an amateur free agent in 1963. Player B is "Lefty", Steve Carlton.

Phillies General Manager John Quinn had seen the fortunes of his squad slowly deteriorating. After narrowly missing the pennant in 1964 due to a painful late season collapse, Quinn's squads would finish no higher than fifth in the newly-created NL East, winning just 67 games in 1971.

In a July 25, 1989 interview with the *Philadelphia Daily News'* Stan Hochman, Wise recalled he wanted a 100 percent raise from Quinn: "After seven years with the Phillies I was only making $25,000. And then I led the league in fielding, in hitting, hit six homers, threw that no-hitter, led the Phillies' pitchers in every major category... John Quinn offered me a $10,000 raise."

Out in St. Louis, Cardinals' owner Augie Busch was playing the same game with Carlton. According to Wise, Busch said "he wasn't gonna give (Carlton) one more red cent." Strangely, both players were traded for each other on February 25, 1972 as pitchers and catchers began to report to Spring Training and got the raises each desired but from different teams.

Wise had been an asset to the Phillies for the bulk of his seven seasons in Philadelphia. 1971 was Wise's first All-Star season, winning 17 games for a team that had only won 67, posting a career-best 2.88 ERA under manager Frank Lucchesi. Wise hit a career-high six homers including a pair during his June 23 no-hitter at Riverfront Stadium and retired 32 batters in a row on September 18, falling four shy of Harvey Haddix's Major League mark.

Meanwhile, Carlton had made three All-Star teams as a young man on talented St. Louis Cardinals teams. Carlton won a World Series ring in 1967 with the Cardinals, tossing six innings in a Game 5 start. Carlton was on the precipice of becoming an upper echelon pitcher but had a rocky 1970 season, seeing his ERA jump from 2.17 in 1969 to 3.73 in 1970, going from 17-11 in '69 to 10-19 in '70. But in 1971, Carlton was an All-Star once more, winning 20 games but posted an ERA of 3.56.

Tim McCarver, who had caught both pitchers, is cited by Rob Neyer in his 2006 book *Big Book of Baseball Blunders* characterized the trade as a "real good one for a real good one". Until the beginning of the 1972 season, McCarver was right. By the time 1972 was over, it was very clear that the trade had become a real good one for a really great one.

In 1972, Carlton was unlike any pitcher in baseball history. On a historically-bad Phillies team that won just 59 games, Carlton won the NL Cy Young and pitching's Triple Crown with an MLB-best 27 wins and an NL-best 1.97 and 310 Ks while pitching an NL-best 346.1 innings. The Phillies scored just 503 runs and reached base at a .302 clip, both worst in the NL. Yet somehow, Carlton was that good to make up for a lousy Phillies offense that regularly featured .222-hitting third baseman Don Money, .222-hitting catcher John Bateman, .225-hitting right fielder Roger Freed, and .213-hitting back-up Deron Johnson.

Amazingly, General Manager Quinn wouldn't last the season to see the fruits of his trade. Quinn was fired on June 3, 1972 and would be replaced by "The Pope" Paul Owens. Despite Carlton's one-in-a-lifetime season in 1972, the trade had its detractors following the 1973 season. The Phillies would win 12 more games, seeing increased contributions from Greg Luzinski, Willie Montanez, and Del Unser, but Carlton would take a major step backwards while Wise would remain consistent and earned an All-Star birth. In 1973, Wise went 16-12 with a 3.37 ERA versus Carlton's 13-20 mark with a 3.90 ERA.

By 1976, however, it was clear that the trade was a clear win for the Phillies. The Cardinals had traded Wise to Boston following the 1973 season while Carlton would average 18 wins a season with a 2.97 ERA from 1976 through 1984. Carlton would win his second Cy Young in 1977, third in 1980, and fourth in 1982, ultimately leading the National League in wins four times, innings pitched five times, and strikeouts five times.

Initially, Carlton would struggle in the postseason with the Phillies until 1980. In four starts from 1976 through 1978, Carlton would go 1-2 with a 5.53 ERA with his best result coming in Game 3 of the 1978 NLCS when Lefty threw a complete game, striking out eight against the Los Angeles Dodgers. From 1980 on, however, Carlton began one of the top postseason pitching runs in Major League history.

Carlton would win three games in the 1980 postseason, beating the Astros in Game 1 of the NLCS, pitching well enough to lead to an eventual win for the Phillies but a no decision in Game 4 of the NLCS, and beating the Royals in Games 2 and 6 of the World Series. He struck out a combined 17 in the World Series en route to the Phillies' first World Series championship. Lefty would put the Phillies on his back once more in 1983, beating the Dodgers in Games 1 and 4 of the NLCS en route to their second World Series appearance in four seasons.

Over his parts of 15 seasons with the Phils, Carlton led baseball in wins while ranking second in WAR, games started, innings pitched, and strikeouts. Carlton's time with the Phillies would conclude at age 41 when the Phillies released him on June 24, 1986. However, he would play through 1988, spending time with the Giants, White Sox, Indians, and Twins. Carlton's 329 career wins rank 11th all-time, fourth in strikeouts, sixth in games started, 75th in complete games, and 14th in shutouts. Carlton was inducted to the Baseball Hall of Fame in 1994 as a first-ballot selection and on to the Phillies Wall of Fame in 1989, when his number 32 was also retired.

While Carlton became one of the greatest baseball players ever, Wise became a serviceable starter on some winning ball clubs. Wise would win 19 games for the 1975 AL Pennant-winning Boston Red Sox winning Game 3 of the ALCS while vulturing a win in relief in the 12th inning of the historic Game 6 of the 1975 World Series by keeping the game tied before Carlton Fisk ended things with a walk off homer aided by his mojo. Wise would win 113 games with a 3.74 ERA in 11 seasons after being traded. While the numbers pale in comparison to Carlton's 252 wins with a 3.25 ERA in 17 seasons after being traded, Wise was a fine pitcher in his own right. It's just unfortunate for Wise that he was traded for one of the finest pitchers ever.

Phillies' Top 10: **Strikeouts, Career as Phillie**

Despite joining the Phils in his seventh Major League season, "Lefty" was dominant enough to finish his tenure in Philadelphia as the Phils' all-time leader in strikeouts.

1. Steve Carlton	3031, 1972-1986
2. Robin Roberts	1871, 1948-1961
3. Cole Hamels	1844, 2006-2015
4. Chris Short	1585, 1959-1972
5. Curt Schilling	1554, 1992-2000
6. Grover Cleveland Alexander	1411, 1911-1917
7. Jim Bunning	1197, 1964-1968, 1970-1971
8. Curt Simmons	1052, 1947-1960
9. Brett Myers	986, 2002-2009
10. Randy Wolf	971, 1999-2006

Bonus
The Top Ten Trades in Phillies' History

The Phillies have made some pretty solid trades over their 130+ years existence. They have acquired in-their-prime Hall of Famers for player near the end of their careers and prospects. Here are the Top 10 trades in Phillies History.

10. Phillies receive RHP Brad Lidge and UTL Eric Bruntlett from Houston for OF Michael Bourn, INF Mike Costanzo, and RHP Geoff Geary from Houston on November 7, 2007.

9. Phillies receive OF Bobby Abreu from Tampa Bay for SS Kevin Stocker on November 18, 1997.

8. Phillies receive RHP Roy Halladay from Toronto for C Travis d'Arnaud, RHP Kyle Drabek, and OF Michael Taylor on December 16, 2009.

7. Phillies receive RHP Jim Bunning and C Gus Triandos from Detroit for OF Dom Demeter and RHP Jack Hamilton on December 5, 1963.

6. Phillies receive CF Dave Hahn, LHP Tug McGraw, and OF Dave Schneck from New York (NL) for LHP Mac Scarce, C John Stearns, and CF Del Unser on December 3, 1974.

5. Phillies receive OF Lenny Dykstra, RHP Tom Edens, and RHP Roger McDowell from New York (NL) for 2B/CF Juan Samuel on July 27, 1989.

4. Phillies receive OF Garry Maddox from San Francisco for 1B Willie Montanez on May 4, 1975.

3. Phillies receive OF Ben Francisco and LHP Cliff Lee from Cleveland for RHP Carlos Carrasco, INF Jason Donald, RHP Jason Knapp, and C Lou Marson on July 29, 2009.

2. Phillies receive RHP Curt Schilling from Houston for RHP Jason Grimsley on April 2, 1992.

1. Phillies receive LHP Steve Carlton from St. Louis for RHP Rick Wise on February 25, 1972.

Mike Schmidt

Third Baseman

Years as a Phillie: 1972-1989
Line as a Phillie: .267/.380/.527 with 548 HR, 174 SB in 10062 PA
fWAR Phillies Rank: 1st among position players, 1st among Phillies
rWAR Phillies Rank: 1st among position players, 1st among Phillies
First-Ballot Hall of Fame Selection, 1995
Signature Stats: Franchise leader in games played, PA, HR, runs, RBI, BB, IBB, and FanGraphs' defensive runs saved. Leads all third basemen in HR (15th all-time), SLG%, RBI (35th all-time)
Signature Stretch: Eight-time NL HR King, ten-time NL Gold Glove winner, and six-time NL Silver Slugger winner. 12 NL All-Star Selections and won three NL MVP Awards (1980, 1981, 1986).
Signature Series: Hit .381/.462/.714 against the Kansas City Royals in the 1980 World Series en route to the Phillies winning their first World Series and Schmidt winning the World Series MVP award
Signature Game: Hit four HR in April 17, 1976 game against the Cubs
Signature Moment: 500th HR at Three Rivers Stadium hit on April 18, 1987

Michael Jack Schmidt was drafted in the second round of the 1971 amateur draft, a senior-sign out of the University of Ohio. Before Schmidty could play one full season in the minor leagues, Schmidt was called up to be a piece of one of the worst teams in recent Phillies' history, the 1972 squad. Winning just 59 games, the 1972 team featured the newly-acquired Steve Carlton and not much else.

Schmidt, like the Phillies themselves, would struggle, often mightily, in his first two years in the Majors. Schmidt would hit just .197/.324/.367 in his first 483 PA across 1972 and 1973. Regardless, the Phillies stuck with the Ohio native and were rewarded mightily in 1974: Schmidt would lead the league in strikeouts while also leading the Majors in homers and the NL in slugging. Schmidt earned his first of 12 NL All-Star selections in 1974, posting a triple-slash line of .282/.395/.546.

Often, even in retrospect, it is hard to recognize just how great Schmidt was due to a number of factors. When the Phillies reached the postseason in 1976 for the first time since 1950, Schmidt once again led the Majors in homers but fell behind teammate Greg Luzinski in MVP voting. When Schmidt won his first of an NL-record-for-third-baseman ten Gold Gloves in 1976, Larry Bowa had already established himself as the defensive presence on the team. When Schmidt blossomed, the team blossomed, but he was better than the rest.

Schmidt asserted this in 1980, hitting a then-club-record and Major League-leading 48 homers, while leading the NL in SLG% and OPS, en route to his first of three NL MVPs, carrying the Phillies back into the playoffs after a one-year hiatus. Schmidt would lead the Phillies to the first World Series' title in club history after hitting .381/.462/.714 against the Kansas City Royals. Schmidt was named the World Series MVP.

Schmidt's all-time marks are legendary: ranked 15th by FanGraphs and 19th by Baseball Reference in their respective WARs, Schmidt ranks 15th all-time in HR and 35th in RBI, while leading all third baseman in those categories as well as slugging. Schmidt ranks as the all-time Phillies leader in games played, PA, HR, hits, runs, RBI, BB, IBB, and FanGraphs' defensive runs saved.

Schmidt was among baseball's greatest and that point is reflected in other spots in the Phillies' leaderboards, including his somewhat surprising ranking of 15th in steals. From 1972 through 1989, FanGraphs' indicates he was the best player of his time by their version of WAR, leading baseball in HR, runs, and RBI, ranking fourth in SLG%, 12th in FanGraphs' version of defensive runs saved, and 14th in hits.

Schmidt's number 20 was retired in 1990 and he was inducted on to the Phillies' Wall of Fame the same year. Schmidt was inducted as a first-ballot choice to the Baseball Hall of Fame in 1995 alongside Richie Ashburn. Schmidt is considered to be the greatest third baseman of all-time in the Baseball Historical Abstract by Bill James and is the definitive number one choice for the Greatest Phillie of All Time.

Bonus

Building a 25-Man Roster from the PN 100

Well, if you are reading this, you have reached the end of the book and the debate is likely to have begun. But there is still some unfinished business.

I have always wondered what the ultimate, all-time 25-man roster would be. If you take the Phillies Nation Top 100, here is how it would shake out based on the following criteria:

1. It can only contain folks that made the PN Top 100 and the highest ranked player at each position will get the nod. As an example, despite having one of the greatest pinch-hitting runs in club history, Del Unser would not be able to take a bench spot. Matt Stairs is not eligible, either.

2. You must carry five starting pitchers even though starters like Robin Roberts and Curt Simmons frequently started on shorter rest.

3. Unless a starting pitcher has been used in a swing-man capacity in his career and has over 50 relief appearances as a Phil, he must remain a starter and not be slotted in the bullpen.

4. Starting position players must have spent most of their career at their position. For instance, even though Mike Schmidt played first base, he would only be eligible for third despite the fact that Schmidt and Scott Rolen or Schmidt and Dick Allen in a line-up could potentially be more potent than Schmidt and Ryan Howard, depending on your point of view.

5. You must take a back-up catcher, at least one left-handed reliever, and at least one bench middle infielder.

Let's begin.

<u>Starting Infield</u>

C Carlos Ruiz (#32)

1B Ryan Howard (#27)

2B Chase Utley (#4)

3B Mike Schmidt (#1)

SS Jimmy Rollins (#9)

This one is pretty cut and dry with the possible exception of Chooch. The Phillies have a run of half-decent catchers in their history (Darren Daulton at #34, Jack Clements at #35, Mike Lieberthal at #46, Stan Lopata at #48, and Andy Seminick at #49) so this one could go in a few different directions after some debate but according to our rankings, this is how it shakes down.

<u>Starting Outfield</u>

LF Ed Delahanty (#5)

CF Richie Ashburn (#6)

RF Bobby Abreu (#11)

This one will probably turn some heads. Some will probably prefer Chuck Klein (#13) and his MVP but Abreu played in a tougher environment (CBP v. the Baker Bowl) and put up a similar OPS (.928 as a Phillie v. Klein's .935) with significantly more steals (254 v. 71) and the highest OBP in club history for those with over 1500 PA.

<u>Bench</u>

C Darren Daulton (#34)

1B/3B Dick Allen (#10)

2B/SS Nap Lajoie (#51)

OF Chuck Klein (#13)

OF Sherry Magee (#14)

Wow – there are some big names left off the list, here. The notably excluded include Billy Hamilton (#15), Roy Thomas (#18), Johnny Callison (#19), Garry Maddox (#22), and others. But this is a pretty amazing bench: a left-handed hitting catcher, one of the best left-handed power hitters of his time, one of the best right-handed power hitting corner infielders of his time, and a pair of speedy, great-glove players that can get on base at will. Not bad.

Starting Rotation

LHP Steve Carlton (#2)

RHP Robin Roberts (#3)

RHP Grover Cleveland Alexander (#7)

LHP Cole Hamels (#8)

RHP Jim Bunning (#12)

Nothing too much to debate here, although some of the game's biggest big-game pitchers of all-time are out in the cold for this one (Curt Schilling, #16 and Cliff Lee, #26). On a side note, the Phillies may have one of the best MLB all-time 1-2-3 top pitchers, ever.

Bullpen

Closer: LHP Tug McGraw (#56)

Set-Up: RHP Brad Lidge (#62)

Set-Up: RHP Ron Reed (#68)

Middle Relief: RHP Ryan Madson (#96)

Middle Relief: LHP Billy Wagner (#93)

Middle Relief: RHP Eppa Rixey (#36)

Long Man: LHP Curt Simmons (#17)

A little creativity with both Rixey and Simmons is needed, but both were starting pitchers who had a number of relief appearances with the Phillies (Rixey 55, Simmons 62). The roles, other than Simmons in the long-man role, may appear to be somewhat arbitrary but this is likely the best combination based on their skillsets.

Index

2

3

4

6

7